A TWO REEL MURDER

A Maisy Malone Mystery

Starring

Mabel Normand and Mack Sennett

LARRY NAMES

USA

ISBN: 0910937443

ISBN-13: 978-0-910937-44-3

To my nephew and niece,

Randy and Kathy Hodges

Two wonderful people
Who truly understand the meanings
Of Love, Tolerance, and Forgiveness

Leslie Clover stood in front of a full-length mirror on the closet door in the master bedroom of his Hollywood bungalow admiring himself. On the one hand, his overall form pleased him. Although his sallow face remained on the fleshy side, his torso certainly appeared to be trimmer, which was the desired effect of donning a theatrical corset. He turned to the left: no belly protruding from that view. He turned to the right: no midriff bulge to be seen this way either. A smile of satisfaction curled the corners of his lips.

"Haven't looked this lithe since my early youth, don't you know? Yes, quite fit and proper. This should do the trick and get me a bigger role or two at Keystone."

To celebrate the moment, Clover reached for the pack of Chesterfields on the dressing table that doubled as a nightstand. He flipped up a pair of fags, drew one with his lips, and dropped the pack back on the vanity. From a pocket of his gray trousers crumpled on the bed, he withdrew the Sterling silver Eveready cigarette lighter he had brought with him from England. As he so often did, he admired the engraving on the German made petrol lighter before removing the lid. He thumbed the wheel to make the spark to ignite the wick and then put the flame to the tip of the cigarette. One quick inhale brought the tobacco to life. Before taking a deep drag, Clover replaced the lid on the Eveready, effectively smothering the tiny fire. As he returned the lighter to his trouser pocket, he drew hard on the cigarette to fill his lungs with the addictive smoke. Before the tar- and nicotine-laced gas could complete the inflation, Clover's breath suddenly deserted him in a blasting cough. He jerked the Chesterfield from his mouth instinctively. As a natural reaction to the abrupt and excessively violent tussive spasm, his lungs panicked for oxygen; air that would not come because his diaphragm was now out of synchronization with his pulmonary system.

Clover hacked several more times. Between coughs, he tried to breathe, but nothing came of his efforts. The harder he tried to inhale, the more his skin reddened with the struggle. He dropped the burning cigarette on the hardwood floor and reached for the ends of the strings of the man's corset binding his torso. He caught one and gave it a good pull, but only succeeded in creating a knot instead of untying the bow. Worse, he tightened the laces, which only made his panic-stricken effort to breathe more difficult and eventually futile.

Now without life-giving air for too long, Clover clutched his throat, brown eyes bulging, mouth agape, and crumpled to the floor. He rolled onto his back, and in the next instant his eyes rolled up in their sockets. Complete unconsciousness overtook him.

The other person in the room who had been sitting quietly and watching Clover for several minutes rose from the armchair, walked over to the supine and comatose actor, and stooped over to check to see if Leslie had yet begun breathing again. Certain of that eventuality, the visitor straightened up, went to the bed, retrieved a pillow, and returned to Clover. Quite deliberately, the watcher knelt beside the unconscious body, placed a knee onto the actor's solar plexus, put the pillow over his face, and pressed firmly.

Feeling the pillow against his nose aroused Clover. He opened his eyes, but was unable to see anything with the cushion covering them. Realizing he was being attacked, he reacted by thrashing about. Touching his assailant stimulated his senses all the more. He kicked his feet and swung his arms, but the defensive moves exhausted the remaining oxygen in his lungs. In spite of the hormonal injection from his adrenal glands, he failed to fend off the assault.

Knowing there was no turning back now, the visitor held the cushion in place for several minutes to make damn certain Leslie Clover was dead.

* * *

Most people remember 1912 as the year the *Titanic* struck an iceberg, sank in the North Atlantic, and fifteen hundred people perished at sea. One of them should have been Susan Delaney Deaton, but she failed in her attempt to stow away on the ill-fated ocean liner. This put her in trouble with the law, which was why she was known by another name when she arrived at 7:30 a.m. Thursday, September 26, 1912 in Los Angeles aboard the Santa Fe Railroad's *California Limited*.

The La Grande Depot bore a stronger resemblance to a Baghdad mosque than it did to an American railroad station. Passengers debarked the various cars at all speeds. Our girl took her time, pausing at the top step of a coach exit when she heard her name called out.

"Miss Malone?" queried a dapper young man on the station platform. He held up a sheet of typing paper with the name Maisie Malone printed neatly in large black letters on it.

Hearing her recently adopted *new* name spoken by a stranger — *and a man at that, a handsome man, a very handsome man neatly attired in a dark blue suit with gold pinstripes and wearing a black bowler* — Maisy appeared quite taken aback, especially when she read the sign.

"My name is spelled with a 'Y' like in daisy. Not with an 'I E' at the end."

The fellow looked at the sign, shrugged, crumpled it, and then casually tossed it aside. "Sorry."

"Fair enough."

Clutching her French silk purse by its silver chain, Maisy started to disembark from the coach but caught a shoe heel on the top step, stumbled, and lurched forward directly at the gentleman. He reacted instantly with athletic reflexes, throwing his arms around her, as if he had expected her to fall into his embrace. The collision had no effect on the navy blue chapeau crowning her naturally wavy auburn coiffure. She made no effort to remove herself from his strong but gentle hold, clutching her against his chest until her amber-flecked, whiskey-brown eyes met his roguish blues.

With a devilish grin, he spoke in Ivy League English. "I had hoped you would be glad to see me, Miss Malone, but this is much more than I expected."

"Well, I'm not exactly in the habit of throwing myself at men." The slightest hint of a Southern drawl lilted Maisy's voice. "But all things considered, I could get used to it."

"Could you now?"

"You could stick around and find out."

"I just might do that."

"Fair enough then."

He tipped his hat at her. "Milo Cole … at your service. Mr. Sennett sent me to meet you and see that you get to the right hotel and then to the studio. He actually lives there, you know."

"No, I didn't know."

The alluring scent of her French perfume paralyzed Cole for the eternity of six seconds, until he replied slowly, "Well, he does." Then he realized he still held her in his arms. "I suppose you want me to let you go now."

Maisy smiled precociously. "For now, but who can say about later?"

Cole grinned to one side of his face with eyebrows raised. "You don't say?" Then he withdrew his arms from around her.

A porter waited patiently on the steps of the car, holding a suitcase in each hand. He caught Milo's eye with a toothy grin and a gentle nod.

Cole smiled back at him. "Is that Miss Malone's luggage?"

"Yes, sir, it is."

"I have an automobile waiting in front of the station." Cole proffered a bent arm to Maisy, who took it. "Right this way, Miss Malone."

They made their way through the train station crowd with the porter trailing behind them until they emerged from the depot.

Maisy held back for a second as she admired all the palm trees that seemed to be everywhere in southern California. "Are you Mr. Sennett's assistant or something, Mr. Cole?"

"No, I'm one of Mr. Sennett's actors."

"Really? But I don't recall having heard of you before."

"That's because I haven't had a real role yet. I've just played very minor bit roles so far. You might say I'm a background actor."

"Oh, I see. You're an extra."

He frowned at her. "And what about you, Miss Malone? Is this your first time in Los Angeles?"

"Yes, it is. It's my first time in California, to be perfectly honest."

"Oh, don't do that, Miss Malone. Not here. It'll only get you into trouble."

"Trouble? What will get me into trouble?"

"Honesty. We don't get much of that here. There's not a whole lot of room for it in this business."

"I'm not quite sure I understand, Mr. Cole."

"It's Milo, if you don't mind, Miss Malone."

"I won't, if you'll call me Maisy."

A wave of confidence flowed over Cole. "All right, Maisy it is."

"So what were you trying to tell me about honesty, *Milo?*"

"Oh, yes, honesty. I don't think too many people around here do understand about honesty, so you're not alone on that one."

"Are you being honest with me, Milo?"

Cole gave her a wink. "Now you're catching on already, Maisy."

They arrived at the curb where a liveried chauffeur waited beside a dark blue Cadillac Model 30.

"Edendale is some distance from here, Maisy. We could take a Red Car, but Mr. Sennett thought you would prefer riding in an automobile."

"That was very thoughtful of Mr. Sennett."

The driver opened the rear door for Maisy, and Cole assisted her courteously into the back seat. As soon as she was situated comfortably, he slid in beside her. The chauffeur closed the door behind the actor, then assisted the porter with loading Maisy's luggage on to the front passenger seat before taking his own place behind the steering wheel.

"Here you go, pal." Cole held out a dime to the porter through the window. As soon as the man accepted the gratuity, the actor turned to Maisy. "Willie will drive us out to Hollywood first. Mr. Sennett had me reserve a room for you at the Hollywood Hotel. You can stay there until we can find an apartment or a house for you to rent."

Willie started the engine, then maneuvered the car into the bustling weekday traffic, a mixture of combustion engine, electric, steam, and horse-drawn conveyances plus trolleys and street cars, both Pacific Electric Red Cars and Los Angeles Railway Yellow Cars.

"I'm not sure I'll be here long enough to rent a house or an apartment."

"Oh, really?"

"Oh, yes. My deal with Keystone is only for one month with an option for a second one … if Mr. Sennett likes my work."

"Well, Mr. Sennett must be planning to pick up that option or he wouldn't be going to all this trouble and expense. The owners back in New York are really tight with their money. Keystone is the lowest paying studio out here in California."

"Is that right?"

"Unfortunately, it is."

"What did you mean by 'all this trouble,' Milo?"

Cole sighed. "Yes. The car? And me? I've never known him to go to such lengths for anybody before. You must be very talented."

"Well, that remains to be *seen*."

Cole laughed softly. "Yes, of course."

Maisy smiled at him, impressed that he had understood she had made a pun. Pleased by his response, she patted his hand. "You're all right, Milo."

"Thank you, Maisy. So are you."

"Have you been out here long, Milo?"

"I came out here back in April."

"From New York, I'll bet."

"That's right. I was trying to break into the business back there, but there was too much competition. So I scrounged up the train fare to come here where I figured there would be more opportunities for me. So far, Keystone has been the best place for me. I worked at Polyscope before coming down the hill to work for Mr. Sennett."

For the moment, Maisy focused her attention on the sights and sounds of the burgeoning city. "Los Angeles is much bigger than I thought it would be."

"It's not New York or Chicago, but it's catching up fast."

"Yes, I can see that. It looks like there's a new building going up on every block."

"Pretty much."

"No wonder Mr. Sennett wanted to move out here."

"So how do you come to know Mr. Sennett? Did you work for him in New York?"

"No, we met in Chicago when he and Miss Normand were passing through town on their way to coming out here last month. They had a day's layover to change trains and had plenty of time to kill, so they took in a show at the Majestic. I was doing a comedy act with Eddie Foy. Actually, I was just a walk-on for his act. He had me make a joke that he used as a straight line for a joke of his own, and when he'd come off funnier than me, I'd stomp off the stage in a huff. That was the whole bit.

"Mr. Sennett and Miss Normand came backstage to see Eddie and make him an offer to come out and film comedies with them. He turned them down, so they asked me if I'd like to be in the movies. They said I was pretty funny and they were planning to make a lot of comedies. They said they could use someone with my—how did he put it?—with my 'sense of the comic.' Sense of the comic. Can you believe that?"

"That sounds like Mr. Sennett, all right."

"Well, I told them I'd think about it and let them know. Mr. Sennett offered me thirty bucks a week, if I'd come out here to work for him. I said forty, and he said, 'Let's see how you look on camera first. Then we'll talk about a raise.' I said not enough dough. Then he said okay to forty, and I said I should have asked for fifty. He laughed, and I asked him what so funny. He said he would have gone to fifty, and then they left.

"Last week, I sent him a telegram saying I wanted to come out here to work for him, and the next day a guy comes to the Majestic and tells me Mr. Sennett sent him the money to buy me a one-way ticket to Los Angeles. He asked when I wanted to leave, and I said as soon as I can give notice to Eddie and get my bags packed. Now here I am."

"And here we are. Welcome to the Hollywood Hotel, Maisy."

Willie pulled the Cadillac into the horseshoe driveway in front of the three-story hotel and stopped in front of the main entrance. A smiling, middle-aged doorman came to Maisy's side of the car and opened the door for her, while a bellboy did the same thing for Cole on his side.

"Welcome to the Hollywood Hotel, miss."

Maisy and Milo exited the automobile at the same time. Then he hurried around the rear of the Cadillac and stopped beside Maisy. "Miss Malone's bags are in the front seat."

The doorman snapped his fingers at the bellboy and pointed to the front passenger door; the order to get Maisy's luggage. Still smiling, he tipped his hat to Maisy. "Edgar Wilson at your service, Miss Malone. Will you be staying long with us?"

Cole answered for her. "Until the end of the month … or longer."

"I hope you enjoy your stay with us, Miss Malone."

Maisy scanned the building and the landscaping, replying to the man absently. "I'm sure I will." She turned Cole. "This is some swanky joint, Milo. Are you sure Mr. Sennett wants me to stay here?"

"That's what the man said."

"Fair enough."

The doorman motioned toward the entrance. "This way, Miss Malone."

Maisy took the lead with Cole behind her and Wilson walking slightly to her left. The bellboy brought up the rear. When they reached the door,

Wilson grabbed the handle and pulled it open for Maisy, Cole, and the bellboy to enter the lobby.

"Should I tell your driver to wait?"

Again Cole answered for Maisy. "No need. He already knows. As soon as I get Miss Malone checked into her room, I'll be taking her to Edendale to meet with Mr. Sennett. Miss Malone has come to Los Angeles to make moving pictures for Mr. Sennett's Keystone Motion Picture Company."

Wilson tilted his head and smiled with approval. "Very good to have you with us, Miss Malone. What's that phrase you picture people use to wish someone good luck? Break an arm or something?"

"It's 'break a leg,' not an arm. But that's for the stage. I don't know what they say in the moving pictures for good luck. Maybe you can help me out with that, Milo."

"You know, I don't believe we have an expression like that in the movie business. I suppose it's because if we don't get the scene right the first time, then we can do it over and over until we do."

Maisy grinned at him. "Or maybe moving picture people aren't as superstitious as theatre people."

"That could be as well."

"Fair enough. Let's get me checked in. I'm anxious to see Mr. Sennett and Miss Normand again."

They entered the lobby and approached the front desk.

"I'll take care of this, Maisy. How do you want me to sign you in?"

"May Zelda Malone will do just nicely."

* * *

After completing the registration in the baroque style lobby, Cole and Maisy followed the bellboy to her room on the second floor. Seeing inside the room took Maisy's breath away. "This is some swell place." She brushed a hand over the sea green satin spread of the double-bed. "I've never slept in a bed this size by myself. I'm afraid I might get lost in there in the night." Another gasp. "And a nightstand and lamp on each side. Wow! This is the lap of luxury." She flopped down on the bed and fell backward to enjoy the comfort.

As soon as the hotel worker departed with his ten-cent gratuity in hand, Cole had to ask Maisy the question that had been tickling his curiosity since they had stood before the desk clerk signing in.

"May Zelda?"

Maisy sat up. "Sure, why not?"

"May ... I can understand. But how does an Irish girl get the middle name of Zelda? I've heard of Jewish girls named Zelda. Even some German girls. But never an Irish girl."

"Who said I was Irish?"

"Your last name is Malone. That's Irish, isn't it?"

She winked at him and fell into a brogue. "It's the name I gave Eddie Foy so he would give me a job in his act. The Foys are Irish, you know, and you know how clannish the Irish can be, don't you?"

"I certainly do. But even so—"

"I can do a pretty good brogue as well. Good enough to fool Eddie into giving me that part in his act anyway."

"Okay, I can buy that, but where does the Maisy come from? Is that Irish as well?"

"May ... Zelda? May ... Z?"

Cole thought for a few seconds, quite perplexed. Then the light went on, and a smile burst over his face. "Oh, I get it. May ... Z. *Maisy.* Pretty clever of you, Maisy."

"I thought so. Now what do you say we get out of this joint and you take me to meet Mr. Sennett?"

"Of course, but we have to make a stop along the way. We have to pick up a chum of mine. Another actor. Leslie Clover. His house is along the way. Normally, Leslie would be at the studio, but today Mr. Sennett is planning to do a screen test with you and Leslie. So there was no need for Leslie to go into the studio at the usual time."

"A screen test?"

"Yes, to see how you act together."

"That should be interesting. Me and a total stranger acting together in a business I know practically nothing about. Yessiree, Bob! That should be real interesting to say the least."

* * *

Many lots in the subdivision between Hollywood Boulevard on the south, Vermont Avenue on the east, Franklin Avenue on the north, and Normandie Avenue on the west were still vacant. Every street had at least two properties currently under construction. The completed houses had been built over the last three years. They included the bungalow on Alexandria Avenue belonging to Leslie Clover.

By the time Willie halted the Cadillac in front of Clover's modest home, Maisy thought she knew as much about the English actor as she cared to know. She expected to learn even more about him on the ride to the Keystone studio in Edendale.

"Just sit tight, Maisy, while I get Leslie." Cole opened the rear door on his side of the touring car and climbed out. He leaned through the window. "I shouldn't be long. Leslie is usually quite punctual. I'm surprised he's not sitting on the porch steps waiting for us and complaining that we're late. Back in a flash." He dashed around the rear of the car and up the gravel walkway to the yellow bungalow constructed from Sears Catalog floor plan #155. Still in stride, he bounded up the five steps two at a time, then slowed for the last two paces to the screen door, where he rapped the knuckles of his right hand on the sash three times. Noting the inner door was ajar, Cole shouted through the wire mesh.

"Leslie, old bean! It's Milo. We're here to take you to the studio with us, don't you know?" Cole chuckled under his breath, thinking himself rather clever with his mock English accent. "We've got that new actress Mr. Sennett sent for from Chicago. She's a real peach. You've just got to meet her. So shake a leg, chum."

Cole stepped back from the door, turned around, and waved to Maisy with a bit of boyish confidence.

To hide the annoyance she was feeling for the delay in continuing to Keystone, Maisy forced a smile and waggled the fingers of her left hand at her escort.

No sound came from within the bungalow, raising Cole's curiosity. Now peeved for having to wait, he thought he should knock a second time. He turned, stepped up to the door again, but held off rapping on the sash. Instead, he opened the screen door and struck the inner door firmly, widening the gap between it and the doorway a few inches more.

"I say, Leslie, are you about?"

No response from Clover, but a squeaky hinge in the rear of the house did interlope on the quiet, stirring Cole's curiosity. He pushed the door completely open with his right forearm and entered the house cautiously.

"Leslie?"

Again absolute quiet.

"The door was open, so I just came on in. Hope you don't mind."

Still nothing.

Cole scanned the living room. Sofa ahead slightly to the left fronted by a coffee table and facing the fireplace. Armchairs in the middle facing the fireplace. Writing desk against the wall and between the windows to the right with a Model 20B Western Electric telephone on the right side close to the wall. A bit sparse in furnishings, although not so much for a house occupied by a single man. Newspapers and magazines littered the room. A copy of *The Motion Picture World* and the latest issue of *Photoplay* on the coffee table caught his eye. He shook his head, wishing he had had a role in the film featured on the cover, *Queen Elizabeth*, a real dramatic film, a six-reeler produced in France. The ashtray on the coffee table had several cigarette butts in it.

Being reminded that Clover had played a minor part in the picture caused Cole to talk to himself. "Lucky bastard got to act with Sarah Bernhardt. And all I get are bit parts as a walk-on extra with unknowns. One day, Milo. One day."

Remembering why he was there, Cole continued into the dining room, which he immediately noted as being in the same disarray as the parlor had been. An oak table with four matching chairs was strewn with more magazines and newspapers, including the morning edition of the *Los Angeles*

Times, its pages scattered around the breakfast dishes and an ashtray with only two cigarette butts, all left in place by Clover and a guest, making Cole think someone had spent the night in the extra bedroom, which was adjacent to the dining room.

Cole peeked into the spare room and saw the bed in perfect order, not a single wrinkle on the spread. He heaved a sigh and hung his head slightly.

"He's such a lucky bastard. I can't even get a dog to stay over at my place. But then again, I don't live in a house or even a decent- sized apartment."

He moved on to the kitchen, which appeared to be in the same condition as the living room and dining: clean but very untidy with cooking utensils on the stove and dirty dishes in the sink and on the counter.

"The man needs a maid … or a wife."

This left only the master bedroom for Cole to check. Aware that Clover might be in there with a woman, he thought it best to knock before entering. He tapped the main knuckle of his right hand twice on the door, which pushed the door open a few inches.

"Leslie, are you … entertaining this morning?"

No response from within.

Quite curious now, Cole nudged the door open a few more inches with his forearm and peered ever so carefully around the edge of it. He couldn't see the bed along the outside wall, but he could see the dressing table between the closet and entrance to the shared bathroom in the opposite wall. One more gentle push brought a pair of bare feet on the floor between the bed and dresser into full view. Their ashen color struck Cole as more than odd. He elbowed the door wide open to see Clover face up and motionless on the floor.

"Good God, Leslie!"

Cole burst into the room and dropped to a knee beside Clover. In a heartbeat, he realized his friend was dead. His first thought escaped his lips.

"How did this happen, old bean?"

T

ired of waiting in the car, Maisy thought of sending Willie up to the bungalow door to see what was keeping Cole and his friend Clover, but she discarded the idea because she had just met the driver and felt she had no right to be giving him any orders. So she went herself, taking her purse with her. Peeking through the screen door, she saw Cole facing the writing desk and holding the telephone transmitter up to his mouth with his right hand and the receiver to his left ear with the other.

"Milo, what's the hold up?"

Cole pressed the mouthpiece to his chest. "Maisy, be a good girl, would you please, and look for the house number outside, and then come inside and tell it to me?"

"The house number? Whatever for?"

"Please, Maisy. Just do it. It's rather important."

Uncertain of what to think of his request, Maisy stared at Milo with disbelief for a few seconds before she realized he was absolutely serious. After an exaggerated shrug, she moved back from the doorway and scanned the walls to either side of it in search of the address numerals. None there. She stepped down to the walkway and looked up at the façade of the porch roof. They were there on the cross beam. Making a mental note of their sequence, she climbed the steps again and went into the house in time to hear Cole speaking to someone on the telephone.

"Yes, I'm pretty certain of it." Then he saw Maisy standing a few feet inside the living room. "Could you wait a moment please? My friend has come back inside, and I hope she found the house number." He paused, then thanked the person on the other end of the line before pressing the transmitter against his chest again. "Did you find the number, Maisy?"

"Yes. One, seven, five, five."

Cole repeated the four digits aloud but to himself. "Thank you."

"Say, what's this all about?"

Cole ignored her and spoke into the mouthpiece again. "The address is one, seven, five, five, officer." He paused. "Yes, Alexandria Avenue." Another pause. "Yes, we'll stay right here until your man arrives." Pause.

"No, we won't touch a thing. I promise." One final pause before he said good-bye and replaced the receiver on its hook and returned the telephone to its spot on the desk.

While she waited for Milo to finish the call, Maisy surveyed the disorderly living room. As soon as Cole turned to face her, she focused on him again.

"Are you going to tell me what that was all about? Or are you going to make me try out some kind of mind-reading act on you? Why did you need the house number?"

"*I* didn't need it. The police did."

"The police? Whatever—?" A tingle on the nape of her neck interrupted Maisy and redirected her line of thinking. "Say, where's your friend? Is he here or not?"

"Oh, he's here all right." Cole held up a hand to stop Maisy from asking the next obvious question. "He's on the floor in the rear bedroom. He's dead."

Maisy flinched with the news. "He's dead? Are you sure?"

"Go see for yourself, if you don't believe me."

After a second's thought, Maisy headed toward the dining room and the rear of the house. "I have got to see this."

Cole took an agile sidestep and intercepted her. "I wasn't serious about you seeing for yourself. Just take my word for it. He's as dead as yesterday's mackerel."

"Oh, I believe you, Milo, but I still want to see for myself."

"Good grief, Maisy! That's rather morbid of you, don't you think? Wanting to see a dead man you don't even know."

"Is he all bloody or something horrific like that?"

"No, nothing like that."

"Okay, so how did he die?"

"How should I know? I'm not a doctor or an undertaker. I'm an actor, for goodness sake. He's just lying there on the floor ... all ... dead."

"Well, he must have died from something. Let's go have a look at him and see if we can figure it out."

"Maisy, you're unbelievable. That's what the police are coming here to do. And I promised them we wouldn't touch anything."

"Okay, we won't touch anything, but we can still look. So come on. Let's take a look at him before the police get here."

Cole frowned. "I don't want to look at him again." Then another thought occurred to him. "But I suppose I'd better, if only to make certain *you* don't touch anything and get *me* into trouble with the law."

Maisy pointed toward the kitchen door. "Is that the way?"

"Yes, it's back there. Come on. I'll show you."

"And don't worry, Milo. I do fair enough at getting myself into trouble, but I never get other people into trouble."

"There's always a first time for everything."

"Yes, I suppose there is that."

As they walked past the first bedroom doorway, Maisy looked in and noted how neat and tidy the room was compared to the living room. She glanced at the dining room table and thought how much it resembled the parlor. The only thing different was the ashtray; only two butts instead of two dozen.

"Looks like he had company for his last meal here."

"I thought so, too."

They entered the kitchen.

Maisy saw the sink with dirty dishes. An ashtray on the counter to the left had several butts in it. "Not much of a housekeeper, was he?"

"How many men are?"

"A few I've met over the years. Usually, those gents who are more like their mothers than their fathers, if you know what I mean."

"Yes, I do know what you mean. Believe me. Leslie was no—" The image of Clover lying on the floor in the bedroom popped into Cole's mind, cutting short his remark as he reconsidered his estimation of his friend's sexual orientation. He stopped at the far side of the bedroom doorway. "Well, I might be wrong about that."

Maisy came to the center of the doorway and looked inside the master bedroom at the corpse lying in the middle of the room. "So that's your friend Leslie Clover?" She turned an intentionally suspicious eye on Cole, more to tease him than to question his heterosexuality. "Did he *always* wear a corset?"

Truly offended, Cole snapped to attention. "How the hell should I know? I've never seen him in anything other than trousers, shirt, tie, shoes, and coat. I have no idea what he might have worn underneath."

Maisy giggled. "Relax, Milo. I was only fooling. From the moment you caught me at the train depot, I knew which team you were playing for." She looked back at Clover. "But your friend here? I'm not so sure about him. One thing's for certain, he had help getting into that thing."

"How do you know that?"

"The laces are in the back. Unless he was triple-jointed, there's no way he could reach back there and tie those laces himself. Somebody else had to do it."

"Yes, but he could have tied those up first and then hooked the front when he put it on."

"Not if he wanted it really tight. That takes somebody else tying the laces in back. I know. I've worn corsets on and off the stage. On stage, you get help from one of the other girls in the dressing room. At home, you're on your own. Someone else pulling on those strings can get them a lot tighter than you can by yourself. And if you do it by yourself, there is no way you can get the corset as tight without someone else's help."

"So you're saying he's dead because somebody tied the laces too tight on the corset?"

Maisy shook her head. "No, I'm not saying that. When the laces are too tight, you can't breathe as deeply as you can when they're loose or when you're not wearing a corset. If they're too tight and you get a little excited, most women just faint from not getting enough air. But after a minute or two of being out cold, the excitement goes away, and you start to breathe normally again. That's when you wake up, and everything is okay again."

"Okay, I can see that, but what happened to Leslie? If he got excited about something and wasn't getting enough air and then fainted, why didn't he wake up when the excitement passed and he started breathing normally again?"

"That's a very good question, Milo. Why didn't he start breathing normally again?" She entered the bedroom.

Cole grabbed her by the arm. "Hey, we can't go in there."

Maisy glared at his hand holding her back. "Sure we can. At least until the coppers get here." She smiled when he released his grip on her. "Come on and help me turn him over."

"We can't touch him, Maisy. I promised—"

"We'll put him back the same way we found him. Relax, will you, Milo. We're just doing a little snooping around here. That's all." She bent over the corpse, reaching for his right arm to roll him on his front side. Suddenly, she popped erect. "Hey, I know this guy. I worked in the same music hall with him a couple of years ago when I was in London."

"You worked with Leslie in London?"

"No, I said I worked at the *same* music hall with him. His name didn't ring any bells, but I never forget a face. This is the same guy. He did a comedy act. Pretty funny guy."

"What were you doing in London?"

"I told you. I was playing the music hall circuit. I saw your pal here at the Royal Comedy Theatre in London. Of course, I wasn't Maisy Malone then. I was ... Well, never mind that now. That's in the past, and your dead pal is the present. So let's focus on him, all right?"

Cole eyed Maisy with suspicious curiosity, but he decided not to pursue questioning her past for the time being. Something told him he would have plenty of time in the future to learn a lot more about her personal history.

The two of them knelt down beside Clover, one to each side, and rolled the deceased man onto his left side with a slight degree of difficulty, which did not go unnoticed by Maisy.

A shiver coursed through Maisy. "I haven't touched a dead person in a long time. I forgot how cold a body feels when it's no longer a living, breathing person. You ever touch a dead person, Milo?"

"My mother made me kiss my grandmother's cheek when she was in her coffin. I was a boy of six, if I remember correctly." He thought about the memory for a second. "Can't say I particularly enjoyed the moment."

"Did you know your grandmother very well?"

"Not really. She was pretty much a stranger to me. What about you? Ever have to kiss a dead relative?"

"I'd already run off from home when my grandparents died, so I missed that. I missed my father's funeral, too. Didn't miss some other relatives and family friends though. Wish I could have. Hate funerals."

"It's the sadness around them that disturbs all of us. When my time comes, I—"

"It'll come sooner than you think, Milo, if you don't stop yapping." Maisy frowned at Cole. "Can we get back to business ... before the police show up and stop us from snooping here?" She leaned forward to inspect Clover's back. "See there? Those laces are as tight as you can get them. No way *he* did that by himself. Somebody stood behind him, put a knee on his tailbone, and pulled those strings tighter than a drum."

"All right, I'll take your word for it."

"Untie the bow, Milo. Let's loosen the laces and then unbutton the front so we can look at his chest."

"Not on your life. I told the police we wouldn't touch a thing in here, and already we've rolled poor Leslie on his side to look at the backside of his corset. Now let's put him back the way we found him and go back out in the living room to wait for the police."

"Aw, come on, Milo. I only want to look at his chest."

"No, I'm not helping you any more with this. Now let's put him back the way we found him and back to the living room."

Maisy grimaced, but she went along with Cole. They eased Clover onto his back, and both of them stood up again. Milo stepped over the body and went to the doorway, but Maisy stayed put.

"I said let's go back to the living room to wait for the police."

Maisy surveyed the room again. "Does anything in this room strike you as being odd?"

"Certainly. Leslie's lying on the floor dead. How much stranger can it get than that?"

"No, I mean everything except him. Look at the bed, at the clothing valet, at the dressing table. The ashtray is clean as a whistle. Everything is in perfect order in here."

"So?"

"Did you look at the rest of the house?"

Cole thought about it for a second before answering. "Well, the other bedroom was nice and neat as well."

"Yes, it was, but the living room, the dining room, the kitchen. All cluttered just like a single man lived here." Maisy looked around the room again. "Does this place have an inside toilet or a bathroom?"

Cole pointed to the doorway in the corner. "The bath is through there. The toilet is in there, too."

Maisy stepped over the corpse and opened the door to the lavatory. A quick look inside revealed a space in the same condition as the two bedrooms; everything clean and in the proper place. She moved back into the bedroom, stepped over the deceased, stopped, and stared at the floor.

"Do you see this?"

"See what?"

Maisy pointed at a spot directly in front of her. "There's a nicotine stain on the floor about the length of a regular cigarette. Come here and see for yourself."

Cole did as she bade him to do. "All right, there's a nicotine stain on the floor. So what?"

"Didn't you notice the ashtrays in the other rooms?"

"Yes, I did. Why?"

Before Maisy could answer, the rumble of an Indian motorcycle reverberated from the street, growing louder as it came closer to the house. A few seconds later the noise ceased.

Agitation gripped Cole. "That would be a member of the Los Angeles Police Department's Speed Squad. We need to get out of this room, Maisy. Now!" He grabbed Maisy by the arm and pulled her from the bedroom into the kitchen and from there into the dining room.

"Let go of me, Milo."

"Don't you get it? The police are here."

"Are you sure?"

Cole pointed toward the screen door. "Look for yourself."

Reluctantly, Maisy did as she was told and saw a policeman wearing a blue tweed riding cap, blue tweed coat, leather riding gloves, and leather trousers tucked into black riding boots approaching the steps to the porch. The officer carried a Colt's .45 in a holster on his right hip and held a nightstick in his right hand.

"He certainly got here fast, didn't he?"

"Those guys sit by call boxes and wait for a call from the main station downtown. Hollywood Boulevard is the busiest street around here. He was probably only a few blocks from here when he got the call."

Maisy sneered at him. "Thanks for the tip. If I ever decide to rob a bank here in Los Angeles, I'll keep that in mind."

The patrolman stepped on to the porch, came to the door, and opened it without knocking. He squinted in the dimmer interior light.

"You the gent who called in about finding a dead body?"

"Yes, officer, I am. Milo Cole … at your service."

"You know, Milo, you sound like a butler when you say that."

"That's because I played a butler on stage once. Longest job—"

The patrolman interrupted Cole. "Where's the body, sir?"

A bit peevish at the policeman for cutting him short Cole jabbed a thumb over his shoulder. "He's in the back bedroom. His name is …"

The officer stormed past Cole and Maisy to the kitchen.

"I guess he doesn't care about your friend's name."

"I guess not."

Stopping in front of the bedroom doorway, the patrolman leaned forward slightly, nodded, tightened his jaw, and abruptly marched back into the dining room.

"Where's the telephone?"

Cole pointed to it. "Over there on the desk."

No gratitude, no courteous acknowledgement of any kind. The cop simply went to the telephone and placed a call, speaking loud enough for Maisy and Cole to overhear him from where they stood in the dining room.

"Yes, Sarge, he's dead all right. Better send a hearse for him." Pause. "No, I don't have any idea how he died. He's just lying there on the floor … dead." Another pause. "Just a minute and I'll ask them." He turned to Cole and Maisy. "How'd that guy die?"

The actors answered simultaneously.

"Suffocated," said Cole.

"Murdered," said Maisy.

The policeman glared at them one at a time. "What did you say?"

Maisy and Cole peered at each other.

"Ladies first."

Maisy wanted to respond with "Who are you calling a lady?" Instead, she took the higher road. "No, you first. He was your friend."

Cole shrugged and turned his focus back to the officer. "He suffocated."

Maisy's turn. "And I said he was murdered."

The patrolman grimaced at them with his jaw jutting outward. "So how do you know he suffocated to death, mister?"

Annoyed now, Cole glared back at the officer. "His name is Leslie Clover. He was my friend. I know he suffocated because he's wearing a corset that was too tight on him."

"He was you friend, eh? A dead man wearing a corset, and you say you're his friend. You some kind of freak like him?"

Cole stiffened to attention, burning with the urge to punch the cop squarely in the nose, but before he could take any such action, Maisy stepped in front of him.

"Officer, Mr. Clover was an actor, and whether you know it or not, lots of actors, including men, wear corsets on stage for one reason or another.

I'm sure that's why the deceased is wearing a corset."

"But he ain't on stage now, is he, miss?"

Cole stepped up beside Maisy and addressed the lawman through clenched teeth. "That still doesn't mean he's what you're thinking about him."

"You better change your attitude, mister, before I tell the sergeant here to send the wagon for you." Then realizing his superior was waiting on the other end of the telephone line, he spoke into the mouthpiece again. "Sorry, Sarge. These two nuts can't get their stories straight. The gent says the dead guy suffocated, and the lady says he was murdered." Pause. "Okay, I'll ask her." He aimed a cold stare at Maisy. "Okay, miss, if he was murdered, how was it done? I don't see no blood on him."

Irritated by the officer's tone of voice, Maisy heaved a sigh to calm herself before answering. "He was suffocated to death."

"But you said he was murdered."

"Yes, he was. *Somebody* suffocated him, probably with a pillow or with their hands."

"And how do you know that? You got some kind of woman's intuition that tells you he was suffocated with a pillow or somebody's hands?"

"No, I just took a look at the body, and I know he wasn't killed from the corset being too tight."

The patrolman frowned at her a second before speaking into the telephone again. "Sarge, the lady says the dead guy was suffocated all right, but it was done by somebody using a pillow or their hands." Pause. "No, I didn't see no signs of anything like that. The room's as neat as a pin, and there's no blood anywhere to be seen." Another pause. "Okay, Sarge. Do you want me to wait here for him?" One more pause. "Okay, I'll do that. 'Bye, Sarge." He replaced the telephone on the desk.

"Sarge says for me to wait here and for you two to stay here as well. Detective Browning is coming out here from downtown to question the two of you and inspect the premises. Until then, the two of you can have a seat on the couch there. Something tells me there's a lot more to this guy croaking than you two are letting on." He winked at them. "And you can rest assured, if there is, Detective Browning will get it out of you."

Maisy took one last look at the dining room table before she followed Cole into living room and sat down beside him on the sofa.

"I can't wait for that detective to show up. Have I got an earful for him."

Cole grimaced at Maisy. "Just who do you think you are? Sherlock Holmes?"

Maisy smiled back at him. "No, Dr.Watson, I'm not *Sherlock* Holmes. I'm *Shirley* Holmes, Sherlock's *smarter* sister."

Dressed to the nines in a slate gray suit with a navy blue vest, white shirt, maroon cravat, and navy blue bowler, Detective Sergeant James Edward Browning entered the house on Alexandria Avenue as if he owned the place.

Maisy took one look at Browning's olive green eyes, nudged Cole sitting beside her on the sofa, and leaned close to the actor to whisper to him. "Now there's a charmer, if ever I saw one."

Cole whispered back. "Down, girl. I'm the fellow who brought you to this dance, remember?"

"Well, if this is your idea of showing a girl a good time, then—"

The patrolman interrupted. "Quiet, you two! This is Detective Sergeant Browning. He's in charge here now."

"Thank you, Kronchie."

Maisy giggled. "Kronchie? What kind of name is that?"

"It's Officer Kronschnable to you, miss, and don't you forget it. Only my friends and superiors in the department get to call me Kronchie. Got it?"

Browning patted the patrolman on the shoulder. "Take it easy, Kronchie." He spoke with a distinct southern drawl. "I'm sure the lady meant no disrespect." He focused on Maisy, an inviting smile on his handsome face distinguished by a full umber brown mustache. Doffing his hat to her, he revealed a thick head of wavy hair combed straight back that matched his whiskers in color perfectly. "Detective Sergeant Edward Browning, ma'am. And you are?"

Maisy squirmed away from Cole and smiled coyly at Browning. "I am anything you want me to be, Detective Browning."

The policeman grinned at her. "Right now, I would like you to be co-operative with me as I investigate this … unfortunate occurrence. So would you mind telling me your name please?"

"May Zelda Malone, but my friends call me Maisy. That's with a 'Y' at the end, not an 'I E'."

"I shall call you Miss Malone."

"No need to be so formal, Detective Browning."

Browning aimed his left hand in her direction to show her the gold wedding band he wore. "I'm afraid there is, Miss Malone."

Maisy feigned a pout. "You're not much of a sport, Detective."

"I'm not paid to be a sport, Miss Malone. I'm paid to investigate crimes in our fair city."

"You're fair city? You're not from around here." She tilted her head to the left as she studied him. "You're from the South." She bent it the opposite way. "Georgia ... from the sound of your voice."

Browning jerked backward with surprise. "Now how in the world did you guess that?"

"No guess, Detective. One of my grandmothers is from Georgia, and your drawl is almost identical to hers. Besides that, I've made it a practice of listening to people's voices to try to figure out where they come from. I've known a few mentalists in Vaudeville who do the same thing. Really shakes up the rubes when you get it right."

"And you think I'm a rube?"

"Not now, but you were when you lived in Georgia. Couldn't wait to get off the farm, could you?"

Browning studied her for a moment, then smiled, refusing to let her get the upper hand on him. "You are the clever one, Miss Malone."

"Maybe more than you think. Stick around for the next show, why don't you?"

"Wouldn't miss it." He turned to Cole. "And you, sir, are ...?"

"Milo Cole ... at your service, Detective Browning."

"I understand you made the report of finding a dead body on these premises. Is that correct, Mr. Cole?"

"Yes, sir, it is. My friend Leslie Clover lives here. Or I should say lived here. He's in the back bedroom on the floor. Dead."

"Dead? Are you certain?"

"Pretty sure, Detective."

"Well, I'll see about that in a moment, but first I'd like to know if that Cadillac with the colored driver belongs to you, Mr. Cole."

"No, it belongs to the Keystone Moving Picture Studio in Edendale where I work."

"So why are you two here this morning?"

"We came to pick up Leslie and take him to the studio with us."

"You're both moving picture actors? You and Mr. Clover, I mean."

"Yes, we are."

Maisy smiled and batted her eyes at Browning. "And I hope to be."

"So what prompted you to enter the premises, Mr. Cole? Do you live here as well?"

"No, this is Leslie's house."

"Does he own it or rent it?"

Cole shrugged. "I don't know."

"And you say he's a moving picture actor like you?"

"Yes, sir."

"You moving picture actors must be paid quite well, Mr. Cole."

"I wish we were, but we're not. I can barely afford a one-room apartment at the Beverly."

"But your friend could afford to live here? He must have been doing well in your business."

"I guess he was."

"Yes, of course." Browning paused for a second before resuming his original line of questioning. "So tell me what prompted you to enter the premises uninvited, Mr. Cole."

"When I was at the front door, I thought I heard a noise inside, but Leslie hadn't answered me."

"You heard a noise? What sort of noise?"

"A hinge creaking."

"A door hinge?"

Cole nodded. "Yes, that's right."

Maisy leaned away from him. "You didn't tell me about hearing a door hinge creaking."

"You didn't ask. Detective Browning did."

Browning glanced toward the rear of the bungalow. "Would you folks mind waiting a bit, while I examine the body and have a look around the house?"

Maisy popped to her feet. "May I come with you? I'd like to show you a few things."

The detective inclined his head toward her, a patronizing smile turning up the corners of his mouth. "If you don't mind, Miss Malone, I'd rather you left the police work to me."

"But I can show you how I know he was murdered and didn't die accidentally from the corset being too tight."

"I believe I can determine that on my own, Miss Malone." Browning replaced his bowler on his head and gave Maisy another denigrating grin. "Now if you will excuse me, Miss Malone, I have my job to do." He nodded at Cole and disappeared around the corner.

Perturbed at being snubbed, Maisy plopped down on the sofa again and leaned against Cole. "I'll bet you a three-cent nickel he won't figure out your friend was murdered."

Cole looked askance at her. "A three-cent nickel? They don't make those anymore."

"I know, but my daddy has a stoneware crock full of three-cent nickels. He got them from our postmaster who didn't like handling them. Adding up all those threes was too much for him. He could count by ones and even by twos, but counting by threes was outside the limits of his smarts. Daddy would trade the postmaster a shield nickel for every two three-cent pieces he had. Daddy had just a few more smarts than the postmaster." She picked up her purse, opened it, and withdrew a three-cent nickel from a side compartment for coins. "I keep a few in here just in case someone else has one and wants to take me up on the bet."

"Has anybody ever accepted a bet with you for one of those coins?"

Maisy smiled. "I never bet on anything that I know isn't a sure thing." She replaced the coin in her purse. "How do you think I got the extra ones?"

"You're that positive Leslie was murdered?"

"I am."

Cole sighed. "On the one hand, I hope you're wrong. But on the other, if you're right, I hope they catch the bastard who did it and soon. Leslie was a good chap as they say in England. He knew comedy, and I think he would have done well in motion pictures. Mr. Sennett only saw him the one time in New York when Leslie was with the Fred Karno Troupe from England. When the troupe went back to England in April, Leslie came out here hoping to get a job in the movies with Carl Laemmle's Independent Motion Picture Company in Hollywood or with Selig's Polyscope studio, but Polyscope already had plenty of heavyset actors hanging around the lot hoping to get a chance at a role in a comedy. Leslie worked as an extra and sometimes as a bit actor doing small parts occasionally at whatever studio would give him a job. That paid just enough for him to make ends meet. Sometimes he rented out his extra room by the day to help out another actor, but he never wanted anybody staying here for too long. Interfered with him romancing the young ladies."

Browning emerged from the master bedroom to the kitchen and came back to the living room. He turned the closest armchair to the sofa toward the actors, took a small notebook and pencil from an inside pocket of his jacket, and sat down to talk to them again.

"Well, it certainly looks to me like your friend in there died from asphyxiation. I figure he tied his corset a lot too tight, and it gradually deprived him of the air he needed to stay alive."

Maisy groaned. "Aw, come on, Detective. Didn't you notice how nice and neat he was laying there?"

"Sure, I did. I figured you two put him in that position."

"Do we look like a couple of undertakers?"

Cole jumped into the conversation. "We found him that way, Detective Browning. We did roll him onto his side once, but we put him back exactly the way we found him."

"You touched the body?"

Maisy poked Cole in the ribs with an elbow. "Why'd you go and tell him that? Now he's going to think we did other stuff in there."

"You're exactly right, Miss Malone. What else did the two of you do in there before Officer Kronschnable arrived?"

"Nothing except look around like you just did. The only thing we touched was the body just like Milo said."

Browning wrote in his notes. "You said your name is May Zelda Malone, right?"

"That's right."

"And people call you Maisy with a 'Y' at the end?"

"Correct again."

"And your full name, Mr. Cole?"

Feeling under pressure here, Cole cleared his throat before answering. "My real first name or my stage name?"

"Let's start with your real first name."

"Milos Radek Kolar."

Curiosity struck Browning. "What kind of name is that?"

Before Cole could reply, Maisy interrupted. "I know."

The detective smiled with surprise. "You know?"

"Sure, I do. I told you already—"

Browning's head bobbed. "Yes, I remember. You make it a practice to study people's voices. So I suppose you also make it a practice to study people's names as well."

"Among others. You can never learn enough in this life, my mother always said."

"Your mother sounds like a very smart lady."

"Maybe the smartest lady in the Blue River valley."

"Okay, Miss Malone, what do you know about his real name?"

"It's Bohemian, isn't it, Milo."

Cole was totally taken aback. "Now how in the world did you know that?"

"Yes, Miss Malone, how did you know that?"

Maisy turned to Cole. "I'll bet you a three-cent nickel all four of your grandparents came to America before the Civil War and your mother was either born here or she was just a little girl when her parents came here."

"That's incredible, Maisy. How did you know that? I mean that my mother was born here."

"In the first place, you don't have any kind of foreign accent, which tells me you were born in America and your mother grew up here, whether she was born in America or in the old country. Children learn to talk mostly from their mother's because they are around her more when they're small. Since you have absolutely no accent, I'd have to say your father also grew up here as well as your mother. They still knew the language they learned from their parents, but they didn't speak it as much. English was their first language, while whatever Bohemian dialect they learned from your grandparents became their second language here in America.

"And you're educated. You went at least through high school, and you might have attended an eastern college because you sound a bit like some of the college boy snobs who were always waiting for me at the stage door to try sweet-talking me into stepping out with them. For some reason those rich college boys think women in show business are easy. Well, not this one."

Milo cleared his throat, slightly embarrassed by Maisy's insinuation. "You're right again, Maisy. I did graduate from high school. New Haven, Connecticut, Class of 1907."

"I thought you sounded an awful lot like some of those Yale boys, but I'll bet you couldn't get in there because of your family, right?"

Cole shrugged off the remark.

Browning shook his head. "I must admit I am impressed, Miss Malone. But how did you know his name was Bohemian and not some other European name?"

"Oh, that was easy. I knew a stagehand in Chicago whose name was Milos Kovac whose parents were from Bohemia. As soon as Milo said his real name, I knew he had to be a Bohunk of some kind." She nudged Milo in the ribs and winked at him to show him she was only teasing. "Actually, Milo here is a pretty classy guy. A real gent, if you know what I mean, Detective Browning."

"Yes, I believe I do. So what is your full *stage* name, Mr. Cole?"

"Milo Randolph Cole. I tried to make it sound as American as I could. Did you know Mr. Sennett's real name is spelled S-I-N-N-O-T-T and his real first name is Mikall and is spelled M-I-K-A-L-L and he's an Irish-Canadian? He changed his name for the stage as well."

"I'm getting the impression all you show business people change your real names to some stage name."

Maisy nodded. "You'd be right about that. I don't know hardly a soul in the business who goes by his or her real name. How about you, Milo? Do you know anybody who goes by their real name?"

"Oh, there's a few, although I can't think of any right at this moment … except poor Leslie in the other room. That was his real name, Detective Browning. He told me so. But he never told me his middle name, if he had one."

"Now getting back to you, Miss Malone. I take it your real name is not May Zelda Malone."

"Yes, it is. I only go by Maisy professionally."

"Malone is your real last name?"

"It is now."

"What was it before it was Malone?"

"McGillicuddy."

"How do you spell that?"

Maisy spelled it for him. "That's Irish as well. Taking another Irish surname made it easier for me to remember what country my people came from."

Browning nodded. "And your real first name is May?"

Maisy shook her head. "No, actually, my real first name is Zelda and my middle name is May. I switched them around because too many people kept asking me if I was Jewish. Not that I have anything against being Jewish, because I know a lot of Jewish people and nearly all the ones I know are my friends. Good, decent folks all of them."

The policeman looked at Maisy suspiciously, wondering if she was telling him the full truth or just spreading horse manure all over the south forty. Before he could decide which, an idea struck him.

"You know what, Miss Malone? I think it would behoove me—in light of how you knew I am originally from Georgia and how you figured out Mr. Cole's people came to America from Bohemia—I believe it would be in the best interests of my investigation into Mr. Clover's death to hear your theory on how he died."

Maisy's face suddenly glowed as if the morning sun had just begun to shine on her. "For real, Detective Browning? You want to hear why I think he was murdered?"

"I would be remiss in my duty, if I didn't."

"Well, come on then." She popped up from the sofa. "Let me show you what makes me think he was murdered."

Browning stood up slowly. "Kronchie, while Miss Malone and I have another look around the place, why don't you call into the Hollywood Station and have them send out a wagon to pick up the deceased and take him downtown to the county morgue?"

"Sure thing, Lieutenant."

"Mr. Cole, I hope you don't mind waiting a bit longer."

Milo threw up his hands. "Why should I mind? My good friend is dead, and the man I'm hoping will give me a regular acting job in his studio is probably pacing up and down wondering why I haven't shown up yet with Maisy and Leslie. Wait a little longer? Why not? Take all day, if you must. I'll be right here on the sofa when you're done." He folded his hands behind his head and leaned back on the couch.

Maisy frowned at Cole. "You're becoming a grouch, Milo. This won't take long. I promise."

Browning winked at Cole. "I promise as well, sir." He waved a hand toward the kitchen. "After you, Miss Malone."

"We'll start in the dining room."

"The dining room?"

"Yes, the dining room." Maisy peered at him with incredulity in her eyes. "Do you mean you didn't inspect the dining room?"

"Never mind that, Miss Malone. You just tell me what you think is so important in the dining room."

Maisy glared at him. "Just look at the table and tell me what you see."

"I see a mess of newspapers and magazines and some dirty dishes."

"It's what you don't see that matters here, Detective Browning."

"What I *don't* see? I don't follow you, Miss Malone."

"What's missing from the table, Detective?"

Browning stared at it for several seconds. "I give up. Tell me, what's missing from the table."

"There are two plates, but only one has any flatware with it and only one has a cup *and* saucer with it. The other one only has a saucer."

"So?"

"So both plates have egg yolk on them."

The policeman mulled over her remark for a few seconds. "Are you trying to tell me the deceased had a guest for breakfast?"

Maisy shook her head. "Boy, you're a real quick study, Detective. Yes, that's precisely what I'm trying to tell you."

"If he had a guest for breakfast, then where are the flatware and the cup *you think* was on that saucer?"

"I don't think, Detective. I know it was there. Can't you see the ring of a coffee stain on the saucer?"

Browning leaned over the table for a closer view. "Yes, I see what you mean. There is a coffee stain on the saucer. But that still doesn't mean he had a guest for breakfast."

Maisy heaved a sigh. "Moving right along, Detective. Take a look in the spare bedroom and tell me what you see."

He poked his head through the doorway. "I see a room as neat as a pin without a thing out of place."

"Very good, Detective. Now let's go into the kitchen." She led him through the doorway. "What do you see in here?"

"Another messy room and a sink full of dirty dishes."

"Yes, but not all the dishes are dirty, Detective. Do you see that cup, fork, spoon, and table knife on the counter?"

"Yes. What about them?"

"They're spotless, Detective."

"So?"

"What was missing from the table?"

Browning hesitated a second before replying. "You think that cup and flatware are the missing items from the dining room table?"

"Don't you?"

"It could be mere coincidence, Miss Malone."

"Really?"

Browning nodded.

"Okay, let's go in the bedroom." Maisy turned to enter, glancing furtively toward the rear door of the house and through the window to see a house under construction on the next street over. She nodded in its direction and blinked simultaneously, as if she were taking a mental snapshot of the scene outside.

Browning followed Maisy into the bed chamber. "So what's out of place in here, Miss Malone? Curtains closed too tight or something like that?"

"Did you see the nicotine stain on the floor?"

"What about it?"

"It's brand spanking new, that's what about it."

"How can you tell that?"

"Compare the sheen on it to the rest of the floor. This was made just this morning."

Browning frowned. "Or it could have been made last night or sometime yesterday. How else would you explain that there are no ashes on the floor?"

"Somebody cleaned them up, Detective."

"Of course, someone cleaned them up." A hint of triumph accented Browning's voice. "The deceased cleaned them up."

"Have you really looked at this place, Detective? The bedrooms are neat as pins, and the rest of the house looks like a twister blew through it. Mr. Clover here was not that meticulous about his housekeeping. Ask Milo. He'll tell you the same thing. Did you look in the bathroom?"

"Yes."

"See anything out of place in there?"

"Nothing."

"Then why don't you get it, Detective? Someone was here this morning and had breakfast with Mr. Clover and then cleaned up some after he was dead."

"Now why would someone do that?"

"To hide the fact that he or she was here, which is why the cup and flatware were washed."

"Now why would *he or she* do that?"

"To get rid of any trace that *he or she* was here this morning."

"And how do you know *he or she* was here this morning and not last night?"

"The corpse was still limp when Milo and I rolled him on his side."

Browning bent down and lifted Clover's arm. It moved fairly easily. He released it, came erect again, and pulled his pocket watch from his right vest pocket.

"A little past eleven o'clock. Rigor mortis hasn't begun yet, so he couldn't have died any earlier than eight this morning. And since there's some definite lividity, I'd have to say he's been dead over an hour. This means he died between eight o'clock and ten o'clock this morning."

Browning shook his head. "You still have no proof that he was murdered, Miss Malone." He held up his left hand to keep her from interrupting him. "I will admit that it's possible he was murdered, but until I have at least one piece of evidence to prove he was murdered, I have to take the point of view that his death was an accident. He died of asphyxiation, that much is certain, and it was caused by the corset being too tight."

"There you go, Detective Browning. The corset was too tight. Now how in the world did *he* get the corset too tight all by himself?"

Browning replaced his watch in his vest. "I've watched my wife don her corset, and I can tell you she gets it pretty darn tight sometimes."

"Yes, but does she get it so tight that there's a good inch of fat bulging over the top of it?"

Browning glared at Maisy. "I'll have you know my wife is not fat, Miss Malone."

"I didn't mean to imply that she is. I'm only trying to make a point here. Does she ever get it so tight that there's *any* fat bulging over the top of it?"

Browning had to think about that for a moment before answering. "I can't say that I've ever seen that much of her bulging over the top of her corset."

"Well, there's at least that much bulging over the top of this man's corset. Wouldn't you agree?"

"I can't rightly tell, Miss Malone. With the corpse on his back like that—"

"Then let's sit him up and see how he looks then."

"Sit him up?"

"Sure. You get on one side, and I'll get on the other. We'll sit him up together."

"All right, we'll do it, but only to prove the point."

They knelt down, one on each side of Clover. Each took him by an arm with one hand and placed the other hand under the shoulder on the same side.

Browning made eye contact with Maisy. "Ready?"

"On the count of three?"

"On three."

Together, they spoke the numbers and then lifted Clover into a sitting position, although with a mild degree of difficulty.

"He's getting a little stiff already," said Maisy.

"Yes, rigor mortis is beginning to set in."

"So he died closer to eight than to ten, right?"

Browning nodded. "I have to agree with you there, but it still doesn't mean he was murdered. You still have no proof of that. Therefore, I have to stick to my original determination that his death was an accident from the corset being too tight."

Maisy was incredulous. "You really believe that, don't you?"

"I have to go by the facts at hand, Miss Malone. Until I get a piece of evidence that confirms your suspicion, I have no choice but to assume Mr. Clover died accidentally."

Browning's preliminary determination that Leslie Clover's death was an accident totally riled Maisy and put her in a most disagreeable mood to say the least. And with Maisy that meant speaking her mind until she felt her point was made and made again, which she was doing as she and Cole rode in the Cadillac to Edendale.

"I'm telling you, Milo, that man wouldn't recognize a murder, even if he had a smoking gun in one hand and a corpse with a bullet hole in the other. He'd probably call it a suicide or say the victim *accidentally* shot himself."

"Oh, I don't know, Maisy. He seemed like he knew what he was doing."

"Are you kidding me? The man is totally incompetent. Asphyxiation by *accident* from a corset. Unbelievable. One person cannot get a corset tight enough all alone by himself or herself, no matter how hard he or she tries. The strings will come loose before you can tie the bow, providing, of course, that you can tie a bow behind your back in the first place. You can get one on by yourself simply by lacing up the strings before you put it on and then doing up the hooks-and-eyes in the front. But if you do it that way, you can't get it tight enough to keep you from breathing normally. If you want it really tight, then it takes another person to help you. I know. I've tried it by myself. It can't be done. Somebody pulled those strings so tight that he passed out, and then whoever that person was smothered him with something. Probably a pillow."

"A pillow? Really?"

Hearing Cole repeat the word banged the gong in Maisy's brain. "Yes, a pillow. Milo, we didn't look at the pillows."

"We were told not to touch anything."

"Not you and me *we*. Browning and me *we*. Browning and I didn't look at the pillows. Come on. We have to go back there right now and have a look at those pillows."

"You and Browning?"

"Of course not, me and Browning. You and I need to go back there right now."

"Maisy, we're almost to the studio. We can't go back now. Mr. Sennett will probably be furious with us as it is for being so late. We were supposed to be at the studio by ten-thirty, and now it's already past noon. We're late, and Leslie, who is supposed to be going with us to Edendale, is probably on his way to the county morgue by now. And most of all, his death is police business, not ours."

"But, Milo, Detective Browning is positive your friend's death was an accident, and I know it was murder. Don't you care enough about him to make certain it was one or the other?"

"Sure, I do, but not right now. Now we have to get to the studio and see Mr. Sennett about you working for him."

Willie turned the Cadillac off Sunset Boulevard onto Allesandro Street and drove a short distance up the hill where he turned the car through the gateway to a dirt driveway to the left front of a small, somewhat dilapidated bungalow on the west side of the street. A recently painted sign next to the front door read: *Mack Sennett, Keystone Pictures.*

"Well, this is it."

Unimpressed, Maisy frowned as she peered through the car's window. "This little house is the studio?"

"No, this is Mr. Sennett's living quarters. The studio is out back." Cole pointed to a large barn behind the house. "The New York Motion Picture Company bought this place three years ago because it was so close to Mr. Selig's studio just up the street from here. That's it with all the Spanish architecture buildings, including the arched entrance to the lot. Pretty impressive, isn't it?"

"It certainly is."

"The New York company sent Fred Balshofer out here to make westerns under the Bison Motion Pictures name. Last November, he went back to New York, and Mr. Thomas Ince came out here to replace him. Mr. Ince only made three films here before moving the outdoor part of his operation to the Bison Ranch out in the Santa Monica Hills. He's building a whole new studio complex out there. This studio here sat empty and unused for several months until Mr. Sennett and his comedy ensemble arrived here at the end of last month to reopen it under its current name."

Maisy sighed. "Well, are we just going to sit here and wait for someone to come out and meet us?"

"No, of course not." Milo opened his door and dashed around the rear of the Cadillac to open Maisy's door for her. "Right this way, Miss Malone. Your future awaits you." He bowed facetiously with a flourish of a wave toward the house.

Maisy emerged from the car and marched up to the bungalow's porch steps without waiting for Cole. She had every intention of storming the place unassisted.

"Maisy, wait!"

Sensing urgency in his voice, she complied, stopping a heartbeat before taking the first step up to the porch. She turned to see him hurrying up to her.

"I told you the bungalow is where Mr. Sennett lives. The office and studio are in that big barn behind the house. Now come with me."

Cole offered her his arm, which she took with some reservation, and he led her around the smaller structure to the larger one in the rear. They turned the corner to the north end of the building and discovered dozens of workmen—carpenters, electricians, painters, masons, plumbers, and all their apprentices and general laborers—sitting in the shade, eating their lunches. Many of them whistled and some made crude remarks about Maisy's looks and shapely hips when she came into sight with Cole.

Maisy stopped to let them get a good look at her, and she smiled to show her appreciation for their good taste in the gentler sex. "Afternoon, gents. Anybody got a pastrami on rye he'd like to share? A girl can't live on love alone, you know."

To a man, they all stopped chewing and went totally silent for several seconds until one youthful apprentice jumped to his feet. "I got pastrami on rye, ma'am."

"With mustard and pickles?"

His head drooped forward. "Naw, just sauerkraut."

"Fine meat … like pastrami … should never be *eaten* without putting the mustard and relish to it." She winked at the kid as all the others broke out in raucous laughter. "Don't ever forget who told you that first, sonny. The name is Maisy Malone, and I'm here to make moving pictures with Mr. Sennett. See you all in the movies."

Amid a jumble of friendly replies from the workmen, Cole tugged her into motion again and guided her toward the entrance to the studio. He opened the door and let her pass through it ahead of him.

The interior seemed more like a dark cave than a motion picture studio; at least until their eyes adjusted from the bright sunshine outside to the dimmer light inside.

"Mr. Sennett is making a lot of changes and additions to the property. This place was really a mess when he got here. Mr. Ince took everything of use with him to the new studio he's building up in Santa Ynez Canyon between Santa Monica and Malibu."

"You said that already."

"Oh, yes, of course. Anyway, the carpenters here have already remodeled the dressing rooms inside the old barn for both men and women actors as well as the costume room, the storage room, the laboratory, and a cutting and viewing room. Mr. Sennett likes to be able to see everything, so they built him a temporary office in what used to be the hayloft. That's it up there. That's the first thing Mr. Sennett added to the place. All of this is temporary. Mr. Sennett already has plans to expand the studio to cover the whole lot. As soon as the new building is done, the old barn here will be torn down and replaced by a bigger and better studio building." He pointed to a large room at the top of a wide flight of wooden stairs. A single window faced the rest of the studio. "He and Miss Normand and the other lead actors usually take their lunch break up there."

"Should we go up now or wait until they're done eating?"

"I think we should go now. If we wait, I think it will only upset him all the more. Mr. Sennett is not a very patient man. Besides, as soon as they finish their meal, he'll want to go back to work immediately. So let's get up there."

Maisy and Cole climbed the stairs side-by-side. When they reached the landing at the top, they stopped to straighten their clothes. They could hear one muffled voice from within.

"That would be Mr. Sennett," whispered Cole. "Ready?"

"Ready as I'll ever be."

Cole nodded nervously, then tapped a few knuckles on the door's frosted glass window, which had "Mr. Sennett's Office" painted in gold leaf on it. The voice inside said a few more words before going silent. They heard a couple of footfalls, and then the door opened, revealing a muscular man with a square jaw and matching head. Blocking their view of the room's interior, he gave Maisy the once-over before he even noticed Cole. Having seen dozens of moving pictures, especially comedies, Maisy recognized him as Henry Lehrman, actor and director.

"We were just talking about you, Milo," he said with a slight German accent. "You must be Miss Malone."

"Yes, I am."

Lehrman turned to someone inside. "It's Milo and Miss Malone." A half second more and he opened the door completely to allow them to enter the office. As soon as they stepped inside, he closed the door behind them.

Maisy made a quick survey of the people looking back at her. Mack Sennett sat behind the only desk in the room. Mabel Normand sat to his left in a leather armchair. Comic actor Fred Mace sat in a straight-back wooden chair to Sennett's right. Close to Mabel in another straight-back sat Alice Davenport, and to her left was Ford Sterling.

Lehrman returned to his straight-back near Mace.

Sennett appeared to be very displeased at the moment. "Where have you been, Milo? You should have been back here a couple of hours ago."

Cole cleared his throat before speaking. "Mr. Sennett, we're sorry to interrupt your lunch."

"*We're sorry?* Why are you apologizing for Miss Malone? *You* were in charge of picking her up at the depot and bringing her out here with your pal Clover. Speaking of Clover, why isn't he with you? Is he why you're late?"

Cole's head bobbed from one side to the other a couple of times as he searched nervously for the right words to say to Sennett.

Maisy had no such difficulty. "Mr. Clover is dead, Mr. Sennett."

This was the last thing Sennett or any of the other five people in the room expected to hear. Their faces paled and appeared frozen with shock at the dreadful news.

Mabel was the first to regain her composure. "He's dead?"

Maisy looked her straight in the eye as if she had known the actress for years, which she had, if only on the motion picture screen. "Yes, Miss Normand. He was murdered just this morning."

To a person, the six seated people gasped, and then muttered the questions Mabel asked clearly succinctly above all their chatter.

"Murdered? How?"

"Now we don't know that for certain, Miss Normand," said Cole, almost stuttering.

"You might not know for certain, Milo," said Maisy testily, "but I know he was murdered. Nobody dies from a corset being too tight. They only faint. Isn't that right, Miss Davenport? I'm sure you've worn a corset a time or two like the rest of us women have. Have you ever seen or heard of anybody dying from their corset being too tight?"

"No, I can't say that I have."

"Detective Browning said he died accidentally from his corset being too tight," argued Cole.

Sennett straightened up in one jerk of his body. "Did you say *Detective* Browning? Are the police involved in this already?"

Cole's color left him. "Well, we found Leslie dead and—"

Maisy cut him off. "*You* found him dead. Not me. Get your facts straight, Milo, or let me tell it."

"All right, you tell it then since you think you know so much."

"I know more than you do, that's for damn sure."

Sennett slapped a hand on the desk, startling Cole and annoying Maisy. "Christ Almighty, you two act like you're married and you just met this morning. Knock off the bickering and one of you tell me what the hell happened to Clover."

Maisy took the lead. "We stopped to pick up Mr. Clover at his home. Milo went to get him. When he didn't answer the door, Milo went inside and found Mr. Clover on the floor of his bedroom. He was dead. Milo called the police. A motorcycle cop showed up first, and he called for a detective to come out and investigate. He made us wait for the detective to show up. Then this Detective Browning came to the house about twenty minutes later. He did some snooping around, and he questioned us about Mr. Clover and what we were doing there. I told him Mr. Clover was murdered, but he didn't believe me, even though I showed him all the evidence I had found. He said that wasn't enough to prove a murder, so he determined Mr. Clover died from asphyxiation from his corset being too tight. Then he sent us on our way, and now here we are."

Sennett frowned a second before looking straight at Mace. "Looks like we'll have to put *A Double Wedding* on the back burner for now, Freddie, while we find you another groom. Let's start looking right away. Time is money, don't you know? Start by taking a look at the extras who've been hanging around. Maybe we'll get lucky and find somebody there." He focused on Maisy. "I had hoped to get you in here earlier, Maisy. You and Leslie Clover. The plan was to get the two of you in makeup and Henry here would do a screen test to see how you two would look and act in front of the camera. That was supposed to happen while the rest of us were having our lunch, but as you can see it's too late for that now. With Clover dead, poor fellow, God rest his soul, that won't be happening."

"I'm sorry, Mr. Sennett," said Cole.

"Forget it, Milo. It's not your fault Clover is dead." Sennett twisted his head to one side. "It isn't, is it? I mean you didn't kill him, did you?"

The question stung Cole so sharply that his lips quivered too much to form a reply.

Maisy recognized Sennett was only joking and decided to add her own spark to the gag. "You know, Milo, you were in the house by yourself several minutes before I came in. Plenty of time to smother him with a pillow if he was already passed out."

Her remark revived Cole's senses. He turned on Maisy in an instant. "You and Detective Browning proved Leslie had been dead long before we got there."

"Relax, Milo. Mr. Sennett was only pulling your leg, and so was I."

Cole could only sputter a response. "I know he was, but you were dead serious."

"You know, Mack," said Alice, "I think you're right. These two stopped off somewhere along the way here and got married. Will you listen to how they bitch at each other?"

Sennett laughed for the first time. "Take it easy, Milo. Maisy's right. I was only pulling your leg. We all know you're too much of a Nancy boy to murder anybody."

This brought a round of laughter from the others in the room.

Maisy saw the blush in Cole's face. "Again, Milo, he's only joking with you. Right, Mr. Sennett?"

The studio head nodded with a broad smile. "Of course, I'm only joking."

"Milo, how are you ever going to act in a comedy if you don't have a sense of humor?" asked Mabel.

"Milo's got a sense of humor," said Mace. "He keeps it under his pillow and only takes it out when he's dreaming of becoming an actor in a comedy. Ain't that right, Milo?"

More laughter all around.

Cole finally realized their teasing came from their good natures. "Yes, Fred, that's right. I keep it under my pillow at home, but you're mistaken about when I take it out."

Mace played along. "Oh, is that right?"

"Yes, it is. I only bring it out when I dream about you complaining so much about Miss Normand's cooking that she hits you in the face with a cream pie."

"Now that's funny." Mace followed up his words with a loud guffaw, leading all but Sennett and Mabel in the merriment.

"You know, Mabel," said Sennett quite seriously, "that's not a bad idea. I wonder if audiences would go for it."

"Sounds like a dandy idea to me. When do we do it?"

"First chance we get."

Mabel looked at Cole. "Got any other ideas like that one, Milo?"

"A few, I guess."

"Well, write them down whenever they come to you," said Sennett. "I pay good money for good ideas. Keep that in mind. For now, let's all get back to work. Maisy, you can hang around and watch what we do here, or I can have Willie take you back to the Hollywood Hotel right away if you'd rather do that."

"Oh, I'd like to stick around here and see how you make motion pictures, Mr. Sennett. There's no time like the present to start learning this business."

The studio head appeared pleased with her decision. "Milo, you continue to show Maisy around and explain things to her, but make sure you stay away from the workmen. They don't need any distractions."

"Wait a minute, Mack," said Mabel. "Why not have Milo take Maisy to get made up and then to wardrobe instead? And when she's done there, he can bring her to the set and you can use her as an extra. That will save Henry from having to do a screen test on her."

Sennett nodded. "That's a better idea. Okay with you, Maisy?"

She smiled at him. "Fair enough."

"Got that, Milo?"

"Yes, sir, Mr. Sennett. Makeup first, then wardrobe. Got it."

* * *

When Tom Ince moved the Bison operation to the Santa Monica Hills to make his westerns appear more authentic, he cleaned out all the makeup and costumes, which were primarily for horse operas anyway. Keystone had no trouble restocking the makeup shelves, but replacing the tables, chairs, and mirrors was another matter. The costuming department was pretty much the same. Hangers, racks, shelves, and furniture all had to be purchased and built from the floor up. Fortunately, they brought the small collection of furniture, accessories, and costumes the company had back in New York with them on the train.

While Katy Killoy, a pudgy woman nearing forty, who did makeup occasionally and managed the costume department all the time, applied greasepaint and powder to all the right places on Maisy's face, the newest member of the Keystone ensemble sat as still as possible, although she really wanted to chat with Cole. She had lots of questions for him and not all of them were about the motion picture business. The murder of his friend kept picking its way through the network of her brain synapses and pushing aside any thoughts of appearing in a real film for the first time in her life. Much to her disdain, Cole went outside to out of the stuffy, hot barn instead of hanging around to watch Maisy get made up.

Katy worked on Maisy, chatting so fast the whole time with a distinct touch of old Ireland in her voice that she sounded like a whole sewing circle all by herself. "Ain't it tragic about Mr. Clover that English actor dying this morning over in Hollywood? And he was so young, too. Almost twenty-five, I heard."

"How did you hear about it so soon?"

"Darlin', this is the moving picture business. Everything travels fast around here, especially something like an actor dying all sudden like. Willie Lopez the driver told the boys as soon as he brung you and Mr. Cole here to see Mr. Sennett. Pretty soon everybody on the lot knew about it. If you don't want nobody to know something around here, you best keep it to yourself because as soon as you tell it to one person it'll come back to haunt you before you know it. Of course, I'm telling you, and I hear you was there at his house this morning and helped find the body. One of the boys said Mr. Clover died from having his corset too tight."

"No, he was smothered to death."

"Well, ain't that the same thing?"

"No, it's not. Have you ever heard of anybody dying from their corset being too tight?"

Katy thought for a second. "Can't say that I have. I can tell you I've tied up many an actress in her stays during my time, and I can tie 'em as tight as anybody. But I ain't never known of one single girl to die from the corset being too tight. Faint maybe, but never kicked off from it."

"Me neither."

"So if he didn't die from the corset being too tight, then what do you suppose killed him?"

"He was probably smothered with a pillow."

"You don't say? Now why would anybody want to kill a nice young man like Mr. Clover?"

"That's a very good question, Katy, and I intend to find out."

The sometimes makeup artist chuckled. "Hey, you ain't some kind of Sherlock Holmes, now are you?"

Maisy winked at Katy. "No, I'm Shirley Holmes, his smarter sister."

The older woman gazed into the younger's eyes. "Yes, Darlin', I believe you are."

"Did you know Mr. Clover very well, Katy?"

"I can't say that I did. I did have him in this chair a time or two these past few weeks. He was an extra, don't you know? I believe it was only this past Tuesday that he was sitting right where you are now. He was sure in a good mood that day. He was saying something about getting a real part in one of Mr. Sennett's upcoming films. He said something about having to trim down a bit to play the part."

"Then that would explain why he was in a corset this morning when we found him. He was supposed to audition for a part that required a slimmer man. That rules out him being a Nancy boy like somebody suggested."

"Mr. Clover a Nancy boy? Oh, I don't think so."

"No? Why not?"

Katy shook her head. "I get a lot of the extra girls in this chair, and there's not a one of them can keep her yap shut while she's sitting here. They ain't all as polite as you, Darlin'. I guess it's because they're rather excited about getting to work that day or they're nervous about getting in front of the camera. Anyway, the general talk was Mr. Clover had a nice way with the girls. All of them seemed pretty happy with the … attention he give 'em."

"Then you'd say he was a ladies' man?"

"For sure, I would. The girls was all taken by him being from England and all."

"I lived in England for the better part of three years. None of those Limeys did it for me."

"Your people must have come from the grand isle then."

"No, I'm not Irish, Katy. My daddy's family was mostly Scottish with a little German and Swiss thrown in."

"The Scots came from Ireland first, so that explains why you don't fancy the Limeys."

Maisy shrugged. "Fair enough."

"But these girls waiting in the extras line all day to get a bit of work, so many of 'em down on their luck, they'll go to dinner with just about any man who asks them. And who knows what other kind of mischief they're willing to commit to get a decent meal?"

"The studio has only been open … how long now?"

The costume manager tilted her graying head skyward, as if the answer was written somewhere above her. "Let me see now. Mr. Sennett and Miss Normand came here on the twenty-eighth of last month, and Mr.

Sennett was here the next day telling all the workers what he wanted done with the place. He started shooting the first picture that afternoon because there was already some extras lining up looking for work. So that was four weeks ago today."

"Do you recall whether Mr. Clover was giving his *attention* to any one girl in particular?"

Katy gave the question a few seconds of thought. "I do recall seeing him with a couple of the girls more than once." She paused to admire her work. "You're all done, Darlin'." She winked at Maisy. "You're gonna knock 'em dead, kid, once you get in front of the camera. I know. I've been in this business for more than three years now. I started with the Bison Studio and made up all those cowboys and Indians for Mr. Balshofer and Mr. Ince when he came out last November and took over the studio. When Mr. Ince moved the business to the Santa Monica Hills, I quit because I've got a family and we live in Pasadena. It's just too far from my home for me to work for Mr. Ince. The Red Car goes out to Santa Monica, but not all the way to the ranch. It's too far to walk and all uphill in the morning. A body would be good and tired before even going to work every morning. So you have no idea how happy I was to read in *The Motion Picture World* magazine that Mr. Sennett and Miss Normand were going to reopen this studio. I was practically waiting here for them to arrive. I was one of Mr. Sennett's first re-hires. Now you go over to wardrobe, and I'll be over in a minute to get you in a proper costume."

"Just one more thing, Katy. Do you recall the names of the two girls you saw more than once with Mr. Clover?"

"No, not off hand." She winked at Maisy. "But I can sure-as-there's-a-God-in-heaven find out for you."

"Fair enough, Katy."

"Remember what I said, Darlin'. This is the moving picture business and word gets around quicker than lightning. Be careful *what* you say, and especially be careful *who* you say it to."

Much to Maisy's surprise she had company on the ride back to the Hollywood Hotel after sundown. She thought Milo would be riding with her, but since he lived in the Bunker Hill neighborhood, which was in a different direction, he took the Red Car home. So instead of Cole, she rode with Mabel Normand, Fred Mace, and Ford Sterling who were also guests at the luxurious resort. Mace and Sterling sat in front with Willie, both of them dozing, while the girls chatted in the back seat.

"You've had quite a day, Maisy. Arriving in Los Angeles on the train. Being driven around town in a big Cadillac. Discovering a murder. Being an extra in your first moving picture. That's a lot for a lady in a single day, and you handled it so well. How old did you say you are?"

Maisy felt a need to be honest with Mabel. "I turned nineteen only twelve days ago."

Mabel smiled. "Really? You seem so ... worldly for someone barely older than I am. I won't be nineteen until November."

"Really? But you seem so much more ... worldly, too. I mean—"

The film actress giggled. "I know what you mean, Maisy. Honestly, I thought you were well past twenty from the way you speak and behave. I'll bet you thought the same about me, didn't you?"

"I cannot tell a lie, Miss Normand. I did."

"Please call me Mabel. At least when we're together like this. At the studio, you might want to continue calling me Miss Normand. Mack kind of prefers that everybody who works there should address me so."

"Fair enough with me."

"You've been around, haven't you, Maisy? Vaudeville must have really taken you to a lot of different places, I suppose."

"I got around some. I spent the better part of three years in London."

"London? London, England?"

Maisy nodded. "I worked at the Royal Comedy Theatre, among other places, as a dresser mostly. Sometimes I got on stage as a stand-in when some girl was sick or something or just plain didn't show up in time to do her bit."

"Oh, how grand! And here I've never been more than fifty miles from New York until we came out here last month. And you've been to England. Did you get to any other countries in Europe?"

"I spent a short time in France, but it was so short it's hardly worth talking about."

"Did you go to Paris?"

"No, Cherbourg was the only place I went to in France."

"Cherbourg? Why does that sound familiar? Is it famous for something that I just cannot remember at this moment?"

"I don't know that it's famous for anything. It's just a town on the coast of France."

"Oh, I remember now. The *Titanic* stopped there before sailing for New York. That's where I know the name from. Did you get to see the *Titanic* while you were there?"

This was not a question Maisy wanted to answer, but she did anyway, in hopes that Mabel would be impressed rather than judgmental by the truth of it. "Well, yes, I did see the *Titanic*."

"Did you get to go aboard?"

"Yes, I did."

"Was it as grand as the newspapers said it was?"

"It certainly was that. What I saw of it, I mean."

"How thrilling that must have been! And to think how fortunate you are that you didn't sail on the *Titanic!*"

"Oh, I sailed on the *Titanic* all right. From Southampton to Cherbourg. That's how I got to France."

"You were a passenger on the *Titanic?*"

"Well, not exactly a passenger. More like a … an uninvited guest."

Mabel's brow furrowed with perplexity. "An uninvited guest? I don't quite follow you there."

Maisy sighed dreadfully. "I was a … stowaway."

Mabel gasped. "A stowaway?" Then she giggled. "Really? A stowaway? How exciting! And you were caught? How did you do it?"

"I bought a maid's uniform and cape in London, and when the rich people were boarding at Southampton, I pretended I was with one of them. When I was asked for my ticket, I told the officer my mistress had it, and he let me go aboard. Once we were at sea I went down to the third class level and mingled with the common people like me. I was doing all right until the same officer who had questioned me at the gangplank saw me in a passageway on my way to the washroom. He hauled me up to the bridge to see the captain, and he told the officer to lock me up until we docked in Cherbourg where I was to be handed over to the French police."

"What did the French police do?"

"They threw me in *la geôle*. That's one French word I'll never forget. Lucky for me, French men are suckers for *l'amour* and a pretty face. I promised the night guard—who was old enough to be my father—that he could have his way with me, if he would let me just slip away in the night."

"You didn't!"

"I certainly did."

"That's shameless!"

"You haven't heard the whole story yet. He let himself into my cell, and I asked the randy old coot if I could play with his … nightstick. He got this great big naughty grin on his face and said, '*Mais oui, mademoiselle.*' He started to unbutton his fly, and while he was doing that, I started playing with his policeman's club hanging from his belt. By the time he had his personal nightstick out of his pants, I had the wooden one out of the thing on his belt. He started to laugh when I waggled it front of his nose, so I hit him with it."

"On his head?"

"No, on his tallywacker. Folded him up like a Murphy bed. Before he could let out another yelp, I cracked him a good one on the head and put him out until next Tuesday. Just to make sure he learned a lesson from his lechery, I gave him another whack on his pecker."

"Ouch! That was mean."

"Do you really think so? Ever since that night I've wondered how he explained the condition of his *thing* to his wife."

Both girls erupted in laughter so loud that it awakened Mace and Sterling. Not that it mattered because Willie was just then turning the Cadillac into the driveway of the Hollywood Hotel.

Edgar Wilson, the doorman, met the car along with a pair of eager bellboys. This had become a daily routine for the trio of hotel employees. Mace and Sterling got out of the car on the passenger side. Each of them handed a nickel to the bellboy who opened their door for them. Mabel gave Wilson a quarter for the same service because she knew her fellow actors were not good tippers, each of them having spent a lot of time working in other forms of show business which were not nearly as lucrative as the motion picture industry. Not knowing how much to tip, Maisy gave the bellboy on her side two dimes and whispered in his ear.

"Please give one to the other young man. Okay?"

The lad grinned gratefully and nodded to assure Maisy that he would do exactly that.

Wilson closed the car door behind Mabel. Then he hurried to the hotel entrance to accommodate the four arrivals there. "Have a pleasant evening, Miss Normand, Miss Malone, gentlemen." He tipped his hat to them.

As usual, Mace went to the registration desk to check for their mail and to get their room keys.

"Would you like to join us for dinner, Maisy?" asked Sterling.

Mabel spoke before Maisy could reply. "If you don't mind, Georgie, Maisy and I were just getting to know each other on the way here, so would you and Fred be okay if we dined alone?"

"Aw, gee, Mabel. If I eat with just Fred at the table, I might actually have to talk to him."

Mabel gave him a mock punch in the arm. "Here I was feeling sorry for Freddie because he might have to talk to you."

Mace returned with their keys and some mail. "The usual for each of us except you, Maisy." He handed a two-inch thick bundle of letters and postcards to Mabel and another about half that size to Sterling. He kept an even smaller packet of post for himself. "Nothing today, but I'm sure that once people start seeing on the screen you'll be getting lots of mail every day from all over the country. Don't you think so, George?"

"I don't know, Fred. She might be too pretty for comedy."

"You're right, George. She might have to ugly up a little to get the same kind of attention Mabel gets."

Mabel pushed Mace gently. "Hey, I like that." When he laughed, she pushed him harder. "Now go on, you two, and let us be." She took Maisy by the arm and pulled her toward the restaurant.

Mace nudged Sterling in the elbow. "What's that all about?"

"No men allowed, old boy. Girl talk, don't you know?"

"No, I don't, but it doesn't matter anyway. Leaves more opportunity for you and me to scout around for some new talent." He scanned the lobby. "See any potential extras in here."

"Freddie, you're worse than that Clover fellow, God rest his soul. Come on. Let's go eat. I'm starved."

* * *

Over supper, Maisy and Mabel compared some more personal notes about their lives and discovered they had only one other commonality. Besides being born in the same year, both of their fathers worked with wood; Mabel's being a carpenter and a partner in a house building operation and Maisy's being a sawyer and owning his own lumber business. While one talked, the other ate and drank.

After washing down a large bite of buttered bread with a mouthful of red wine, Maisy changed the subject. "Why did you and Mr. Mace call Mr. Sterling George. I thought his first name was Ford"

"His real name is George Ford Stich Junior. Ford Sterling is his stage name."

"Is Mabel your real first name?"

"Oh, yes, Mabel is my real name. Mabel Ethelreid Normand from Staten Island, New York."

"What did you do before you started acting in moving pictures?"

Mabel smiled. "I was a poser."

Maisy scrunched up face. "A poser? What's that?"

"I posed for Mr. Charles Dana Gibson, the artist."

Maisy gasped. "You were a Gibson girl?"

"I was."

"I am impressed."

"What about you, Maisy? What did you do before you got into Vaudeville?"

"I was a runaway."

Mabel took her turn at squeezing her eyebrows together and staring at her dinner partner with perplexity. "A runaway?"

"Yes, I ran away from home. I had just turned thirteen, and a Vaudeville show came to the theatre in our town for a couple of shows. There was a boy in the show who caught my eye, and I caught his. His name was Jake. Before I knew what hit me, I was on the train with him and his folks, and we were off to see the country. Every couple of weeks or so, I would send my mama a postcard to let her know I was safe. Of course, I always mailed it the day we left some Podunk town for another Podunk town. We went to every state east of the Mississippi and south of the Mason-Dixon Line until we finally got onto a better circuit that included bigger towns like Atlanta, Charleston, Richmond, and finally Baltimore. That's when Harry, Jake's father, met an English song and dance man, who said we should take the act to London to play the music hall circuit over there. Harry begged, borrowed, and stole every nickel he could to get us the price of four fares to England. Only three of us got there, though. Harry died from apoplexy the day before we docked at Southampton. When Harry died, so did the act. Diana, the widow, had been holding out on Harry and saving money for years for when they got old and had to get out of the business. She used enough of it to pay to have Harry embalmed so he could be shipped back to the United States with her and Jake and they could bury him in his own country. Funny, but she didn't have enough saved to buy me a ticket, too. Jake talked her into giving me five pounds in English money, and then he gave me a kiss good-bye and wished me good luck. And that's how I got to England."

"On the one hand, that's a sad story, but on the other, it's really exciting because you were in England and not in Podunk any longer."

"Yes, I did get to England, but I had to work my way to London. When I got there, things really got interesting, especially after I started working at the Royal Comedy Theatre. All the best acts in the country played there, and all the best people came and sat in the audience. Before every show, a bunch of us would peek out through the curtains to see if there was anybody famous in the crowd. Most of the time I didn't know who this person or that person was, so somebody would tell me who he or she was and why they were important. The only one that ever impressed me was Sir Arthur Conan Doyle.

I read a few of his stories when I was still living on the farm, and—"

"But I thought you said your father was a sawyer and owned a lumber mill."

"Yes, he did, but we lived on a farm with my grandparents. They did the farming with a couple of uncles on my daddy's side because I didn't have any brothers."

"Oh, I see."

"I also saw the late Leslie Clover at the Royal Comedy as well, although I didn't remember his name until I saw his body this morning. Actually, I never knew his name. I'm really bad with names, but I never forget a face." The memory of the interview with Detective Browning interjected itself into Maisy's consciousness. "I tell you that man was murdered. He was smothered with a pillow. I just know it, and I might be able to prove it, if I could only get back in his house and have another look around."

"Whatever are you going on about, Maisy?"

"Oh, sorry. I was just thinking about the police detective who questioned Milo and me this morning at Mr. Clover's house. He insists that without any solid evidence he has to rule Mr. Clover's death was accidental from asphyxiation due to the corset being too tight. Have you ever heard of such a thing, Mabel? I mean someone dying from a corset being too tight?"

"I've never heard of anybody dying from it, but I passed out more than once when I was posing for Mr. Gibson. He insisted every beautiful woman had to have a tiny, tiny waist, and the only way we could look like that was to wear the stays so tight that we'd finally lose our breath and faint."

"See? There you go right there. I tried to tell that to this Detective Browning, and he still wanted to call Mr. Clover's death an accident. If I could only get back in that house again—"

Mabel interrupted Maisy by grabbing her forearm. "I've got an idea. Why don't we take a taxi over there right now and have that look around you want so badly?"

Maisy frowned. "Sounds all right to me, but won't that cost a lot?"

"Not for a ride this short."

* * *

Maisy had seen a taxi sitting outside the hotel earlier in the day and again that evening, but she thought it was a just another big automobile. Not in Los Angeles. Here a large car with the word TAXI painted on its doors was more like a bus. For a dime, the driver would take passengers wherever they wanted to go within the city limits. The system had only one serious drawback. No matter when you got into the cab the person dropped off next was always the one whose destination was closest. During the day, this could present a problem for some riders. But in the evening? Not so much, especially after dark, and even less so in the quiet, sedate Hollywood section of the burgeoning metropolis where the native residents were accustomed to a more rural way of life, one where the lights went out in every house by nine. The transient populace staying at the new hotels and the newcomers settling in with the motion picture business had yet to create any real night life along Sunset or Hollywood boulevards. So when the driver saw Maisy and Mabel approach his vehicle, he was quite surprised.

"Are you still in service, sir?" asked Mabel.

"Until nine o'clock, young lady."

"Where are we going, Maisy?"

"The house is on Alexandria Avenue, just a few doors north of this street out here."

"Driver, we would like to be taken to the corner of Alexandria and Hollywood please."

The man held out his hand. "That'll be ten cents … each."

"Get in, Maisy. I'll pay him." Mabel reached into her purse and gave the driver a quarter. "Keep the change."

"Thank you, miss."

When Mabel sat down beside her, Maisy leaned close to her to whisper a question. "Why aren't we going up to the house? I know the address."

"Wait a second."

The driver started the engine. It popped and growled before settling into a steady rumble.

"Do you hear that?" asked Mabel.

Maisy nodded. "I get it. The noise from this monster will wake up the neighborhood, if we have him drop us in front of the house."

"That's right. This ain't New York, you know."

"And it ain't Chicago neither."

The girls giggled as they settled in for the ten-minute ride to the corner with Alexandria Avenue. Only a few gentleman pedestrians walked the sidewalks of Hollywood Boulevard that evening, but none of them hailed the taxi to pull over for them, which satisfied Mabel and Maisy, both of whom became aware that they were two unescorted young women out after dark in a new place for both of them.

"You know, Maisy, maybe we should have him take us up to the house after all."

"No, we'll be all right. Remember, this ain't New York or Chicago or even really Los Angeles from what I saw of it this morning. This is more like most of those hick towns I saw while on the Vaudeville circuits. Most people in those places don't even have locks on their doors. And I'll bet you a three-cent nickel there won't be any street lamps on Alexandria Avenue. If you think it won't be safe, you can stay with the taxi and I'll go up to the house by myself."

"No, that's all right. If you think we'll be safe, then I'll go along with you to the house."

Maisy patted Mabel's hand. "We'll be just fine. I promise." Then a thought struck her. "How do we get back to the hotel? Walk?"

"Do you think this will take long at the house? What you have to do there, I mean."

"Shouldn't take us more than ten or fifteen minutes. Why?"

Mabel tapped the driver on the shoulder. "Sir, would you mind waiting for us on the corner until we come back from taking care of our business on Alexandria Avenue?"

"Taking care of your *business*? What kind of *business* would that be now?"

Getting his drift, Maisy answered for them. "Well, sir, it's not actually any kind of business. We're going to look at a house on that street. We won't be more than fifteen minutes. Will you please wait?"

"It'll cost you another ten cents each for the ride back to the hotel."

"Fair enough. And if we take longer than fifteen minutes, we'll give you fifteen cents each. Deal?"

"I'll wait for you, but remember, I go off duty at nine o'clock." He checked the time on his pocket watch by the dim glow from the electric street light. "It's already a quarter after eight, so you'd better hurry." He turned the taxi around in the intersection with Alexandria and brought it to a halt just past the northwest corner. After shutting down the engine, he faced the girls and wagged a finger at them. "Now don't be late getting back here or I won't be here waiting for you."

Both of them nodded and spoke simultaneously. "Yes, sir." Then they exited the taxi and walked quietly up Alexandria Avenue toward the house previously occupied by the late Leslie Clover. Just as Maisy had suspected, not one streetlamp along the entire block. The farther up the hill they went, the darker the night became.

"This is it," said Maisy when they reached the end of the walkway to the porch steps of the bungalow.

"There aren't any lights on inside."

"Of course not. The place is empty. Come on. Let's go inside."

"But it will be darker in there than it is out here."

"Then we'll turn a light on."

"And what if one of the neighbors looks out and sees there's a light on in the house of a man who just died today? Then what?"

"They'll probably call the coppers, and we'll get arrested and go to jail for burglary or something."

"Oh, my goodness, I can't have that hap—"

Maisy bumped Mabel to quiet her. "I was only joking. We'll be in and out of there before you can say Jack Robinson. Now come on, let's go inside."

They walked up to the porch and climbed the five steps as quietly as they could. Maisy pulled the handle of the screen door and hoped it would open just as silently as they had been so far. It creaked a little, and the spring reverberated dully. Still, the two sounds weren't enough to be heard more than a few feet away. So far so good. She turned the knob on the inside door. Not even a click. She pushed it open, and happily the hinges failed to make a sound. She turned to Mabel and whispered.

"Don't let the screen door slam. Close it as quietly as you can."

"Yes, of course. Quietly."

Maisy went inside, and Mabel followed her, remembering to close the outer door as gently as possible. Maisy then closed the inner door without a sound.

"It's awfully dark in here," said Mabel.

Maisy felt the wall alongside the door until her hand came to the light switch. She felt for two buttons and pushed the upper one. The ceiling light came on.

"It's about time you showed up."

Maisy and Mabel spun around together and saw Milo Cole sitting at one end of the sofa across the room. Sitting at the other was Detective Ed Browning.

"Good evening, Miss Malone. We've been expecting you. And you brought a friend, too. How nice!"

Cole stood up. "Detective Browning, I'd like to introduce you to Miss Mabel Normand, the lead actress at Keystone Motion Picture Studios."

Being a gentleman, Browning stood in the presence of two ladies, even if they were still teenagers. "How do you do, Miss Normand? It's an honor to make your acquaintance." He tipped his bowler to her.

Mouths agape, Maisy and Mabel were speechless.

T he cat finally released Maisy's tongue. "What are you two doing here?"

"I might ask you the same question," said Browning, "but I already know the answer."

Mabel was still quite shaken by the presence of Cole and Browning, especially the detective. "Maisy, are we in trouble?"

Browning smiled at the actress. "No, Miss Normand, I assure you, *you* are not in any trouble. Miss Malone, on the other hand …"

The hackles sprang up on the nape of Maisy's neck like the hair on the back of a cat. "How can I be in any trouble? I haven't done anything wrong."

"You're interfering in a police investigation of a possible homicide."

Maisy replayed his words in her head before speaking. "What do you mean, 'possible homicide'? Are you telling me you're finally seeing the light here? That Mr. Clover was murdered?"

Browning smiled and nodded. "Yes, I have concluded his death could have been something other than an accident."

"Other than an accident? Meaning it was a murder."

"We still don't have any positive proof that he was murdered because we don't know for sure how he was murdered … if he was murdered, that is."

"Well, if it's not murder and it's not an accident, what else could it be? Natural causes?"

"No, it could be manslaughter."

"Manslaughter? Do you mean you think someone *accidentally* killed him?"

"It's possible, don't you think?"

"Possible, but not very likely."

"So you're still convinced Mr. Clover was murdered, even though we still don't have any positive proof that he was murdered?"

"Yes, I do because I think I can provide you with that proof."

"So I've been told by Mr. Cole here."

"Milo, you rat. You called him?"

"I didn't tell him anything, Maisy, except you might be coming here tonight to look around again because you think you might know a way of proving Leslie was murdered. That's all I told him, I swear."

"But you're still a rat for calling him."

"Now simmer down, Miss Malone. Mr. Cole was only doing his civic duty."

"Civic duty, my eye! He ratted us out."

"Oh, no, Maisy. Not Miss Normand. Just you. I didn't know—"

Browning interrupted Milo. "I think you've said enough, Mr. Cole. I'll deal with Miss Malone now. You just have a seat again."

Although unhappy about being bossed around, Cole plopped down on the couch and folded his arms in a pout, refusing to glare at anything except the floor.

"Now, Miss Malone, what is it that makes you think you can prove Mr. Clover was murdered?"

"Why should I help you with your 'police investigation of a possible homicide'? What's in it for me?"

Browning shrugged. "Nothing, but helping *me* might keep *you* out of jail for the night."

"Are you threatening me?"

The detective smiled and shook his head. "Oh, no, Miss Malone. That's not a threat. That's a promise. Help me by telling me what you suspect is the cause of Mr. Clover's death, and I promise I won't arrest you and take you to jail tonight for interfering in my investigation."

"You tell me first why you think Mr. Clover's death is now a *possible* homicide and not an accident."

Browning studied her face for a moment in search of any guile that might be hidden there. One last delve into her eyes, and he was satisfied she wasn't up to any shenanigans.

"All right, I'll tell you why. When we got Mr. Clover's body back to the morgue this afternoon, the coroner and I took a good look at it. We discovered two contusions on—"

Maisy interrupted him. "Contusions? What's that?"

"Bruises."

"Well, why didn't you say that in the first place?"

Although annoyed by her attitude, Browning maintained his composure and resumed his explanation. "We found two bruises of the same size but in totally different locations. One was at the coccyx, and—"

"The what-six?"

"Coccyx, the base of his spine, the tailbone."

"You could have said tailbone, you know."

Browning sighed and then continued. "One was on his tailbone, and the other was on his solar plexus."

Maisy frowned. "Solar plexus? What's that? Or where is it?"

Mabel knew the answer. She showed Maisy by pointing to herself. "It's right here, Maisy. It's this spot at the base of your sternum."

"My sternum?"

"Yes, your breast bone."

As the anatomy lesson sank into her brain, a smile lit up Maisy's face. "That proves I'm right." She turned to Browning. "The bruise on his spine was probably from the person who tied up the corset for him."

"Yes, we figured that already. But what about the other one?"

Maisy poked Browning gently on the shoulder. "Come on, I'll show you." She immediately brushed by him, heading for the rear of the house.

Browning turned to watch her pass through the dining room and into the darkness of the kitchen. "Where are you going?"

"Come back here, and I'll show you."

Mabel had finally calmed down. "May I come, too?"

"Why certainly, Miss Normand."

Cole stood up. "What about me?"

"Yes, Mr. Cole, you may come as well."

Mabel and Milo followed Browning toward the rear of the house. A light came on in Clover's bedroom, illuminating the way for them.

"Hurry up, will you?"

No sooner were the words out of Maisy's mouth than Browning was standing in the bedroom doorway. "No need to shout, Miss Malone. The bungalow isn't that big."

Mabel and Cole crowded behind the detective, each peeking over a shoulder into the room.

Maisy went to the bed, which was still neatly made. She pulled back the spread to reveal the pillows and stared at their cases for a moment. Then one at a time she gingerly turned them over to reveal their undersides. Without turning around, she waggled a finger over her shoulder in her audience's direction.

"Come here, Detective Browning, and look at this."

Browning obeyed Maisy, stepping up behind her, yet staying a good two feet away from her. "All right, what am I supposed to be looking at here?"

Cole and Mabel edged into the room and placed themselves at the foot of the bed. Like Browning, they stared at the pillows, neither knowing why.

"Compare the two pillowcases, Detective. Do you see anything different about them?"

Browning squinted as he studied the left one for a moment and then the right one. "Yes, I think I see what you mean. There is a slight difference in them. A stain of some sort." He shifted his focus to Maisy. "Is that what you're seeing, Miss Malone?"

"It looks like a spit stain, Detective Browning."

Excited, Mabel blurted out, "Yes, I see it, too. Right there on the one on the left."

Browning looked over his shoulder at the comedienne. "Yes, that's right, Miss Normand. The one on the left." He turned back to Maisy. "But that doesn't mean anything, Miss Malone. It only proves Mr. Clover drooled in his sleep."

"Oh, really? Then why aren't there any stains on the other side or on the other pillowcase?"

The policeman frowned. "Would you mind standing aside and letting me take a closer look at these pillows please?"

Maisy backed off. "Be my guest."

Browning examined the pillowcases closely for a good minute. "All right, I agree with you about the saliva stain, but—"

Maisy's brow furrowed. "Saliva?"

"That's the proper word for spit," said Mabel.

Maisy shook her head while smiling wistfully. "Contusions, coccyx, solar plexus, sternum, saliva. Maybe I should read more and when I come across a word I don't know, I ought to look it up in a dictionary instead of guessing what it means."

"As I was saying, Miss Malone, I agree with you about the *saliva* stain, but that still doesn't prove anything other than he drooled on that pillow last night."

"You want more proof, do you?"

"It would be helpful, yes."

"Mabel, would you help me here?"

"Sure, I will. What do you want me to do?"

"First, I'm going to turn the pillow over." Maisy gently reversed the pillow on the bed. "Now you take the pillowcase by the corners and hold them tight while I pull the pillow out of the case."

Browning grimaced. "What good will that do, Miss Malone?"

"You'll see in a second. Ready, Mabel?"

"Ready."

As they performed the procedure, Maisy had a caution for her new friend. "Be careful not to fold or wad up the case or touch it anywhere except by the corners. Okay?"

"Okay."

Once the cushion was free of its cover to her satisfaction, Maisy nodded at Mabel. "Now let's do the same thing to the other one."

They repeated the process with the other pillow.

"Now look at the two of them, Detective, and see if you can see any difference in them?"

Browning looked them over for a half minute. "The left one looks like someone slept on it last night."

LARRY NAMES

"Yes, it does, doesn't it? But tell me this, Detective. How does someone sleep on both sides of a pillow at the same time?"

"Now what are you talking about, Miss Malone?"

Maisy bent over and looked at the pillow from its side. "Bend down here with me, Detective, and have a look for yourself."

Curious now, the policeman did as he was bid to do, the top of his head quite near the top of Maisy's as they studied the pillow from that angle. After several seconds, Browning popped erect again.

"That means nothing, Miss Malone. It only proves he slept on one side, then flipped it over and slept on the other side."

"If that's so, then why is there only one saliva stain on one side of the pillowcase?"

A smile of triumph spread across Mabel's face. "She's got you there, Detective. Good going, Maisy."

Browning tightened his jaw as he looked from Mabel to Maisy to Cole and back to Maisy again. His face reddened with a combination of anger, frustration, resentment, and embarrassment. A girl with no police training whatsoever had bested him, and it galled his ego.

Confusion colored Cole's face. "Then he *was* murdered?"

"That's right, Milo. Somebody murdered your friend. Now that we know how it was done we—"

Cole interrupted her. "Exactly how what was it done, Maisy?"

"Yes, Miss Malone, how exactly did the murder happen?"

Maisy frowned at Browning. "You don't have to be so snide about it, Detective. You know exactly how it happened."

"Yes, but I'd still like to hear your version of it. Please proceed."

"Yes, go ahead, Maisy," said Mabel. "I think I know, too, but you tell it anyway."

Maisy nodded at the actress. "Well, okay." She focused on Browning again. "Remember the cigarette burn on the floor?"

"Yes, go on."

"I figure Mr. Clover was smoking a cigarette when he started to cough. Mabel, have you ever coughed when you've been wearing a corset? Takes the wind right out of you, doesn't it?"

"It sure does. You get light-headed, and if you don't catch your breath soon enough, you faint." Mabel suddenly saw where Maisy was headed with this line of reasoning. "Then you think Mr. Clover fainted from coughing while smoking a cigarette, right?"

"You're getting it now. Anyway, Mr. Clover fainted and dropped on the floor like a limp dishrag. Whoever was in the room at the time then straightened him up to give him a chance to breathe again. But then whoever the killer … *was* … suddenly figured out this was a golden opportunity to do away with Mr. Clover and let the police think it was an accident. He … or she

… then grabbed the pillow from the bed and smothered him with it." She knelt down where the corpse of Leslie Clover had been earlier that day. "He … or she put his or her knee in his solar plexus to hold him down, which explains how he got that *contusion* on his chest. Once the killer was certain Mr. Clover was dead, he or she replaced the pillow on the bed. Then to hide his or her presence in the house this morning, the killer tried to do away with every trace of being here, such as making up the bed and … Hey, wait a minute. I just thought of something else to prove that nobody else was here last night." She stepped past Browning toward the doorway. "Come with me, everybody."

The detective, Cole, and Mabel followed Maisy into the other bedroom off the dining room. She pushed the light switch and waited for the others to join her.

"What are looking at in here, Miss Malone?"

"The bed. I'll bet you a three-cent nickel when we pull back the covers we won't see a single wrinkle in the bottom sheet."

"So what does that prove?"

"It'll prove nobody has slept in it since the bed was made with a clean sheet."

Mabel added an observation of her own. "Just look at the pillows. Both look nice and fluffy, as if nobody has slept on them in quite some time."

"Good call, Miss Normand."

Maisy took exception to Browning's patronizing Mabel. "Hey, how come she gets a 'good call, Miss Normand' when she throws in her two cents and all I get out of you is a lot of snottiness?"

"You're not a leading lady of the moving pictures, Miss Malone."

Mabel stuck in her opinion. "Not yet, she isn't, but I've got a feeling she will be before long."

This caught Maisy off-guard. "Do you really think so, Mabel?"

"Oh, I know so, Maisy. You've got that thing … that charisma … that charm … that magnetism … that *je ne sais quoi* … that flair for the dramatic and the comic. That's what Mack and I saw in you in Chicago, and that's why we sent for you to come out here and make motion pictures with us. You've got what it takes, Maisy, and we plan to make the most out of it."

Irritated now, Browning folded his arms against his chest. "All that is beside the point. We're talking about a murder here. You've proven your point about Mr. Clover being murdered and not dying by accident. That leaves two questions."

Before the policeman could reiterate his statement by holding up a finger, Maisy interrupted him. "We don't know *who* murdered him or *why* he was murdered."

Flustered, Browning could only say one word. "Exactly."

Cole stared at Maisy. "So what happens now?"

Browning answered for her. "Now I try to figure out *why* someone wanted Mr. Clover dead, and once I do that, I'll figure out *who* killed him." He looked askance at Maisy. "Unless you beat me to it, Miss Malone, as I believe you intend to do."

Maisy had to smile at him. "Fair enough, Detective Browning. Want to bet me a three-cent nickel on it?"

"You know, Miss Malone, I wish I hadn't made you that promise not to take you to jail tonight for interfering in a police investigation."

Mabel waved a finger at Browning. "Yes, a promise is a promise."

"I wasn't finished, Miss Normand. I said tonight. I never promised not to arrest her in the future."

"Hey, that's not fair."

"Don't worry about it, Mabel. Detective Browning knows that in the end he'll get all the credit when the time comes to make an arrest in this case. Isn't that right, Detective?"

"That attitude is *not* helpful, Miss Malone."

"Look, Detective, as soon as I solve this case for you, I'll give you the lowdown on who and why and you can make the arrest. Fair enough?"

"Sounds like a good deal to me," said Mabel.

Browning tilted his head and gave Maisy a good study for a few seconds. "All right, Miss Malone. Since Miss Normand is so favorable to this arrangement, I suppose I'll go along with you and make that bet."

Maisy produced one of her three-cent nickels from her purse. "Here's mine. Where's yours?"

"I don't have one."

"Well, you don't look like the kind of guy who would welch on a bet, so I guess I'll have to trust you."

"And I you, Miss Malone."

Maisy grinned. "Fair enough, Detective Browning." She winked at him. "What do you say about you calling me Maisy?"

"That wouldn't be appropriate for a gentleman, Miss Malone."

"But I insist, and a gentleman shouldn't deny a lady a simple request such as calling her by her first name."

Browning sighed. "All right then. Maisy it is."

"And I think I'll call you Eddie."

"It's Edward, not Eddie."

"How about you, Mabel? Don't you think he's an Eddie?"

"Yes, Maisy, I do. He's definitely an Eddie."

Browning refused to continue arguing with them about his name, but he had to take his frustration out on someone. "It's still Detective Browning to you, Mr. Cole."

Suddenly, Mabel remembered the time. "Oh, my goodness! The taxi! What time is it?"

The policeman took his watch from its vest pocket. "It's twelve minutes before nine o'clock."

"Come on, Maisy. We have to hurry or we'll miss our ride."

The two girls bolted from the bedroom and charged for the front door.

Browning scrambled after them. "Hey, hold on there!"

Maisy opened the door to let Mabel go first. She followed a breath behind. The two of them scurried down the porch steps and hit the walkway running.

The policeman tried once more to stop them with his authoritative voice. "I'm not through with you yet!"

Maisy answered over her shoulder. "No time now. I'll be in touch."

Browning shook his head as he watched them scamper off toward Hollywood Boulevard.

Cole joined Browning on the porch. "Don't worry, Detective. I'll make sure she keeps her word to you."

"That's the thing, Mr. Cole. Her keeping her word worries me the most."

* * *

Mabel and Maisy made it to the taxi just in time to get a ride back to the Hollywood Hotel.

"You took more than fifteen minutes," said the driver standing by the front passenger door with his hand outstretched. "Money first."

Breathless from their jaunt, Maisy retrieved two quarters from her purse and handed them to the man.

"I suppose you want change."

Maisy shook her head and then followed Mabel into the back seat.

The driver climbed in behind the steering wheel, started the engine, and drove down the street toward their hotel.

"So what are you going to do now, Maisy?"

"I'm going to get a good night's sleep."

"No, I mean about your bet with Detective Browning."

Maisy chuckled. "I'm going to win it, and Eddie better pay up when I do."

"No, I mean, how are you going to find out why Leslie Clover was murdered and by whom?"

"I'm going to start by finding out who knew Mr. Clover. You know. His friends and acquaintances. Was there any particular girl he was seeing often? Is Milo his only male friend? Was somebody holding a grudge against him? That sort of thing."

"But what good will that do? Isn't that putting the who before the why?"

"Look, Mabel. People commit murder for one of three reasons."

Maisy raised her fingers as she named them. "Jealousy. Revenge. And personal gain. He could have been murdered for one of those reasons, two of them, or all three. Only time will tell."

"You don't suspect anybody at the studio had anything to do with his death, do you?"

"Don't you think that's the first place to start looking?"

Mabel shuddered. "Yes, I suppose you're right."

A new thought disrupted Maisy's calm demeanor. "Mabel, you have to promise me you won't say a word to anybody at the studio that I'm snooping around about Mr. Clover's murder."

"I promise I won't, but what about Milo? Don't you think he'll tell it around about what we did tonight and your bet with Eddie and what you're doing?"

"You're right about that. He will talk. We'll have to do something about that and as soon as possible."

Mabel's face lit up with an idea. "I know what to do. You leave it to me, Maisy. Milo won't say a word. I promise."

"Say, you aren't going to get him fired, are you?"

"Oh, nothing that severe." She patted Maisy's hand. "Don't worry about it. He won't talk. I promise." She leaned back in the seat as Maisy stared at Mabel with great apprehension. "What a grand evening we had, Maisy. The whole thing was so exhilarating. Don't you agree?"

"Depends on your definition of exhilarating, I guess."

"Well, it fits mine."

Maisy sighed with resignation. "Well then, I guess it fits mine, too."

Maisy's second day in California started off at 5:00 a.m., with a bellboy knocking on her Hollywood Hotel room door and practically singing out her wake up call. "Good morning, Miss Malone. Time to get up."

She lifted her head slightly from the pillow but without opening her eyes. "Time to get up?" Her voice rasped softly but quite irreverently. "No-o-o." She buried her face in the cushion.

Another knock; this one much louder. "Miss Malone, you must get up, ma'am. The others will be downstairs soon waiting for you."

"The others?" She raised her head higher, her mussed hair covering half her face. "What others?" When no immediate answer came, she lifted her upper body a few inches off the bed, her eyes still closed, and spoke louder. "What others?"

"The other actors from your moving picture studio, Miss Malone. Miss Normand, Mr. Mace, and Mr. Sterling. They'll be downstairs waiting for you in fifteen minutes. Your car will be waiting outside then as well."

Perplexed, eyes now open in the dark room, she muttered to herself. "My car?" Then louder to the bellboy. "What time is it?"

"It's two minutes after five o'clock, Miss Malone. Better shake a leg, ma'am." For good measure, he knocked once more.

"Okay, already! I'm getting up, I'm getting up."

Realizing it was still dark outside, Maisy turned the switch on the bedside lamp. The sudden bright light hurt her eyes.

A lighter tap-tap on the door. "Maisy? It's Mabel. You need to get up, dear. We have to be at the studio before sunrise, so please hurry."

"Before sunrise? Are you crazy? Why?"

"Mack's orders. Until the interior sets and stages are completely ready, we have to shoot outdoors in the sunlight. It's how we do things in the moving picture business, dear."

Maisy muttered to herself. "Not in Vaudeville."

"Now please hurry and get dressed, dear. We have to get going to the studio as soon as you get downstairs. You don't want to be late on your first day, do you?"

"My first day? I thought yesterday was my first day."

"Please hurry, dear. See you downstairs."

Maisy wobbled to her feet against her will and groggily began doing as she was told.

* * *

Looking handsome, perfectly groomed, and immaculately attired as always when out in public, Ford Sterling met Maisy in the hall outside her room at twenty-three minutes past five. "Come on, sleepy-head. You can go back to sleep with the rest of us during the ride to Edendale. If you're going to work in the moving picture business, you'll need to learn to take catnaps whenever the opportunity presents itself. Now come along. We're almost late already." He helped her down the stairs to the lobby.

"Do we have to get up this early every day?"

"We get up an hour before sunrise every day except Sunday."

Maisy did the math in her head as Sterling guided her toward the front door and the Cadillac waiting outside for them. "The sun rises at six o'clock today?"

"No, today it rises at five forty-four. We let you sleep in because it's your first *full* day at the studio, and we thought you needed the extra sleep."

"A whole fifteen minutes? That was very nice of you. Thank you."

"Don't mention it and don't count on it happening again tomorrow morning. Tonight, when we return from the studio, you will request an alarm clock from the front desk until you can buy one for yourself. You will set it for four forty-five. A bellboy will be around to make certain you are up within five minutes. If he doesn't hear you stirring, he will knock on your door just like one did this morning."

"And when is that going to happen? Getting my own alarm clock, I mean."

"We only work half the day on Saturdays. You can go shopping in the afternoon tomorrow."

"Okay. So when do we get breakfast today?"

"Willie stops at a bakery and brings us fresh rolls, donuts, and small pastries to get us through the morning. Katy makes coffee for us at the studio."

"Katy? The same Katy who did my makeup yesterday?"

"She's very versatile."

Maisy slid into the back seat next to Mabel. She looked at her new friend with astonishment. "How can you look so chipper this early in the morning?"

Mabel giggled a bit. "Oh, you'll get used to it, dear."

Maisy shook her head. "No, I won't. I'm a Vaudeville person. We see the sunrise and *then* go to bed."

Smiling as sweetly as Mary Pickford, Mabel poked Maisy tenderly in the solar plexus. "Not anymore, dear. Moving picture person now. You."

Sterling plopped into the front seat beside Mace. "Getting up this early is only temporary, Maisy. As soon as the new studio is built, we'll be doing the early morning and late afternoon shooting indoors under lights. We're only shooting this early and so late in the day now because the only light we have is from the sun. Once that studio is finished we won't be due into work until seven, and we'll knock off between five and six in the evening. Sometimes later, if we need to get a picture done and on its way to New York. So relax, Maisy, and catch forty winks while you can. Let's go, Willie."

Within seconds, all four actors were peacefully asleep as Willie steered the Cadillac around the potholes in the road all the way to Edendale in order to keep from disturbing his passengers.

* * *

Grizzled Arthur Verring, the night watchman for the studio, stood on the bungalow's porch behind Mack Sennett who sat on the steps, waiting for his acting crew and technical support people to arrive that morning. Old Artie, as he was known to the few on the lot who had bothered to make his acquaintance, marveled at the meticulous organization and work ethic of the moving picture company's director-general. Not once since settling in at the studio had the former horse wrangler have to awaken the big boss and get him started on his day. The man was always up at first light, making his own coffee, which he shared with Verring each morning before everybody else arrived to do the day's shooting.

Sennett held a sheet of typing paper in one hand as he glanced at the horizon to the east across Allesandro Street. The west side of the still quiet thoroughfare remained in shadow. He checked his watch. Seventeen minutes to six. Looking through the open gateway and down the hill toward Sunset Boulevard, he could see the first Red Car of the day coming up Allesandro. Some of his people and some of Bill Selig's Polyscope people would be aboard the electric railroad car. Sennett waited patiently for the streetcar to climb the hill at such a slow rate that people could board it or disembark from it without worrying too much about suffering an injury in the process. The driver waved a friendly greeting at him, and the studio head waved back with equal enthusiasm, although he had no idea about the man's name or why he always acted so friendly.

As the Red Car continued to the Selig Polyscope Studio on the next block, Sennett's workers hailed him one-by-one, and he returned their courtesies, calling each of them by his or her given name, providing he could remember it. If any of them had something special or unusual going on in their lives, he made certain to ask about that situation. The only person he queried today was the manager of his costume department.

"How's the family, Katy?"

"Oh, they're doing just fine, Mr. Sennett. All but the oldest two are back in school for the fall."

"How are Jack and Lizzie doing at their jobs?"

"Jack's doing fine learning the carpenter's trade, and Lizzie enjoys working at that new department store in downtown Los Angeles. The Broadway it's called. Bright and shiny new building. Eight stories high, don't you know?"

Before Sennett could reply, a large taxi, like the one Maisy and Mabel had employed the night before, stopped across the street to drop off more employees. At the same moment, Willie pulled the Cadillac into the driveway next to the bungalow.

The middle-aged night watchman eased himself down the steps past the director-general. "See you tonight, Mr. Sennett."

"See you tonight, Art."

Verring waved over his shoulder at Sennett and nodded to the people gathered around the porch as he hobbled through them toward the open studio gate. He would walk down the hill to Sunset Boulevard and catch the Red Car home to the boardinghouse on South Flower Street just below the Bunker Hill neighborhood of Los Angeles.

The departure of the night watchman was everybody's cue that the time had come to begin the day's work.

* * *

Mabel had to awaken Maisy when they arrived at the studio. "Maisy dear, you really have to wake up now. We're here."

Maisy refused to open her eyes to face the expanding light of day. "Can't I sleep a little longer? Just let me stay here. You can come back for me later?"

After opening the door on her side and exiting, Mabel nodded at Mace and Sterling for some help. Seeing Maisy slump against the door on her side of the car, they understood without any words passing between them. Mace went around to Maisy's side of the car, while Sterling remained stationed on Mabel's side. Should Maisy fall out when Mace opened her door, he would be there to catch her. If she chose to resist and flopped the other way to avoid Mace, Sterling would grab her, pull her from the back seat, and raise her into an upright position.

Sensing a plot against her, Maisy contemplated a plan of escape, but she quickly discarded any such notion as inane folly. When Mace turned the door handle, she leaned away from it to keep from falling out, her eyelids suddenly flapping upward like a pair of roller shades released accidentally. Then he opened the door slowly as he made certain she would not fall out on the ground, which thankfully she didn't. Instead, she begrudgingly put her feet outside and held out her hands to him for his assistance in standing up. The actor chuckled as he firmly enveloped her much smaller hands with his fleshier mitts and pulled her to a somewhat standing position.

"Come along now, Maisy. We mustn't keep Mack waiting." He put his arms around her shoulders and gave her a good jostling to stir her blood, and thus her feet, into motion.

"Okay, I'm right behind you, Freddie."

"No, dear. You're right beside me. All the way." He proffered an arm to her.

"You people are crazy, don't you know?"

Mace sucked on his cheek to make that near clicking sound and tilted his head toward her with a mischievous grin. "You don't know the half of it yet, little sister."

Maisy took his arm. "You know? I think I'm going to like you."

Together they joined the other actors in the half-circle of Keystone employees gathered around Sennett to hear the day's shooting schedule.

* * *

The odor of fresh coffee brewing stimulated Maisy into a feeble locomotion. But seeing Katy Killoy offering her a steaming cup of java really ratcheted her senses up another notch.

"Oh, thank you, Katy."

"You're getting the first cup today, even before his nibs, Mr. Sennett. You need it more than he does at this hour."

Maisy hesitated to take the cup from Katy. "This won't get you in trouble with Mr. Sennett, will it?"

"Me? In trouble with the boss?" She waved off the idea with a flip of a wrist. "It's him who needs to worry about getting in trouble with me." Then she laughed. "Don't you be worrying about it, Maisy darlin'. I can handle his nibs, sure enough. We're both Irish, don't you know?"

Maisy took the cup and sipped the coffee, cooling it just enough so that it didn't burn her tongue once it got past her lips. "Oh, this really hits the spot, Katy. Thank you so much."

"You hang around here, and I'll be right back from taking Mr. Sennett his cup of 'make-me-go-faster' before he starts his grouching for the day. While I'm gone, you might be wanting to strike up a bit of conversation with that girl over there." Katy nodded toward a petite blonde sitting at a makeup table applying greasepaint to her face to hide a few freckles on her cheeks and nose. "She's one of them who I seen with Mr. Clover more than once."

"Thanks, Katy. I just might do that."

As Katy walked away, Maisy sipped on her coffee and eyed the bleached out extra, wondering about the real color of her hair. Her first thought was mousy brown, but she quickly changed her mind to true brunette. Then she contemplated how to approach this girl. Finally, an idea came to her, and she strolled over to a chair only a few feet away.

"Mind if I sit down and watch you do that?"

The extra glanced sideways at Maisy. "Why? You bored or something?"

"No, I'm new here, and I've never had to do that to myself before. I

only thought by watching you do your makeup I might learn something."
When the girl gave her a longer look, Maisy smiled at her. "I'm Maisy Malone,
fresh off the train from Chicago. Actually, I got in yesterday. This is my first
full day with the studio."

"Gloria Newman. I'm from Cedar Rapids. That's in Iowa."

"Cedar Rapids? I played there once."

"Played there?"

"Vaudeville. I was part of a comedy act with this older couple. I played
their daughter. We were only in Cedar Rapids for one day. Matinee and
evening show."

"I thought about trying to do Vaudeville once. But I can't carry a note in
a bushel basket, and I dance like the rear end of a stage horse. I came out here
hoping to get into the moving pictures. So far, I've only been an extra. I tried
Polyscope for a while, but they had so many girls there I came down here
when Keystone opened up. I was fourth in line the first day. Mr. Sennett has
used me sixteen times already. Today will be seventeen."

"You're practically a regular then."

"That's the idea, dearie." Gloria tilted her head to the left and surveyed
Maisy for a second. "I heard you'll be doing supporting roles for Mabel
Normand. Is that right?"

"I don't know what I'll be doing here yet. After yesterday, I'm not sure
this business is for me."

Gloria gasped. "Oh, yes, that's right. You were with Milo when he
discovered Leslie's body at the bungalow yesterday. I'm glad it was you and
not me. I would have fainted dead away right on the spot. I knew him, you
know."

"You knew Mr. Clover?"

"He took me to dinner and a movie a few times. He was English, you
know. A real gentleman who knew how to treat a girl. We met in the extras
line at Polyscope. I could have really gone for him, but when I started getting
a few calls at Polyscope, I was too tired at night to do anything except go
home and sleep, if you know what I mean. Didn't seem to bother him much
when I turned him down the last time. I heard he asked Vivian out after me.
That didn't last long either because Vivian stopped showing up there and
went over to Universal. She was doing better there as an extra. Then she came
here for a few days when this studio opened. But she left and went back to
Polyscope when she learned Leslie was going to be a regular here. You should
have met Leslie. He was a real gentleman." She winked at Maisy. "With nice
hands."

"Oh, I met him once. In England a few years back. I was working at the
Royal Comedy Theatre and saw him perform there one night."

"You've been to England? That's really something. What was it like? Did
you get to Paris, too? I've always wanted to see Paris."

Seeing she had lost Gloria's attention on Clover, Maisy stood up suddenly. "Sorry, but I have to go. Katy's back, and she's going to do my makeup again today for me. It was nice meeting you, Gloria. See you."

"Yes, it was nice meeting you, too, Miss Malone. See you, too."

Hearing Gloria call her Miss Malone taught Maisy something about the pecking order of a motion picture studio. Even supporting actresses got respect from the extras.

Maisy rejoined Katy and sat in the same chair she had the day before to get her makeup done by the costume department manager.

"Did you learn anything from Gloria about Mr. Clover?"

"A little. She went out with him more than once to dinner and a movie. She'd been to his home, too. She didn't say so, but she called it *the bungalow* and not his house or residence or even home. I wonder if that's what all the girls who went out with him call it." Then she remembered another detail of the conversation with Gloria. "Oh, and she mentioned another girl named Vivian who was an extra here for a while but went back to Polyscope. Does that name mean anything to you, Katy?"

"That would be Vivian Vanover. She rides the same Red Car to work that I do. She lives in a room at a boardinghouse just west of the Bunker Hill neighborhood on Beaudry Avenue. We talk on occasion on the ride to work each morning. I usually leave earlier in the day than she does, so I don't see much of her on the ride home in the evening." Katy's face wrinkled up in thought. "You know, I don't recall seeing Vivian on the Red Car this morning or yesterday either. Not like her to miss a chance to get in front of the camera. I can't be sure, but I think she went back to Polyscope about the time Mr. Clover started seeing that red-haired girl named … named … named … it'll come to me." A smile made the lines in her face disappear. "Her name is Alma. Don't know her last name, but you'll know her when you see her. Rusty red hair. In fact, I think I heard somebody call her that. Rusty, I mean. She still comes into the studio as an extra, but she doesn't get many camera calls that I know about. She might be sitting outside right now, if you want to go look."

"No time now. I'm due on the set with Mr. Sennett in twenty minutes. So we'd better get this done, Katy."

* * *

Sennett saw no reason to use the old horse barn as a studio when it was needed more for dressing rooms and the costume department and because the sky was nearly always sunny in southern California. Therefore, construction of a new building had begun the day after the Keystone ensemble's arrival in Los Angeles at the end of August. Until the indoor facility could be completed, all the films would be shot outdoors—weather permitting, of course. To save money on lighting and electricity, the painters spread silver paint on large sheets of cardboard and mounted them on sheet music stands that were easy to move around a set to reflect the sunlight onto the scene.

Maisy had witnessed some filming the day before and had even walked through a set a few times while the camera was grinding. She was in the background, of course, where she wouldn't be a distraction from the stars in the foreground.

Henry Lehrman had her in tow today. "Just like yesterday, Maisy, I'll be using you as an extra. When you're not in a scene, I want you to stand close and observe how we do things here. Mack can tell you personally that making a moving picture is nothing like performing on the stage in Vaudeville. This is a visual medium accompanied by a musical score that complements the action on the screen. We rehearse over and over until the director is confident that the actors have all their moves and expressions exactly as he wants them. Then and only then does the camera start grinding. Film is expensive and is not to be wasted."

And so her morning went. The actors rehearsed and rehearsed and rehearsed some more until the director felt they were ready to perform in front of the operating camera. Their scenes took anywhere from ten to fifteen to twenty seconds to film from the time Lehrman, the associate director of these acts, said, "Action!" until the moment he said, "Cut!" He would then congratulate everybody on doing a good job, and follow that with an order to "Take five!" or "Take ten!" As soon as the break was over, everybody returned to their places to begin rehearsing the next scene.

When the time came to set up the last scene to be shot before lunch. Lehrman left the set, and returned a few minutes later with five extras: three women and two men. One of the female extras had hair the color of a rusty iron pipe. As soon as she saw this girl, Maisy forgot about the filming of a moving picture and wondered if this could be the girl Katy had mentioned, the extra named Alma. She didn't have to wait long to find out.

Lehrman instructed the carpenters to put the set together as soon as the break was over and everybody was back. The background was a false store front. The director explained the scene over the pounding of hammers on nails. One male extra—a short, thin, mustachioed fellow—and one female extra—a somewhat attractive blonde—were to stand in front of the store window, ostensibly admiring some merchandise on display. Another male extra—this one tall and homely—and a female extra—the red-haired girl— were to walk past them and turn their heads toward the same window display as they did. The other female extra—a barely pretty brunette—and Maisy were to do the same thing but from the opposite direction. Maisy would be closest to the camera so the cameraman could get a shot of her profile before she looked at the store window.

"Now that's all you have to do in this scene. Walk slowly and casually just like anybody on any business street in America would when they are strolling along the avenue window shopping. As you extras are doing your part, Miss Normand will come into the set from the right, stop in the center, turn, and look behind her. She will pause for a few seconds and then turn back to continue moving through the set. Then Mr. Mace will come from the same direction that Miss Normand did. He will also stop in the middle of the set, but instead of turning and looking back, he will call out and wave to Miss Normand, whom he is pursuing. Does everybody understand what they are supposed to do?"

The extras voiced affirmatives all around him.

"Very good. Milo, you can tell Miss Normand and Mr. Mace that we're ready for them now."

Maisy had not seen Milo all morning and had not even thought of him until Lehrman mentioned his name.

The director scanned the set. "Where's Milo?" He spun on a heel. "Has anybody seen Milo this morning? He's supposed to be here on this set. Do you know where he is?"

As if cued, Mabel appeared almost out of nowhere with Fred Mace right behind her. "I'm sorry, Mr. Lehrman, but I sent Milo on some errands for me today."

Lehrman's temper showed itself. "Why wasn't I informed of this earlier?"

Mabel walked past Maisy as if she didn't know her. "I said I was sorry, Mr. Lehrman. I thought Mr. Sennett had told you Milo wouldn't be here today. I suppose I'll have to scold him for being so absentminded, now won't I? Or would you prefer to do it?"

Lehrman frowned. "No, Miss Normand, I will leave that chore for you to do. Are you and Mr. Mace ready to rehearse this scene for me?"

Mabel feigned a subservient bow like a feudal damsel before a medieval king. "Your wish is my command, your majesty."

Maisy and a few others snickered.

The director's grimace darkened. "My command then is for you and Mr. Mace to take your places. The same goes for all of you extras, including you, Miss Malone."

Five rehearsals later Lehrman called for the cameraman to be ready. "Places everybody." He paused to affirm he had been obeyed. "Camera! Action!" Fifteen seconds more. "Cut! Good job everybody. Break for lunch, and everybody be back here by one-thirty. That goes for you extras as well."

Mabel, Mace, and Lehrman left the set first and together. As she passed Maisy, Mabel winked at her, as if to say, "See, I told you I'd take care of Milo for you." At least that's what she meant the blink of one eye to convey.

Maisy received the message Mabel intended for her. Then thinking on her feet, she saw this noon break as an opportunity to get close to the red-haired girl. She sidled up to her. "Excuse me, but I'm new to this business.

What do we do about lunch around here?"

"You're Maisy Malone, right?"

"Guilty as charged."

The girl didn't laugh or even smile. "Alma McComb. I hear you're the new feature actress who will be doing foil parts for Miss Normand."

"That's what they tell me."

"Lucky you."

Maisy shrugged. "I suppose you could say that, if you think being in the right place at the right time is lucky. I just happened to be working with Eddie Foy in Chicago when Mr. Sennett and Miss Normand stopped in to see him perform. When Eddie turned them down on joining the Keystone ensemble, Mr. Sennett asked me if I would be interested in coming out to California to be in his moving pictures. I thought about it for a while, decided to take a chance on Keystone, and now here I am talking to you." She offered up her friendliest smile. "Yes, you could say I was lucky."

Alma nodded and beamed back at Maisy. "And now you're lucky again, Miss Malone."

"How's that?"

"I'm going to let you buy me lunch."

"Well, I don't know how lucky that is, but if it's the price I have to pay to learn the ropes around here, then lunch is on me, Miss McComb."

* * *

Alma took Maisy to the grocery on the northwest corner of Allesandro and Effie streets, which was only down the hill a short distance from the studio.

The Edendale store served sandwiches and cold bottled beverages at lunchtime, a practice they had started three years earlier when William Selig opened his Polyscope studio the next block up Allesandro. The film company's workers would rush down the hill en masse to stand in line at the counter to pay fifteen cents for a sandwich and an eight-ounce bottle of ice-cold Coca-Cola, Pepsi-Cola, Dr. Pepper, Chero-Cola, Hires Root Beer, or Vernor's Ginger Ale. After a while, someone at the studio got the idea of asking one person to make the food run for him as a favor. Pretty soon three people paid a nickel each to one person to get their lunch order for them. That practice hadn't carried over at Keystone because the walk back to the comedy studio was not so far up the hill.

Maisy had no problem with paying for Alma's sandwich and soda pop. She would have offered to do it anyway, even if Alma hadn't so insolently made it a condition of taking her under a wing for this one lesson into the routines and customs of the studio. Alma had something Maisy wanted, and the cost of a meal was a small price to pay for it.

As they walked down Allesandro, Alma opened a conversation with a question. "Rumor has it you were with Milo when he discovered Leslie Clover's body yesterday. Is that true?"

"Not quite. Milo discovered Mr. Clover's body while I was waiting in the car."

"Mr. Clover?" Alma giggled. "Oh, of course, you didn't know him like some of us girls around here knew him."

"What does that mean?"

"Now I don't mean to speak ill of the dead and all, but it means he was an S-O-B. Oh, sure, he was nice at first. Aren't they all? They take you to dinner and a movie a time or two, but sooner or later they want something in return. Having been in Vaudeville, I'll bet you know what that is. Men in that business are probably no different than they are in this one."

"I don't know that for certain. No man in this business has asked me out yet."

"Don't worry about that, Miss Malone. It's only a matter of time before lots of them will be asking. You got the looks and the shape they all want ... for a good time." Alma frowned for having said that. "I hope that doesn't offend you, Miss Malone. I meant nothing—"

"Forget it, Alma." Maisy pointed at her bosom. "Ever since these started growing, I've been pinched, pulled, and propositioned by men of all ages. I've slapped so many lechers who have gotten fresh with me that I'm surprised I don't have callouses on my hands from doing it."

Alma studied her for a second. "Hey, you're not one of those Goody Two-shoes who look down your noses at girls like me who have to do whatever it takes to get ahead, are you?"

"I don't look down my nose at anybody, Alma, because someday ... that person might be higher up the ladder of success looking *down ... at me.*"

Alma mulled over Maisy's remark for a few seconds before smiling for the first time since meeting her. "I think I'm going to like you, Miss Malone."

"Thanks, but would you mind calling me Maisy? At least when we're together like this."

"Okay, Maisy."

They went into the store, and Maisy bought their lunches. Then they went outside, found a spot on the curb that was shaded by one of the palm trees that lined Allesandro, and sat down with their legs crossed so their skirts would hide everything beneath them from public view.

"So how long have you been in the moving picture business, Alma?"

"I'm not in the business yet. I'm an extra. We're basically day workers. We show up in the morning and sit on the benches outside the studio, hoping we'll get a call from a director like I did this morning. I'll get a dollar and fifty cents for doing that scene this morning. If I do another one this afternoon, I'll make three bucks for the day."

"What if you're in more than one scene in the morning, do you get paid more?"

"Nope. It doesn't make any difference whether you're in one scene or five scenes or ten scenes before lunch. Extras get one dollar and fifty cents for working in the morning and one dollar and fifty cents for working in the afternoon. But if you leave the studio before lunch, you don't get paid. Same goes if you leave before quitting time in the evening. You don't get paid for the afternoon work."

"How do they know if you leave early?"

"The studio's fanatic bookkeeper, McHatton. He makes sure. He comes around each set throughout the morning and sees who's working and then he checks the extras bench after lunch to see if those people who worked that morning are back there and ready for the afternoon. At the end of the day, he sits on the bungalow porch waiting to see you walk by him. You wave at the little worm to make sure he sees you. Makes us feel like we're sheep being counted or something."

"Hardly seems worth your time to be an extra."

"But it's the best way to get an acting job. Maybe not a lead actor or feature actor job, maybe only a bit player, which is a step up from being an extra. A director sees you on film and you look good to him, and he just might give you a part in his next film. Might not be a big part, just a bit role, but it pays more than an extra makes. Five dollars a day, whether you're in one scene or ten."

Maisy did the math in her head. "That's thirty dollars a week. That's almost as much as I make."

"Maybe so, but you get your money whether you work every day or not, just like Miss Normand and the other lead actors and the featured actors in the ensemble. Bit actors only get paid by the day. No acting, no pay."

There was no mistaking the bitterness in Alma's voice, but Maisy chose to ignore it. "Well, I guess I do have some sort of job security, and that counts for something, doesn't it?"

"It sure does."

They ate the rest of their meal in silence.

Alma finished hers first. She wadded up the brown paper her sandwich had been wrapped in and put it in the hollow her skirt made by crossing her legs beneath it. When she drank the last drop of her soda pop, she placed the bottle in the same place.

When she swallowed the last of her sandwich and soft drink, Maisy tossed the crumpled up paper and bottle into the gutter. She stood up and shook off any bread crumbs that might have fallen on her skirt.

"Well, I suppose we should get back to the studio."

"Sure, but would you mind waiting while I take the bottles back into the store to get back the deposit on them?" Alma stood up, stepped into the street, retrieved the bottle and sandwich wrapper Maisy had thrown there, and then picked up a few other pieces of trash lying there as well. "You don't mind if I keep the penny I get for yours, do you? A penny saved and all that."

"No, you go right ahead. Remember, lunch was on me."

"Thanks, Maisy." She nodded with a genuinely sincere smile. "You're all right. You know, if I get into a scene tomorrow, I might be able to pay next week's rent, eat twice a day, *and* do my laundry."

"How much do pay for rent?"

"Six bucks a week. Twenty-five for a month, if I could ever get that much saved up."

As her new acquaintance returned to the store with the bottles, Maisy could only think of how curious it was that Alma took the two sandwich wrappers and the other pieces of paper with her and dropped the refuse in an outdoor wastebasket near the market's door.

Remembering what **Ford Sterling had** told her that morning about catching a catnap whenever possible, Maisy found a spot in the shade on the east side of the studio and lay down. Her body, tired from the short night and now with food in its stomach, wanted her to sleep, but her mind urged her to stay awake and listen to Alma who was still talking to her.

"I've been an extra for Polyscope and for Bison when they were making pictures here. I also tried to get some work at Independent over in Hollywood a couple of times until I figured out they make westerns mostly and don't have as much call for female extras. Sometimes I'd go to Polyscope one day and come here the next. I got to know Mr. Balshofer a little here at Bison and Mr. Boggs a little up the hill at Polyscope. Real gentlemen both of them, especially Mr. Boggs. Too bad about him. Did you know last year he was shot and killed in his office by the studio's Japanese gardener?"

Maisy almost told Alma she had been in London the previous year, but withheld that episode of her life for no other reason than she felt too tired to talk. "No, I didn't." She yawned.

"Crazy S-O-B also shot Mr. Selig. The newspapers said Mr. Selig was fatally wounded, but it turned out he was only shot in the arm trying to protect Mr. Boggs. He was too late. Mr. Boggs was already plugged in the chest. He died right there in his office. He was the top director for Mr. Selig's story films. He would tell us ahead of time if he would need extras the next day. Mr. Balshofer didn't do it quite the same way because he was only making westerns. He needed more male extras than females. He had the men come every day, and he would post a sign on the days when he needed women. If the sign was up, I'd stop here instead of climbing the hill to Polyscope. If there was no sign in front of the Bison bungalow and I knew Mr. Boggs needed extras that day, then I'd ride the Red Car up the hill. If there was no sign and I knew Mr. Boggs *didn't* need any extras that day, then I'd gripe about it and catch the next Red Car home. I got to act for Mr. Balshofer a few times. I was a saloon girl every time. I guess I have the face and figure of a saloon girl. What do you think, Maisy? Do I look like a saloon girl to you?"

Maisy didn't answer. She was sound asleep.

"Got you up early this morning, didn't they, Maisy Malone? Well, I can't blame you for being asleep then. You go ahead and get your forty winks. I'll wake you when it's time to go back to the set."

* * *

Alma kept her promise and woke Maisy at the right time. They made it back to the set just seconds before Lehrman got there.

Mabel and Fred Mace had also returned to the set. The next scene on the schedule to be shot included them and the same group of extras. Actually, it was pretty much the same scene as the one they had shot in the morning. This time Mabel and Mace would come from the left, although in the same order, Mabel first followed by Mace; and each of them would pause and look behind at a pursuer. The extras were switched around as well. Instead of an extra of each gender standing in front of the store window, this time Maisy and Alma were chosen to stare at the merchandise on display, while the tall and homely fellow and the somewhat attractive blonde passed by behind them from one direction, and the short, thin man and the barely pretty brunette walked behind them from the opposite way.

As they were setting up, Maisy had to ask one question of the director. "Mr. Lehrman, won't the audience notice you're using the same extras in both scenes?"

"They might if they see the film often enough, which is a good thing for us, right? And if they should figure out we're using the same extras in both scenes, then I hope they figure out the joke is really on them."

"Why is that?"

"Because then they will come see more of our comedies to see if we do it again, and that, Miss Malone, is why our pay envelopes are full every Saturday afternoon. *Versteh?*"

"*Natürlich, mein Fuehrer!*"

Maisy's sudden use of German startled Lehrman. He perused her face for a moment. "*Spricht du Deutsch?*"

Maisy held up her thumb and forefinger a mere half inch apart. "*Etwas. Nicht viel.* I picked it up from listening to the German Jews I worked with in Vaudeville. *Gut Leute, ja?*"

"*Ja, gut Leute.*" Lehrman chewed one side of his lower lip as he mulled over a thought. He nodded, but to no one in particular, as an answer came to him. "In this scene, Miss Malone, I want you and Miss … what is your last name, red-haired girl?"

"McComb, Mr. Lehrman. Alma McComb."

"Miss Malone, I want you and Miss McComb to be looking at each other and talking to each other and act like you are excited about buying what is in the store window. Smile and point at the window and point at yourselves. Do you understand?"

Both girls nodded, but only Maisy spoke. "Sure, I get it."

"You don't get it, Miss McComb?"

"Oh, yes, sir, I do. I've done some acting before. I know exactly what you mean."

"Good. And you are sure you get it, Miss Malone?"

"I've spent the last six years on the stage, Mr. Lehrman. I get it."

"You were an actress?"

"Vaudeville in America and music halls in England, where they throw stuff at you when you're not funny or you sing off key." She scanned the other people on the set. "Anybody here got any fruit or vegetables in your pockets?"

Led by Mabel and Mace, everybody except the Austrian-born director laughed and shook their heads.

"Well, at least if I don't get it right here, Mr. Lehrman, I won't have to worry about dodging any rotten tomatoes."

She got another round of laughs, again at Mabel and Mace's instigation, but still not with the director's approval.

"You are funny now, Miss Malone. But let us see how funny you are when the camera is grinding." He clapped his hands together. "Places, everybody. We rehearse now."

* * *

After the scene was filmed, Lehrman gave the cast and crew another short break. Too short for Maisy to say more than a few words to Alma.

"Does this mean you'll get acting pay for today?"

"I hope so, and I owe it to you, Maisy. Thanks a bunch."

Lehrman walked up to them. "You did fine, Miss Malone, but keep this is mind. I have an endless supply of rotten tomatoes, but I don't have to throw them at you. I only have to open my mouth and out they will come. *Versteh?*"

"Yes, Mr. Lehrman."

He walked away slowly, confident that he had made his point.

"I think that was more for my benefit than it was for yours, Maisy. The actors can get uppity on occasion, but the extras don't have that luxury. We do as we're told or we're out in the cold."

"They throw you off the lot?"

Alma shook her head. "Worse! They don't use you anymore, and some of them even tell directors at other studios that you're a troublemaker and then they won't give you any work either. It happened to a guy I was going out with regularly a year or so ago. He had to go back to being a real cowboy for a while, and that ended our relationship."

Mabel approached Maisy and Alma. "I didn't get to watch you two perform, but I know it satisfied ol' Heinrich. Look at him over there talking to Freddie and that extra. He's bragging about what a great director he is for having thought of having you two acting in the background. You know, he's right about that. When Mack sees that scene, he'll pat Henry on the back so much and so hard that he'll raise a welt or two. This could be a break for you, Miss McComb. Henry is sure to tell Mack how well you took direction from him. This could get you more acting scenes."

Alma replied nervously. "Thanks, Miss Normand. I hope so."

Mabel winked at her. "I'll mention you to Mack as well." She turned to Maisy. "As for you, my fine feathered friend, I'd be careful about sparring with Henry. His temper isn't as bad as Mack's, but he can burn you good if you push him the wrong way. The man has a sharp tongue in *two* languages."

"Thanks for the advice, Miss Normand. I'll keep that in mind for the next time."

"You'd better, or there might not be a next time after that one."

Maisy nodded. "Fair enough."

"Well, I've got another scene to shoot with Mack. I'll see you at the end of the day, Maisy. It was nice meeting you, Miss McComb."

"Likewise, Miss Norman."

Mabel toddled off toward another part of the lot, leaving Maisy alone with Alma.

"For a leading lady, she seems really nice. You must have spent some time with her already getting to know each other."

"What makes you say that?"

"She called you by your first name and said she would see you later. That says familiarity to me."

"They put me up at the Hollywood Hotel where she and Mr. Mace and Mr. Sterling are also staying for the time being. I've got until Monday to find another place to stay or start paying for my room at the hotel myself."

"The Hollywood Hotel is some swanky joint, I hear. I've never been in it myself."

"It's only temporary."

Alma winked at Maisy. "It's too bad Leslie is dead. He had a spare room at the bungalow. I'm sure he would have let you stay there for a while."

Before Maisy could ask her to explain that remark, Lehrman called everybody back to the set for the next scene, one in which both girls got another chance to act, this time with the short, thin, man with the pencil mustache—the same extra who had been in the scenes with them earlier and who had been talking to Lehrman and Mace during the break.

"In this scene, Miss Malone and Miss McComb will be joined by Mr. Shannon at the window. The three of them will be having an animated discussion about the display, while the extras pass by them. At the same time, a policeman will enter the scene in pursuit of Mr. Mace who is in pursuit of Miss Normand in the previous scene."

At that moment, feature actor Hank Mann appeared on the set wearing a policeman's uniform.

"Mr. Mann will come from the left, stop in front of the store, shake his nightstick at Mr. Mace, and then proceed across the set." Lehrman rearranged the other extras. He had Shannon change hats and jackets with the taller man. Since Shannon's was too small for him, the larger fellow carried the coat on his arm as he walked through the set. The blonde and the brunette also exchanged hats and walked by the store front individually from opposite directions. "Now does everybody understand what I want you to do in this scene?"

A chorus of positive responses came from the actors and extras.

The director eyed Maisy. "Are you sure, Miss Malone?"

Maisy answered as humbly as she could. "Yes, Mr. Lehrman."

"Good. Places, everybody. Now we rehearse."

After three run-throughs, Lehrman appeared satisfied. "Very good. I believe we are ready to film. Places, everybody. Set the lighting." He waited for a moment while the reflectors were adjusted. "Camera." Seeing the cameraman give him a thumbs-up, the director shouted the final command. "Action!"

Shannon walked up to Alma and Maisy, causing Maisy to move to the middle of their trio so that the camera could see her almost straight on, but not completely because she had to turn her head a quarter to the left to look at Shannon. They immediately engaged in conversation. At the same time, the remaining three extras entered the set. Just as they came to the midway point, Mann raced into view from the left, stopped, shook his nightstick, and then blew his whistle as loud as he could, startling the other six people in front of the camera so much that each of them showed a physical reaction of jumping away from the sound and raising their hands to their ears in one way or another. Mann then raced off the set with the others staring after him.

"Cut!" Lehrman leaped from his chair, a huge smile lighting up his face. He clapped his hands rapidly. "*Wunderbar! Wunderbar!*"

Mann came back laughing as well. "See? I told you it would scare the b'jeezus out of them, didn't I?"

"It certainly did. That was perfect, everybody. You reacted exactly as we had hoped. Mr. Sennett will love what you have done here today. Now take a long break to calm yourselves, while we prepare for the next scene. Be back here in half an hour. That should give each of you time to change your underwear." He and Mann laughed raucously at the director's joke.

Alma leaned close to Maisy and spoke softly to her. "He thinks that's hilarious. I'd like to get him alone for a while. I'll show him what's funny."

Shannon heard her. "Where's your sense of humor, Alma?" His voice still contained a strong hint of his native Ireland. "You can't work in comedy without a sense of humor, you know."

"Watch your mouth, Jackie-boy. I might be a woman, but I'm not always a lady, if you get my drift."

"I meant no insult, Alma."

"You better not have."

Shannon focused on Maisy. "It was a pleasure to do the scene with you, Miss Malone. I hope we get to work together more in the future."

"Now how often do you think that's going to be?" asked Alma.

"You never know, do you, Alma?" He wiggled his eyebrows to accentuate the twinkle in his eyes. "You never know." He bowed to Maisy. "If you'll excuse me, Miss Malone. I need a drink of water. See you on the next set." Then he walked off.

"What did you call him? Jackie-boy?"

"His real name is John Michael Shannon, but he goes by Jack. That's how he wants to be billed, if he ever gets his name listed in the cast."

"You know, Alma, I get the impression you don't like him very much. Do you know him well?"

"About as well as anybody around here does. He showed up right after Mr. Sennett opened the studio. He was always hanging around with Leslie Clover. Beats me why, since Leslie was English and Jackie is Irish. Most Irish natives I know hate anybody and everybody from England. You'd think they'd leave that stuff behind them once they came to America. I guess Jackie and Leslie did."

"Why do you think that?"

"Jackie stayed at the bungalow occasionally. When Leslie would bring a lady guest home with him, if you know what I mean, Jackie would stay elsewhere. That was the situation until last Saturday when Jackie finally got his own place in the same building where Milo Cole lives in the Bunker Hill neighborhood near Phoebe Alden and Vivian Vanover."

"Gloria Newman told me about Vivian, but who is Phoebe Alden?"

"Phoebe is another extra here. You can't miss her. She's taller than most of the men around here, and she's got red hair a couple of shades darker than mine. She keeps it real short because she usually has to wear a wig for a scene. She sometimes plays a man's part because she's so tall. She's a real hoot, too."

"Can't wait to meet her."

"Anyway, Saturday is payday here, and last week Jackie finally had made enough as an extra and a bit player to pay rent for a place."

"So Jackie has played bit roles before today?"

"He's done a few here and there. Leslie had been getting nearly all the male bit and character roles for the past few weeks. Now that poor Leslie is gone, I suppose Jackie-boy will be getting those roles. Milo Cole would get more bit and character roles, but he's usually too busy doing things for Mr.

Sennett outside the studio, like picking you up at the station yesterday and running errands for Mabel Normand today. I hear he gets paid like a bit player on days he does things like that."

"Really?"

"That's what I've heard."

Before the conversation could go any further, Lehrman called them back to work for one more scene with all the same people. Regrettably for Maisy, it was the last scene to be filmed that day with this group of extras. Once it was concluded, Alma, Shannon, and the others were sent back to the extras bench to wait for their next call to a set, leaving Maisy alone to watch and learn more about making moving pictures.

* * *

An hour before sundown Lehrman wrapped up shooting for the day and sent everybody on their way for the evening.

Maisy went to the costume department to return the outfit she had worn that day. She met Katy Killoy at the door as she was coming out.

"So how was your first full day on the set, Miss Malone?"

"It was a real experience, Mrs. Killoy."

Katy gave her a grand smile for being so polite and respectful. "Were you able to get any sleep during the breaks? I thought I saw you at lunchtime with that red-haired extra named Alma. You looked like you were sleeping then."

"I was. That nap got me through the afternoon."

"Did you get to talk much to Alma?"

"We had lunch together. She told me a whole lot I didn't know before about how things are done around here and about some of the people who work here."

"Did she say anything about me?"

Maisy thought this was an odd question coming from Katy, but she kept her curiosity to herself. "No, not a word. We mostly talked about Milo Cole, Jackie Shannon, and Leslie Clover."

"Now there's a trio of trouble for you. The things I could tell you about them three. But it will have to wait, darlin'. I've got to get down to the corner and catch the Red Car for home. The family will be expecting me in time to cook supper, don't you know? Just put your costume on the table inside, and I'll see you in the morning."

Katy scurried away without another word.

* * *

Instead of chatting on the ride back to the hotel that evening, Maisy and Mabel napped just like Mace and Sterling did. When the Cadillac arrived at the Hollywood resort, they awakened to see Milo Cole standing at the door waiting for them. Wilson and the bellhops assisted them as usual, and each of the actors took turns greeting Cole as they passed him and entered the lobby.

He followed them inside.

"Miss Normand?"

Mabel stopped and turned to Sterling and Mace. "George, why don't you and Freddie go ahead into the dining room and get us a table? I've got some business to finish up with Milo. Then Maisy and I will join you as soon as I'm done."

"Okay, Mabel," said Sterling. He and Mace continued to the hotel restaurant.

"I couldn't get everything you wanted me to get for you, Miss Normand. I didn't have enough time."

"Didn't have enough time? You had all day."

"Not exactly. I spent more than half the day at the Central Police Station downtown. Detective Browning sent a patrolman by my place first thing this morning, and he told me to go down to the station or Detective Browning would send a couple of officers to arrest me and bring me downtown for him. I didn't want that because the neighbors might see me being led away and tell the landlord and I might lose my place because of being arrested. So I went downtown voluntarily. Detective Browning questioned me all the way through lunchtime."

"What did he ask you, Milo?" asked Maisy.

"What didn't he ask me? He wanted to know everything about me and everything I knew about Leslie Clover."

"So what did you tell him?"

"I answered every single one of his questions as truthfully as I could, and he had a stenographer write it all down. When he was done, he thanked me and told me I could leave. For a while there, I thought he was going to pin Leslie's death on me and I was going to jail."

Mabel and Maisy exchanged glances before Maisy focused on Cole again. "Milo, you haven't spoken to anybody at the studio about us being at Mr. Clover's bungalow last night, have you?"

"No, of course not. Why do you ask?"

"Well, I have that bet with Detective Browning, and I don't want anybody to know about it. I also don't want anybody at the studio to know I'm trying to figure out who murdered Mr. Clover. If word gets out, nobody will talk to me and I might not be able to figure out who did it and win that bet. So please don't say anything to anybody, will you?"

"No, I'll keep my trap shut, Maisy. After being grilled by Detective Browning today, I really want you to win that bet more than ever now."

"Thank you, Milo."

"You're welcome. Miss Normand, I had the things I did get for you sent up to your room. I hope that was okay."

Mabel dug into her purse. "That's fine, Milo." She handed him a ten-dollar bill. "The extra is for any carfare you had to pay to get around town today."

"You don't have to do that, Miss Normand."

"You earned it, Milo. Now take it. We'll see you at the studio tomorrow."

"You might see Detective Browning there as well. He said something about coming out to Edendale to question some of the people I mentioned to him who might know something about Leslie."

"Whose names did you give him, Milo?" asked Maisy.

"Let me see." He looked skyward as if the names were written on the lobby ceiling. "There was Max Asher, Gloria Newman, Lloyd Bacon, Vivian Vanover, Ed Kennedy, Victoria Forde, George Jeske, Alma McComb, Bobby Dunn, Lucy Ward, Jack Shannon, Katy Killoy, Hank Mann, Phoebe Alden, Slim Summerville, Alice Davenport, big Frank Alexander, Betty and Fritz Schade, Mack Riley, Virginia Nightingale, Fred Mace, Henry Lehrman, Ford Sterling, and Chet Franklin. That's all I could think of at the time."

Mabel shook her head. "Gee, Milo, that's pretty much everybody who works there, including some extras I don't know."

"He did leave out Mr. Sennett."

Milo nodded. "Detective Browning was already aware of who runs the studio. He said he would probably start by interviewing him."

Mabel grimaced. "Oh, swell. That should put Mack in a good mood for the day. It's a good thing tomorrow is Saturday, and we only work half the day. I'd really hate to be on the set with him for a full day that starts off with him being questioned by the police."

"Milo, could you write down the names of all those people you mentioned to Browning? I'd like to talk to them before he does, if I can. Of course, I'm not sure how I can do that because I've only met a few of them."

A coy smile curled Mabel's lips. "I know how you can do it." She took Cole by the arm and snuggled up to him. "Milo can take you around and introduce you to everybody, can't you, Milo?"

Cole blushed. "Sure ... I guess."

Maisy and Mabel winked at each other like two schoolgirls about to pull a prank on the football team's star player.

Rising at 4:45 in the morning still didn't sit well with Maisy, but today she climbed out of bed as soon as she depressed the alarm button on the back of the clock. Knowing she would have to go to the dressing room as soon as the daily shooting meeting broke up, she didn't bother to put on any makeup or even brush her hair. She merely ran her fingers through it to untangle some of the knots that had been made in her coiffure while sleeping. Feeling that was sufficient attention to herself, she dressed and hurried down to the lobby with plenty of time to spare, arriving seconds before the other actors made their first appearances of the day.

"Good morning, everyone."

Sterling peered at Maisy with curiosity. "My, aren't you the chipper one this morning? Sleep well, Miss Malone?"

"Well enough, Mr. Sterling. Thank you for asking."

Mace's mood wasn't so cheerful. "Come on, Miss Sunshine. Let's get to the car so we can all go back to sleep."

* * *

Since he was a little flush with cash, Cole called for a taxi to pick him up and take him to work that morning. Being in a generous mood, he invited Jack Shannon, who lived in the same building, to ride along with him. They waited on the corner of Figueroa and West 3rd Street for their ride.

"Milo, would you mind if we stop by and pick up Vivian Vanover? She lives on Beaudry."

"Sure, why not? We might as well pick up Phoebe Alden, too. She lives on the same block."

"Won't that make it too crowded in the taxi?"

"You're right, Jack. So why don't you take the Red Car and I'll pick up Vivian and Phoebe by myself?"

Shannon caught on. "That's okay. We don't have to pick up either one of them."

The taxi arrived, and the two actors got into the back seat.

"I understand you met our new feature actress yesterday. What did you think of her?"

"Do you mean Maisy Malone?"

"She's the one."

"Yes, I met her on the set. She's got grit, that one. Attractive, too. Don't know how well she'll do in this business, but she showed some promise yesterday. She was quite animated when we were doing a scene together. Mr. Lehrman thought she did well. I heard you picked her up at the Santa Fe station and took her to the Hollywood Hotel. Is that right?"

"You heard right, chum."

"I also heard she was with you when you found Leslie's body the other day." Shannon shivered at the thought. "Glad you found him and not me. I'm not sure what I would have done if I had come across him dead on the floor of his bedroom like that. He was such a good friend. Yours, too, right?"

"Yes, we were friends. I met him when I first came out here from back east. He was trying to break into the business over at Independent before it became Universal. He showed me the ropes over there. He put me up at the bungalow for a while, too, just like he did for you. You know how that went, don't you?"

Shannon smiled. "You bet I do. Lucky sonofagun with the girls, wasn't he?"

"It was that British accent of his that got them. He really knew how to play the ladies with that voice of his. Get them laughing, and the next thing you knew he had them in the kip, as he put it so delicately."

"For a limey, he was all right. He never said a disparaging word to me about me being Irish and all. First one I ever met like him."

They sat quietly for a moment as each contemplated the loss of their mutual friend. Then Shannon spoke again just as the taxi pulled onto Allesandro Street.

"Do you think there will be a wake for him? Nothing like a good wake to give a fellow a proper send-off."

"You know, I hadn't thought about that. I suppose we should give that some thought. A wake and a funeral. We can't let the county or the city bury him in a pauper's grave. We should do something about that, don't you think?"

"Did he have any family here?"

"No, and he didn't mention anybody back in England either."

"Maybe you should talk to Mr. Sennett about it, Milo. He is the director-general of the studio, ain't he? I'm sure he would have something to say about that, don't you think?"

Cole tipped his head to one side as the car arrived at the studio. "I suppose you're right about that, Jack. Somebody should mention it to him."

"Yes, and since you're so close to him, running around all the time doing stuff for him, it should be you who does the talking, Milo."

"Me?"

"That's right, my friend. You."

Cole wasn't exactly keen on the idea, but he knew Shannon was right. He should be the one to speak to Sennett about a wake and a funeral for Leslie Clover, but before he could do that, he had to speak to Maisy and Mabel first.

* * *

Willie drove the Cadillac into the driveway next to Sennett's house on the lot within seconds of Cole and Shannon getting out of the taxi on the other side of Allesandro. Maisy saw the pair of ambitious actors and nudged Mabel.

"Look, there's Milo and Jack Shannon across the street. They're a little early, aren't they?"

"So are we," said Mabel. "We didn't have to wake you up this morning, which is why we were late yesterday."

Cole and Shannon sprinted across the street ahead of the Red Car creeping up the hill at that moment. They came to a sudden halt in front of Maisy and Mabel and greeted them appropriately.

Having been in the moving picture business longer than both men and Maisy combined, Mabel understood the proper studio etiquette when lesser players met studio leads. She acknowledged Cole and Shannon with a slight bow of her head and a single word. "Gentlemen."

Maisy followed Mabel's example, although she had absolutely no idea why she was doing it. "Gentlemen."

Cole cleared his throat. "Miss Normand, do you think you could arrange for me to speak privately to Mr. Sennett this morning at his earliest convenience?"

"May I ask why you wish to speak privately with Mr. Sennett?"

"Yes, ma'am. Mr. Shannon and I were discussing the late Leslie Clover on our way here this morning, and we suddenly became aware that Leslie has no family here to see to the final ... to his final resting place and the manner in which this should be handled. I ... that is, we ... we thought the matter should be brought to Mr. Sennett's attention, seeing as how Leslie was one of his players and all."

Mabel nodded her agreement. "Yes, of course, you're only right, Mr. Cole. You should bring this matter to Mr. Sennett's attention immediately. I will have a word with him right now. Please excuse me."

Cole and Shannon half-bowed to her as she glided past them toward Sennett who had just then come out on the porch.

Maisy stood in awe as she watched this scene unfold before her. She clicked her cheek as her eyes followed Mabel toward the studio head. "I can hardly believe my eyes and ears. You two talking to each other like she was the lady of the house and you were the butler and the gardener."

"She is the lady of the house, Maisy." Cole bobbled his head a little. "Well, rather the studio, not the house. She's a leading actress, and she's the only one at Keystone right now."

"What about Alice Davenport? Isn't she a leading actress, too?"

Cole shook his head. "Oh, no. Mother Davenport is a character actress. She never does leads. At least not so far, she hasn't."

"Mother Davenport? I thought her name was Alice."

"It is, but because she's old enough to be just about everybody's mother, including Mr. Sennett's, we've been calling her Mother around here. Mr. Sennett started it. He said she's been acting longer than any of the rest of us have been alive."

"Really? How old is she?"

"You'll have to ask her. All I know is, she was on the stage when she was only five years old and someone said she was born during the Civil War."

"Then she must be around fifty years old. I guess she is old enough to be everybody's mother around here."

"Have you met her yet?"

Maisy shook her head. "No, not formally. She was in the office when you took me up there the other day, remember? I've seen her around the lot a few times, but we haven't had the opportunity to chat yet."

"Before we leave today, I'll introduce you to her." Cole motioned toward Shannon. "Jack here said he was in a scene with you yesterday."

"Yes, we were, but we didn't get much chance to get acquainted. How are you this morning, Mr. Shannon?"

"I'm doing just fine, Miss Malone. And how about you? How are you this morning?"

"I'm doing better today. The last two days have been such a whirlwind for me. Arriving in Los Angeles, being put up at the Hollywood Hotel, finding a dead body, and all before lunch on my first day in California. I don't know if Milo told you or not, but I saw your friend Mr. Clover on the stage in London. He was really funny. I think he would have been wonderful in moving pictures."

"Yes, he was a very comical man. And you say you saw him on the stage in London?"

Maisy quickly retold the circumstances of seeing Clover at the Royal Comedy Theatre. "And the next time I see him, he's lying on the floor in his bedroom … murdered by someone who knew him."

Shannon became visibly distressed. "Murdered by someone who *knew* him? How do you know that?"

"People don't die from their corsets being too tight, Mr. Shannon. And they can't get them tight enough by themselves to faint from a lack of air. Therefore, somebody murdered him, and it could only have been somebody close to him. Who else would have done it?"

"I don't know. Who else would have done it?"

"Nobody. The murderer had to be whoever it was that laced up his corset and drew the strings so tight on him that he passed out when he started smoking a cigarette."

Her last remark paled Shannon. "How do you know that?"

Before Maisy could answer his question, Mabel returned. "I spoke with Mr. Sennett, and he said he would speak to all of us at once ... during the shooting briefing ... about a wake and funeral for Mr. Clover."

The sun peeked over the horizon, and the entire crew and acting ensemble gathered in front of the porch to hear Sennett. He went over the shooting schedule for the day with the actors and told the extras they would be needed in several scenes. He concluded the meeting with remarks about Leslie Clover.

"It's been brought to my attention that Leslie Clover has no family here in the United States. No family, that is, except us, all of you good people ... and me ... here at Keystone. Therefore, it behooves us to see that Leslie is given a proper wake and funeral. So I'm asking each and every one of you to join me in contributing to the expense of a wake and a funeral. Since today is payday, I'm asking each of you to donate at least one dollar toward those expenses. I will be contributing twenty dollars myself. If we can't raise enough money to pay for the whole thing, then I'll contact Mr. Bauman in New York about the studio making up the difference. In the meantime, Milo, I'd like you to take the morning off and see to all the arrangements for Leslie's funeral and wake."

Cole had a hunch he would be the one to perform this service for the studio. Thus prepared, he replied instantly. "Sure thing, Mr. Sennett. It would be my honor, sir."

"Good. Now let's all get to work."

As everybody drifted away toward their first chore of the morning, Cole cornered Maisy. "I've never had to do anything about arranging something like this before. Where do I start?"

"Well, I think you start by finding an undertaker and a funeral home. It seems obvious that an undertaker would know what to do about a wake and a funeral, don't you think?"

"Oh, yes, of course. An undertaker and a funeral home. Okay, I'd better find Willie and get at it then."

* * *

As the studio car with Cole as the only passenger riding in the front seat with Willie the driver left the lot, a 1911 Ford Model T 5-Passenger Touring Car with its top down turned onto Allesandro Street from Sunset Boulevard. Two uniformed Los Angeles policemen occupied the front seat. As the Keystone's Cadillac passed the Ford, Cole recognized the two people in the back seat as Detective Ed Browning and the stenographer who had taken down his statement the previous day.

"There goes trouble, Willie. Mr. Sennett isn't going to be happy about those cops showing up at the studio this early in the day."

Browning spotted Cole in the front seat of the Cadillac as the cars passed each other. "Did you see who that was, Miss Sharpe?"

The bespectacled police stenographer Nellie Sharpe turned her head to look at the Cadillac as it went down the hill. Returning her focus to the front again, she answered Browning, speaking with an accent that revealed her native country to be England. "Yes, sir, I believe it was Mr. Cole, the man you interviewed yesterday at the station."

"You are quite right, Miss Sharpe. You know, if that man didn't have such an ironclad alibi, he'd be number one on my list of suspects for this murder. He has a lot to gain with Clover dead."

"Looks like he's already getting to enjoy some of the spoils of Mr. Clover's unfortunate demise. He's riding around in a big touring car."

"Miss Sharpe, may I remind you we are also riding in a touring car?"

"Oh, yes, sir, I suppose we are, aren't we?" She touched the bun of her mousy brown hair as if it needed to be put back into its proper place. "But isn't that a Cadillac Mr. Cole is riding in, while we're riding in a Ford?" She batted her brown eyes to accentuate her point.

Browning shook his head in dismay, ignoring her remark. "Pull into the driveway beside the bungalow, Barney."

The long-nosed, sharp-chinned Orville Barney, a former brakeman for the Atchison Topeka & Santa Fe Railroad and now a policeman for the city of Los Angeles, followed the order without hesitation.

"You boys, sit tight until I find the man in charge here. Miss Sharpe, follow me please. And have your notebook out and at the ready. I want every bit of conversation here on record."

Dressed to the nines as usual in a dark suit and bowler, Browning left the car and mounted the steps of the bungalow with the stenographer two steps behind him. He knocked on the door and waited.

A short man wearing spectacles, sleeve garters, and a green eyeshade answered the detective's summons. He looked beyond Browning and saw the uniformed officers in the front seat of the Ford. Grave concern shaded his thirtyish face until he noticed Miss Sharpe behind the detective. Then his expression changed to surprise.

"Why, Miss Sharpe, what brings you to Keystone Motion Pictures Studio this fine morning?"

Browning looked at the man and then at the stenographer. "You know this man, Miss Sharpe?"

Nellie cleared her throat before speaking cautiously. "We once lived in the same boardinghouse on Grant Avenue, sir. However, that was several months ago."

"I see." The policeman focused on the diminutive fellow standing in the doorway. "I am Detective Sergeant Edward Browning of the Los Angeles

Police Department, and Miss Sharpe is one of our department stenographers. I wish to speak to the man in charge of this moving picture studio. I believe his name is Sennett."

"Mr. Sennett is already out on the lot preparing to shoot scenes for a film. Is there something I can help you with, sir?"

"Who are you, sir?"

"I am Hugh J. McHatton, sir."

"And what is it you do here, Mr. McHatton?"

"I am the bookkeeper and paymaster for the studio."

"Is this your office, Mr. McHatton?"

The bookkeeper shook his head. "No, sir, it is not. This is Mr. Sennett's residence … for the time being, that is. I am only here at this moment to get the payroll from the safe. I was in the process of doing just that when you knocked on the door. My office is inside that large building in the rear."

"I am sorry for interrupting you, Mr. McHatton, but it is imperative that I speak with Mr. Sennett as soon as possible."

"It's about Mr. Clover's death, isn't it? I understand from the talk going around the studio that he was murdered."

"That determination has yet to be made official, sir, which is why I am here now to speak to Mr. Sennett first before I start questioning you and everybody else who works here."

McHatton flinched. "You want to question me, sir? But why? I barely knew the man. He was nothing more to me than a name on the payroll record. Other than giving him his pay envelope each of the last three Saturdays, I had absolutely no contact with Mr. Clover whatsoever. He was just another name on the payroll record. That's all he was to me, sir. I assure you of that fact."

"Calm down, Mr. McHatton. I believe you. And you have answered all the questions I was going to ask you anyway. There is one other thing, though. May I see his payroll record?"

"Certainly. It's in my office. If you will allow me to finish getting the payroll from the safe, I'll take you there and show you his record."

"Yes, of course, Mr. McHatton. Miss Sharpe and I will wait for you here on the porch."

The bookkeeper turned to go back into the house.

"Oh, one more thing, Mr. McHatton."

The little man looked over his shoulder. "Yes?"

"I saw Mr. Milo Cole leaving the studio as we were arriving. Do you know where he was going?"

"Mr. Sennett sent him to make arrangements for a wake and a funeral for Mr. Clover."

"Of course. Thank you, sir."

"May I go now?"

"Yes, of course."

The bookkeeper disappeared into the house.

"I hope you got all that, Miss Sharpe. The man did talk rather fast, didn't he?"

"My shorthand is just as quick, sir."

Browning turned away so she couldn't see him rolling his eyes. "Yes, I'm certain it is, Miss Sharpe."

* * *

McHatton's fastidiously neat work space was in the corner beneath Sennett's office. Of course, it was smaller, but for the time being while the new studio office building was under construction, it was adequate for the one-man accounting department.

"Here is Mr. Clover's pay record, Detective."

Browning accepted it. "Thank you. Now would you please inform Mr. Sennett that I am here and that I wish to speak with him *pronto?*"

"*Pronto*, sir?"

"That's Mexican for right now, Mr. McHatton. Apparently, you haven't been living here in California for very long, have you?"

"No, sir, I haven't."

"Well, never mind that. Would you please inform Mr. Sennett that I am here and that I wish to speak with him *immediately?*"

"I can't leave my office, sir."

"And why not?"

"The payroll, sir."

Browning sighed with a touch of exasperation. "Mr. McHatton, have you forgotten that I am a police officer? I will remain here and guard your payroll until you return."

"Oh, yes, of course. I'll find Mr. Sennett immediately and inform him that you are here and that you wish to speak with him."

As soon as McHatton left the room, Browning went over Leslie Clover's pay record. "Make a note of this, Miss Sharpe. Mr. Clover began working here on September third as an extra. He worked every day that week and received fifteen dollars pay on September seventh. The next week he worked as a bit player for four days and as an extra for two other days. He was paid twenty-six dollars on September fourteenth. The following week he worked as a featured actor for two days and a bit player for four days and was paid thirty-two dollars. On Monday, Tuesday, and Wednesday of this week he worked as a featured actor and earned six dollars for each day. Did you get that, Miss Sharpe?"

"Yes, sir." She read back everything he said word-for-word.

"It appears Mr. Clover was headed up the moving picture ladder here at Keystone."

"Yes, sir, it does appear that way."

The bellowing of an angry voice suddenly came within Browning's hearing. "I believe that is Mr. Sennett returning with Mr. McHatton."

"How do you know that, sir?"

"Irate men do not yell at the wind, Miss Sharpe. They only yell at other people, especially those who bring them bad news."

"You would be that bad news, sir?"

"Indeed, I would, Miss Sharpe."

Sennett burst through the office door. "Why in the hell can't this wait until we're done working for the day? I have a shooting schedule to keep. I can't have my actors and crews standing around doing nothing. We only have so many hours in the day when there is sufficient sunlight for us to film. Can't this wait until we're finished for the day?"

"I'm glad to meet you, too, Mr. Sennett. I am Detective Sergeant Ed Browning of the Los Angeles Police Department."

"What do you want from me, Detective? I'm a busy man and don't have time to waste. So get on with your questions. I need to get back to work as soon as possible."

"Mr. Sennett, if you will calm down and let me speak, I can get you back to your work here in less than a minute."

"In less than a minute?"

Browning nodded. "Yes, sir, in less than a minute."

"Fine. Do what you have to do."

"Mr. Sennett, it is my understanding that not all of your people are working every minute they are here. Is that correct, sir?"

"Yes, that's right. What of it?"

"Then could you arrange for those people who are not working at this very moment to come see me one at a time so that I may question them about their relationships with the late Leslie Clover?"

Sennett broke into a smile. "I get it now. Sure, we can do that. Hugh, you start fetching people for Detective Browning., and if any of them balk at coming, tell them they're fired and to get off the lot immediately. Got it?"

"Yes, sir, Mr. Sennett, but what about the payroll?"

"The payroll?"

"Yes, sir. Today is Saturday."

"Oh, yes, I almost forgot. Then get Milo to do it."

"You sent him to make arrangements for Mr. Clover's funeral."

"Then get Katy Killoy to do it. She knows everybody here. She can fetch them for Detective Browning." He turned to face the policeman. "Suit you, Detective?"

"It suits me just fine, Mr. Sennett."

"Good. Now can I go back to work?"

"Where can I meet with your people, Mr. Sennett?"

"Hugh, take him up to my office. I won't be needing it until this afternoon."

"I will speak with you again at the end of your work day, Mr. Sennett. Until then?"

Sennett didn't bother saying another word. He simply bolted from the room.

"So who is Katy, Mr. McHatton?"

* * *

The keeper of the studio's costume department met with Browning in Sennett's upstairs office.

"Why are you so apprehensive, Mrs. Killoy?"

"You're the police, Detective Browning, and I'm Irish. Where I come from, we're all afraid of the police."

"You're from Ireland, aren't you, Mrs. Killoy?"

"I am."

"Well, this is America, and the police here protect and serve our citizens from true lawbreakers. So you have no need to fear the Los Angeles Police Department, Mrs. Killoy. I can assure you of that much."

"Well, you do look like a nice man."

"Thank you, ma'am. My wife thinks so, too."

Katy appeared to be calmer now. "She must be a lovely girl."

"I think she is, but enough about me, ma'am. I need to ask you a few questions concerning the late Mr. Leslie Clover."

"Yes, I know. Little Hugh told me already. And when you're done talking to me, I'm to get someone else from the lot who knew him and bring that person here to talk to you. Is that right, sir?"

"It is. Now about Mr. Clover. How well did you know him?"

"I only met him the first day he came to work here at the studio, and that was the first Monday of the month. I've seen him nearly every day since then. Well, every workday that is. I had no contact with him on Sundays or after work."

"This past Thursday where were you between seven and ten o'clock in the morning?"

"The same place I am every weekday and Saturday morning, Detective Browning, now that the studio is open again. Right here at the studio handing out costumes and helping the actors with their makeup when they need my help." A thought sparked her Irish temper. "Thursday you say? That's the day poor Mr. Clover met his end, and in the morning, too. Surely, you're not thinking I had anything to do with his demise, are you now?"

"Mrs. Killoy, I have to ask everybody that question. But to answer your question, no, I am not thinking that you had anything to do with Mr. Clover's death."

"Well, I should hope not."

"Did you like Mr. Clover, ma'am?"

"Like him? I can't say that I knew the man well enough to like him or to dislike him for any reason. If you're asking if he ever did me a hurt, then the answer is no. For an Englishman, he was all right as far as I was concerned."

"Will you be attending his wake and funeral, Mrs. Killoy?"

"We're a family here, Detective Browning. Of course, I will, and you can believe everybody else who works here will be in attendance as well. We're moving picture folk, Detective Browning. We care for our own, just the same as you police officers care for your own."

"Thank you, Mrs. Killoy. You've been very helpful. You can go now and would you please send in the next person for me?"

"I already sent little Hugh to find you someone, so as you wouldn't have to wait too long for the next person to talk to."

"That was very thoughtful of you, ma'am. Thank you."

Katy left the room.

"Miss Sharpe, did you think she was a little too testy when I asked her where she was on the morning of Mr. Clover's death?"

"As a matter of fact, I did, sir."

"Would you please make a note of that when you transcribe your shorthand for me?"

"Already done, sir."

Almost every actor, extra, and crew member came to Sennett's office one at a time that morning, and Detective Browning asked them all the same basic questions he had asked the first employee of Keystone, Katy Killoy. As he had presumed they would, after giving him their names and addresses for the record, most of them repeated the same stock answers to his questions, almost as if they had read them in a script, the same script that he'd heard Katy recite.

"I barely knew the man."

"I met him when he came to work here at the studio."

"I saw him nearly every day I was here."

"No, I didn't socialize with him."

"The same place I am every weekday, Detective Browning. I was here at the studio working."

"I was here at the studio hoping to work that day so I could earn some money."

"Yes, I liked him. He was a very congenial fellow."

"Of course, I'll be attending his wake and funeral. It's only the right thing to do. We moving picture people stick together."

Only a handful of those questioned expressed anything differently. Just like all the rest, they were led to Browning by Katy Killoy.

"Detective Browning, this is Mr. Hank Mann. Mr. Mann is one of Mr. Sennett's feature actors."

After the usual amenities between strangers, Browning asked Mann a question he had asked only a few of the previous people he had already interviewed. "Mr. Mann, I detect a slight accent in your voice. You're not a native-born American, are you?"

Mann appeared resentful that the detective should make an inquiry into his nativity. "No, I'm not. So what?"

"So where were you born, sir?"

"I was born in Russia. My family came here in 1891. I'm Jewish. So what? Does any of this matter?"

"No, sir, I suppose it doesn't. I was only trying out a new hobby of mine, which is listening to people's voices to determine something of their background so that I might better understand them as a person and treat them with the proper respect."

Browning's remarks calmed Mann. "Oh, I get it. People in Vaudeville would do that so they could imitate them. I even did it. I can do an Irish brogue. Would you like to hear it?"

A smile creased Browning's lips. "That won't be necessary, Mr. Mann. I'll just take your word for it." The detective then proceeded with the same questions he had asked the others. He received the same answers until he asked Mann about liking Clover.

"I didn't know him well enough to like him or dislike him. He was okay here on the lot, but away from here, all he wanted to do was chase some frail. I'd see him flirting with the girls in the extra line. Mack warned him once to stick to business and leave the girls alone when he was here on the lot. I remember Mack saying, 'You're a funny guy, Clover, but funny or not, if you don't leave the women alone when you're on my lot, I'll bounce your butt right out of here.' That's what he said almost word-for-word."

"By Mack, you mean Mr. Sennett?"

"That's right. Mr. Sennett. He's got a lot of pressure on him to produce a lot of films for Mr. Kessel and Mr. Bauman back in New York, and he doesn't have any time for any funny business that ain't on the set, if you know what I mean."

"Yes, sir, I believe I do. Can you recall when Mr. Sennett said this to Mr. Clover?"

Mann stared at the ceiling for a few seconds. "Let me see now. I believe it was last Friday he said that. I had just finished my lunch with Slim Summerville and Mack Riley, and we were returning to the extras benches right outside here when Mack ... Mr. Sennett ... came out of the barn here and saw Clover chatting with the new girl, Betty Schade. At that same time, Betty's husband Fritz came storming up from the other direction, swearing at Clover in German. Fritz and Betty Schade are from Germany, you know."

"No, I didn't know. I haven't spoken to either of them yet."

"Well, as soon as you hear them talk, you'll know they're from Germany. Berlin, I think. Can't be sure about that. You'll have to ask them."

"I will. Now you were saying Mr. Sennett came out of the building at the same time Mr. Schade came from the other direction swearing at Mr. Clover in German."

"Yes, that's right. You see, Fritz doesn't like any of the other men talking to his wife. Of course, Clover backed off right away, and that's when Mack ... Mr. Sennett gave him the what-for about flirting with the girls on the lot." Mann laughed out loud. "You should have been there to see it, Detective. Chubby little Fritz shaking his fist at Clover and screaming, '*Holen Sie sich die Hölle weg von meiner Frau, du Hurensohn!*' I don't think Clover knew what Fritz was saying to him, which is why we would have all laughed, if Mack ... Mr.

Sennett hadn't put a stop to it before things really got ugly."

"What was Mr. Schade saying to Mr. Clover?"

"Get the hell away from my wife, you sonofabitch!"

"Do you know of any other incidents that involved Mr. Clover and Mr. Schade?"

Mann shook his head. "No, none that I know about. As far as I know, that was the one and only time those two knocked heads."

"How about anybody else that works here *knocking heads* with Mr. Clover?"

"I can't really say. I've only been out here a couple of weeks. What went on before I got here I can't say."

That concluded the interview. Mann left, and Katy brought in Gloria Newman for Browning to question.

When the detective asked her if she liked Clover, Gloria smiled and gazed at him wistfully. "Sure, I liked him. He was a real gentleman. He knew how to treat a lady right. He took me to dinner and a movie a couple of times, but then I got so busy here with work that I had to turn him down after that."

"How did he react to that, Miss Newman?"

"I don't think he cared at all, now that I think about it. You know, that new girl Maisy Malone asked me the same thing just yesterday morning when I was putting on my makeup. I hear she's been asking a lot of people questions about Leslie. Kind of nosy, if you ask me." A mischievous grin and a wicked twinkle suddenly changed Gloria's expression from slightly perturbed to naughty. "You know, you should talk to her about what she's doing snooping around like that. She could be getting in the way of what you're doing here, Detective."

"Thank you for the tip, Miss Newman. I'll keep it in mind. Did Mr. Clover ever invite you to his home, Miss Newman?"

"Sure, I went to the bungalow with him after we had dinner and went to a moving picture show. So what of it?"

Browning dismissed the combative question and then sent Gloria on her way.

Katy then appeared as expected with Phoebe Alden in tow.

"Thank you, Mrs. Killoy. Would you see if Mr. and Mrs. Schade can come in next?"

"Mr. and Mrs. Schade? Together?"

"Yes, together."

"I'll do what I can, sir."

Phoebe Alden answered Browning's questions much like the majority of interviewees had until he asked her how well she knew Clover.

"Well, he did take me to dinner a few times. And to the movies. We moving picture people do that, you know. We like to see what other studios are doing."

"But did you like him, Miss Alden?"

Phoebe teared up, turning her blue eyes almost as red as her hair. "He was really nice to me, Detective. Of course, I liked him. Actually, I think I was in love with him."

Browning took a folded white handkerchief from a pocket inside his coat and handed it to her. "Did you accompany Mr. Clover to his home after your evenings out together?"

She burst into a full-blown wail that lasted for a few minutes. When she finally stopped crying and Browning repeated the question, she went from tears to anger. "What kind of thing is that to ask a lady?"

"My apologies, Miss Alden, for being so … inquisitive, but I am investigating the death of Mr. Clover. Would you please answer the question?"

Phoebe exhaled heavily and glared at Browning for a few seconds before finally responding. "Yes, I went home with him, and I spent the night both times in his spare bedroom. Like I said before, Leslie was a real gentleman. He slept in his room, and I slept in the other one. Are you satisfied now?"

"That will do, Miss Alden. Thank you. You may go now."

As soon as Phoebe left, Katy brought the Schades and Henry Lehrman into the office. "Betty and Fritz haven't been in America all that long, Detective Browning, so I asked Mr. Lehrman to come with them to help you with some of the words. He speaks the same language as they do."

Browning nodded, trying not to show his surprise at the incongruity between Betty and Fritz. She stood a good six inches taller than he was, and he had to weigh a good fifty pounds more than she did. Besides their sizes, Fritz appeared to be nearly twice her age. "Good idea, Mrs. Killoy. This should make this easier for all of us. Thank you for coming in with them, Mr. Lehrman."

"I am from Austria, Detective Browning. We speak the same language in my native country as they speak in Germany."

Browning went over nearly all the same questions he had asked the others that morning, learning the Schades real given names were Franz and Frieda. Then he came to the incident of a week ago Friday. "Mr. Schade, would you please tell me about the … confrontation between you and Mr. Clover last week?"

Fritz asked Lehrman to translate the question for him, and the director obliged him. On hearing the inquiry, Schade's face reddened considerably, and then he rattled off his reply in German.

"He says Mr. Clover was flirting with his wife, and this made him so angry that he wanted to punch him with his fist. I saw what happened, Detective Browning. Mr. Clover was flirting with Mrs. Schade when Mr. Schade came around the corner of the building and saw him. He immediately went into a rage at Mr. Clover for being so friendly with his wife. It was a good thing Mack … Mr. Sennett came out of the barn at that exact moment and put a stop to it before the shouting match turned into a fist fight. Mack … Mr. Sennett would have thrown both of them off the lot right then and there if the two of them had exchanged blows. Mr. Sennett won't put up with that sort of thing around here. Losing Mr. Clover at that moment would have been a bad thing."

"Why is that, Mr. Lehrman?"

"Mr. Clover was under consideration to become a leading actor here at Keystone. Mr. Sennett and I were thinking of having him play the groom in a film we had scheduled to make next week. Now we have to delay that film because Mr. Clover is dead and we have to determine which other actor should play the part."

Browning considered Lehrman's statement for a moment. "Was Mr. Clover's advancement to leading actor made public news in the studio?"

Lehrman shook his head. "No, we only told him about it this past Wednesday. He was told to keep it to himself until the film went into production and Mr. Sennett could make the announcement himself."

"Do you know if he told anybody else here that he was being considered for the part?"

The director shook his head again. "No, I am not aware of anybody else who knows besides Mr. Sennett and the other actors who will be in the film."

"And which other actors will be in the film?"

"Miss Normand, Mr. Sterling, Mr. Mace, and Miss Davenport. The regulars in the company."

"Mr. Schade, are you still angry with Mr. Clover for flirting with your wife?"

Fritz shook his head. "*Nein.* I mean no. *Der arme Mann ist tot jetzt.* Clover is dead now. *Ich habe keinen Groll gegen ihn.*"

Browning looked to Lehrman for a translation. "He said he no longer has grudge against Mr. Clover now that he is dead."

"*Nein, nein, Herr Lehrman. Herr Clover entschuldigte sich bei mir, bevor er ermodet wurde, aund ich ihm für sein schlechtes Verhalten, gegenüber meine Frau verzieh.*"

Lehrman didn't wait for Browning to ask for a translation. "He said Mr. Clover apologized to him before he was murdered, and he forgave him for his bad behavior toward his wife."

Schade smiled at Browning and nodded at Lehrman. "*Ja!* Vot he say. Mr. Clover and me better. *Ja?*"

"You're trying to tell me that you and Mr. Clover put the incident with your wife behind you, is that right?"

Lehrman translated.

Fritz's head bobbed up and down rapidly. "*Ja, das ist es.*"

The director started repeat Schade's words in English, but Browning held up a hand to stop him. "I believe I understand what he meant, Mr.

Lehrman." He pinpointed his view on Fritz once more. "So when did this happen, Mr. Schade? When did Mr. Clover apologize to you?"

Fritz glanced at Betty. "*Sontag, ja?*"

Betty nodded. "Yes, Sunday."

"And where did this happen?"

Lehrman translated, listened to Fritz's answer, and then repeated it in English for Browning. "He says Mr. Clover came by their apartment on Sunday morning and apologized to him. To show them he really meant it, he took them to Santa Monica on the Red Car and bought them dinner."

"I see." Browning studied them for a few seconds. "Well, thank you, Mr. Lehrman. You've been very helpful. Thank you as well, Mr. and Mrs. Schade. You may go now."

Browning waited for them to leave before speaking to Nellie Sharpe, the stenographer. "It appears I'll have to create *three* lists of possible suspects now." He enumerated them with his fingers. "Jilted lovers. Jealous husbands and beaus. And now actors who want to get ahead in this business."

Before Nellie could comment, Katy entered the room with Alma McComb. After making the proper introduction, she left.

Expecting to get the same stock answers he had received from a majority of the other people he had questioned that morning, Browning started Alma's interview with the same greeting and initial inquiry.

"Good morning, Miss McComb. I'll begin by asking how well did you know the late Leslie Clover."

"I knew Leslie intimately."

Browning's eyes widened with more than surprise. They expressed hope as well. "Did you say intimately?"

"I did."

"Really? How so?"

"About as intimately as a man and a woman can be, Detective."

Browning could hardly believe his ears. "I have to say, Miss McComb, how refreshing it is to hear someone being so honest and forthcoming with me."

"Look, Detective, I might as well come clean with the whole story. I've already shot my mouth off to Maisy Malone, so I might as well tell you, too. Leslie Clover took me to dinner and a moving picture show a couple of times and I went with him back to the bungalow on both occasions. He was English, you know. A real gentleman who knew how to treat a girl. I met him in the extras line. I could have really gone for him, but when I started getting lots of calls here, I was too tired at night to do anything except go home and sleep, if you know what I mean. Didn't seem to bother Leslie much when I turned him down the last time he asked me out. I heard he asked Vivian out again after me."

"Vivian? Is she another young woman who works here?"

"No, Vivian stopped showing up here last week and went back to Polyscope, I hear. That was probably a good move on her part. She wasn't much for comedy. Too serious, that girl. She's more fit for drama."

"Does Vivian have a last name?"

"Vanover. Vivian Vanover. She lives on Beaudry Avenue in Los Angeles. Ask Phoebe Alden about her. They live on the same block and walk to the Red Car stop together every morning. Phoebe can tell you where Vivian lives."

"You've already answered my next three questions, Miss McComb, so now I'll get to the big one. Where were you on the morning Mr. Clover died?"

"Right here working. Check my payroll record, if you don't believe me. McHatton knows. He makes sure nobody gets paid an extra nickel around here."

"If there is a wake and a funeral for Mr. Clover, will you be in attendance, Miss McComb?"

"Are you kidding? Half the moving picture people in Los Angeles will be there, especially the big shots, the directors and the money men, and all the leading actors and actresses. They'll all be there because they all want to be seen as decent caring folks when the truth is most of them only care about themselves, their careers, and their money."

"That's rather cynical of you, Miss McComb."

Alma burped a laugh. "You haven't been around many moving picture people, have you, Detective?"

"I can't say that I have."

"Well, you just show up at the wake and at the funeral and you'll see what I mean."

* * *

Willie brought Cole back to the studio just as the shooting concluded for the day. Milo met Sennett at the porch of the director-general's bungalow.

"Did you get everything arranged for Clover's wake and funeral?"

"I went to four undertakers. Two on South Flower and two on South Grand. I asked them all about coffins and prices for everything. I thought Pierce Brothers on South Flower had the most to offer for the least amount of money. I gave them your information, sir, and they said they would handle everything from there." Cole took a business card from his coat pocket. "This is their information, sir." He handed it to Sennett.

"I'll call them after all this business with the police is finished for the day. Go ahead back to the barn, Milo. McHatton has the pay envelopes ready to hand out. Don't forget to tell him to check with everybody about him holding back a buck or two to help pay for Clover's funeral."

"Yes, sir."

Cole rushed off to the old horse barn to pick up his wages for the week.

As soon as he went inside, he saw the crew members who hadn't done any acting that day already in line. All the extras and actors were still in the dressing rooms removing their costumes and makeup. As he took his place at the rear of the queue, he saw Alma McComb coming down the stairs from the business office.

"Say, Alma, how did it go with Detective Browning?"

"I told him everything I knew about Leslie and about Leslie and me when we were an item for a short time. I even told him about some of the other girls who went out with Leslie. You know, like Vivian Vanover and Phoebe Alden. I think he already knew about Phoebe, but I know for sure he didn't know about Vivian." Alma paused for a second. "Funny thing, though. He asked a lot of questions, but he never asked me if I might know who would want Leslie dead. You would think that would be his first question, wouldn't you?"

"Yes, you would think so because he asked me that question more than once when he had me in his office yesterday."

"And what did you tell him?"

"I didn't tell him anything. I mean, I told him I didn't know anybody who would want Leslie dead. Can you think of anybody who would want Leslie dead?"

Alma nodded. "A few people come to mind."

"Really? Like who?"

"Fritz Schade for one. Phoebe for another. He broke Gloria's heart. She might want him dead."

"Didn't he break your heart, too, when he took up with Vivian?"

Anger stormed over Alma's face. She kept her voice down and growled out her words through gritted teeth. "Is that what he told you?"

"Well …"

"That S O B! I turned him down the last time he asked me out. What else did the bastard tell you about me?"

"Well …"

"I knew it. You men are all alike. Can't keep a thing to yourselves. And here I thought he was a gentleman. Guess I got that one wrong."

"Well …"

Alma stormed off toward the ladies dressing room, passing Maisy Malone along the way.

"How'd your interview go, Alma?"

"What's it to you?" She kept stomping away.

Maisy got in line behind Cole. "What's eating her?"

"She just found out Leslie spread it around that he jilted her for Vivian Vanover."

"Oh, really? And who told her that?"

Cole blushed. "I guess I let that cat out of the bag."

"Milo, you better learn when to talk and when to keep your trap shut. For a nice looking guy like you, I'm beginning to wonder if there's a brain between those ears of yours."

"Hey, that's not nice. If you were a man, I'd be thinking about punching you one right about now."

"I'm not sure you have that in you to do, Milo." She pinched his cheek. "You're just too sweet to be some kind of ruffian."

"Cut it out, Maisy. Some of the guys are watching."

"Better the guys than the gals. And speaking of gals, do you know this Vivian Vanover? Katy said I should talk to her about your late pal Leslie Clover."

"Sure, I know her. She lives in the same neighborhood as I do."

"Fair enough. Let's grab our pay envelopes, make a donation toward Mr. Clover's funeral, and catch the Red Car to downtown."

* * *

Two Keystone employees that Browning didn't interview that day were Maisy Malone and Milo Cole, but only because he had already questioned them thoroughly. However, he did want to speak them to see if either of them had learned anything new that they wanted to share with him. One problem. Neither of them could be found once he finished with Mack Sennett.

"McHatton said they picked up their pay envelopes and left here like their clothes were on fire."

"Did they go together, Mr. Sennett?"

"That's what McHatton said. Together."

"And you have no idea where they went?"

"McHatton said he heard them talking about catching the Red Car down on Sunset. Who knows where they were going from there? It's Saturday afternoon, and we don't work on Sundays. My guess is they went downtown to do some shopping."

Browning didn't say so, but if he had been a betting man, he would give odds that Maisy and Milo might have gone downtown on the Pacific Electric, but not to go shopping.

"Miss Sharpe, would you look through your shorthand notes for the interview with Phoebe Alden and find her address for me. It's on Beaudry Avenue, I believe."

* * *

Sennett was half-right. Cole and Maisy did go downtown to do some shopping. But first, they took the Red Car from the Sunset Boulevard and Allesandro Street stop to the intersection of 2nd Street and South Beaudry Avenue and walked the short distance to the boardinghouse where Vivian Vanover lived.

"This is it. Two-twenty-two. She lives on the second floor." Cole pointed to a window on the corner. "That's her room there."

"How do you know so much about which room is hers?"

"Leslie told me when we came here one Saturday night a couple of months back to pick up Vivian and a friend of hers from Polyscope. The four of us had a nice evening out, and then Leslie and I brought them back here. That's all there was to it. Dinner and then a little dancing at the Trenton Hotel between 4th and 5th Street. For the life of me, I can't remember the girl's name. Bessie something. Her last name is completely gone from my memory."

"Probably a good thing for her."

"Hey, that wasn't nice."

Maisy rolled her eyes. "Come on, Milo. Let's see if she's come home yet. You lead the way." She pointed toward the clapboard building that needed a good whitewashing.

Cole strolled up the walkway to the steps of the screened-in porch, opened the screen door for Maisy, waited for her to enter, and then followed her inside. He rang the doorbell, and they waited for someone to answer. Nearly a minute passed before the door opened revealing a fortyish woman with jet black hair, almond eyes, and coppery skin and offering them a most gracious smile.

"May I help you?"

Cole gave her a slight bow. "Yes, *Señora*. I am Milo Cole, and this lady is Miss Maisy Malone. We are calling on *Señorita* Vivian Vanover. Is she at home?"

"*Sí, Señor*. I will call her for you. Please come in and wait for her in the parlor." As soon as Maisy and Milo stepped inside, she closed the door behind them. "This way, *por favor*." She led them to the living room. "Sit down, *por favor*. I will tell *Señorita* Vivian that you are here." She left them.

"What's all this *Señora* and *Señor* stuff you're saying to this lady?"

"It's Spanish. She's Mexican. I'm just being polite."

"So where did you learn Spanish?"

"Here in Los Angeles. I don't know very much of the language, but I do know enough to order a drink in a *cantina*."

"I'm sure that will come in handy someday."

"You never know. Mr. Sennett likes to shoot on location. Who knows that one day he might take us down to Old Mexico or one of the *barrios* around Los Angeles to shoot a film or two?"

Just then, the servant returned, her smile gone and the light in her eyes dimmed. "I am so sorry, *Señor y Señorita*. *Señorita* Vivian is still not feeling well and says she wishes not to have any visitors yet."

Suspicious, Maisy took the lead from Cole. "*Pardones por favor. ¿Como se llama, Señora?*"

The smile returned to the lady's lips. "*Me llamo Hortencia Ramos.*"

"*Gracias, Señora Ramos.* You said—"

"*Por favor, Señorita* Maisy, I am Hortencia to you."

"*Gracias, Hortencia.* You said *Señorita* Vivian is not feeling well. Is she ill with an ailment of some kind?"

"*¿Qué es* ailment *por favor?*"

"Ailment? Uh, *enferma*. Ailment, sick, *enferma*."

Hortencia shook her head. "Oh, no, *Señorita*. She has a broken heart."

"A broken heart? *¿El corazón partido?*"

"*No, ella tiene rompe el alma.*"

Maisy peered quizzically at Hortencia. "*¿El alma? ¿No el corazón?*" The servant patted her chest. "*No el corazón. El alma.*"

"*¿Para quién es ella triste?*"

"*El hombre.*"

Maisy nodded. "Of course, a man. What was I thinking?"

Cole was astonished. "How do you know so much Spanish?"

"I spent a little time in Spain and a little more time with a Spaniard."

"In Spain with a Spaniard?"

Maisy waved him off with a grimace. "It's a long story for another time."

"Okay, but what are you two talking about? I heard you say broken heart, but after that, you lost me until you said something about a man."

"Just hold on for a minute, Milo, while I talk to Hortencia some more and get the rest of the story."

Phoebe Alden lived two houses down from Vivian Vanover at 230 South Beaudry. Her building was the newest on the block, sided with red bricks instead of clapboard like all the others, and it was also the tallest at four stories high.

Detective Browning, the stenographer, and the two uniformed officers accompanying them arrived at the address several minutes after Maisy and Cole left Vivian Vanover's boardinghouse. He took Miss Sharpe inside with him. Soon they were sitting in Phoebe Alden's one-room apartment.

"After I spoke with you this morning, I interviewed several other employees. One of them mentioned you in connection with a Miss Vivian Vanover. Do you know Miss Vanover?"

"Yes, I do. Vivian is a good friend of mine. She lives just two buildings up the street from here. We used to ride the Red Car back and forth to work together until she quit Keystone last week. She said she was going back to try Universal over in Hollywood."

"When was the last time you saw Miss Vanover?"

"This past Sunday. We went window shopping downtown and then had dinner together at the Trenton Hotel before coming home that evening."

"And you haven't seen her since, not even on the Red Car?"

"She rides a different car to go to Hollywood from here, Detective Browning. Also, she doesn't have to rise so early now to go to work. Universal has a regular studio building on its lot. However, I did stop by the boardinghouse where she lives to tell her about Leslie's death the other day. Hortencia said Vivian wasn't feeling well and didn't wish to be disturbed. I asked Hortencia to tell Vivian about Leslie's death, and she said Vivian already knew about it. I started to ask her how she knew about it when it only happened that morning, but then I saw a copy of the *Herald* on the hall table and figured she'd read about it in the newspaper."

"Who is Hortencia?"

"She's the housekeeper there. A Mexican woman who lives on the southeast side of the city in the *barrio*."

"Again, Miss Alden, I must ask you a sensitive question."

"If you're going to ask about Vivian's connection to Leslie Clover, you'll have to ask her. I can only tell you that she went out with him before I did. How serious their relationship was never came up in any conversations we ever had. Unlike most men, we ladies don't discuss our personal business with gentlemen with other ladies."

"Yes, of course, ma'am. I'll save that question for Miss Vanover."

* * *

Maisy and Cole caught a Red Car downtown to the new eight-story department store, The Broadway, at 4th Street and Broadway. They encountered Katy Killoy as she was coming out of the building.

"Now isn't this a nice surprise meeting up with the two of you just now and right in front of the store where my daughter Lizzie is working. So what brings you two down here this afternoon? Got a pocket full of money and can't wait to spend some, I'll bet."

"Something like that, Katy. I have to buy an alarm clock, and Milo told me this was the best place in town to buy anything you can't eat."

"I didn't put it that way, but it is the best place to go shopping where you can find just about anything you need for your home or your person, and all under one roof."

"You sound like a newspaper advertisement, Milo."

"Mr. Cole is right. You can find just about anything you might need for your home or yourself right here." Katy glanced up at the tall building. "It is a big place, isn't it?"

Maisy's curiosity jumped in. "So were you here shopping, Katy?"

"Yes and no. I did need a few things, but I thought I would stop and see Lizzie as well."

"So she's working right now?"

"Yes, she is. On the third floor in the girls' clothing area, but you probably won't have any occasion to go up there. I believe alarm clocks are on the fifth floor with other things for the home."

"Sounds like you know this place quite well, Katy."

"I wouldn't shop anywhere else. Now if you'll excuse me, I have to catch the Red Car home to Pasadena. Tootle-loo!"

"Good-bye, Katy. See you Monday morning."

"Good-bye, Katy."

"Well, Milo, shall we go find an alarm clock for me?"

They entered the giant store and went straight to the fifth floor. A young salesman approached them, asking if he could help them. Maisy told him what item she needed, and he led them to the display of alarm clocks. She picked out a simple one that fit her needs, purchased it, and thanked the fellow for his assistance. Then they returned to the elevator and entered it with a few other shoppers.

As the car arrived at the fourth floor, the operator announced the departments located on this level. Then he opened the doors to allow anybody to leave the vehicle. Before anybody else could come aboard, he advised those people getting off on the next floor to move to the front right of the car.

Maisy followed the instruction.

A touch bewildered by her movement Milo edged up beside her and whispered to her. "Why are we getting off on the third floor?"

Maisy smiled and whispered back. "To meet Katy's daughter."

"And why do we want to do that?"

Maisy shook her head. "Milo, don't you hear people when they talk? Or are you only letting their words pass right through your head like a runaway freight train?"

"I listen to people."

"Yes, but you're not hearing them."

The elevator doors closed. The car started down, and in seconds it arrived at the third floor, where the operator announced the departments there before opening the doors again.

Maisy exited the car ahead of everybody, while Milo, being the well-mannered gentleman he had been raised to be, stood aside to allow any other ladies to follow Maisy ahead of him. Then he stepped through the doorway to join Maisy.

"Okay, what did I miss?"

"When we were on the street talking to Katy, she said her daughter worked in the girls' clothing department on this floor."

"So?"

"Then she said, and her exact words were, 'On the third floor in the girls' clothing area, but you probably won't have any occasion to go up there.' Now why would she say that to us?"

"Because we're here to get you an alarm clock?"

"See what I mean, Milo. You don't hear people. On the way up when the elevator stopped at the third floor, weren't you listening when the operator announced what departments were on this floor?"

Cole squinted at her still unsure of her point. "Well, yes, I heard him do that. So?"

"Did he say the only department on this floor is girls' clothing?"

"Well, no, I guess he didn't."

"So why did Katy imply the only department up here was the one her daughter works in?"

Cole shrugged. "Beats me."

"I'm sure it does, Milo. Like a rug on a clothes line. Come on, let's find Katy's daughter. What was her name again?"

"Lizzie."

"Fair enough."

They wandered around the floor. Besides clothing for girls in the pre-teenage group, they saw clothing for young ladies in their teens, for small girls, toddlers, and infants; and of course, shoes for all the same ages and gender. The toy department was also located on this level. Maisy noticed the gleam in Cole's eyes when he saw all of those brightly painted cast-iron trains and automobiles, wooden boats and rocking horses, and the miniature lead soldiers, cowboys, Indians, cows, and horses.

"Now I know why Katy didn't mention any other departments on this floor."

"You do?"

"Come on, junior. You can play with that stuff later."

"Now what does that—?" The answer popped into his head before he could completely speak the question. He didn't like it, and his face showed his disappointment with it. "I guess you don't think too much of me, do you?"

Maisy patted him on the arm affectionately. "Milo, being really smart is not *always* what it's cracked up to be. Be thankful you are who you are. I am certainly glad I know you, and we've only known each other—what?—three days now. You've got more going for you than you might know."

"I do?"

She winked at him. "Yes, Milo, you do." She squeezed his upper arm. "And in all the places that count."

Cole missed Maisy's last words as his attention was drawn beyond her. "Do you think that could be Katy's daughter? She kind of looks like a younger version of Katy, don't you think?"

Maisy turned around and spotted a young woman who did bear a striking resemblance to Katy Killoy. "Only one way to find out. Let's go ask her."

The pair of them strode up to the salesgirl who smiled at their approach and asked them the standard question. "May I help you?" Her eyes locked on Cole for a few seconds before becoming embarrassed for staring at him and shifting her view to Maisy.

"It's quite all right, dear. I think he's handsome, too."

Now Cole blushed and dropped his focus on the floor.

"I'm sorry I…uh…"

"Don't think twice about it, Miss …?"

"Killoy. Miss Killoy."

Maisy turned to Cole. "You were right, Milo. This is Katy's daughter."

"You know me mother?" Her voice slipped out of its learned American English into Irish idiom and accent for the moment.

"This is Mr. Milo Cole, and I'm Maisy Malone. We work at Keystone Moving Pictures with your mother. I'm hoping to become an actress, and Milo is Mr. Sennett's personal assistant and sometime actor. I've only been with the studio for three days now, but Milo has been there from the start, just like your mother. She's very proud of you and your whole family, you know. She told me so herself the first day I was at the studio. She did my makeup and went on and on about Lizzie this and Jack that and Charlie this and Kathleen that. She talked about all her children—what? all seven of you?"

"Yes, that's right. There are seven of us in the family. Eight with Ma."

"You know, now that I think of it, I don't believe she ever mentioned your father. Was there a reason for that, Lizzie? May I call you Lizzie?"

"Certainly, you may, Miss Malone."

"No, none of that now. You call me Maisy. I'm not that much older than you are."

"Well, I'm only seventeen, Miss Malone."

"And I'm only nineteen. So call me Maisy. I insist. Now what about your father?"

"Me pa was killed in a fight back in Ireland. She doesn't like talking about it. It makes her cry every time it comes up. And then she gets fighting mad herself because he died at the hands of a filthy English soldier in a pub back in Cork." She caught her breath. "Oh, I'm so truly sorry, Mr. Cole. You're not English, are you?"

He shook his head. "No, I'm Bohemian. Well, actually, I'm American. My grandparents all came over here from Bohemia."

A short man with a thin mustache walked up to them. "Is there a problem here, Miss Killoy?"

"Oh, no, Mr. Braddock, there's no problem."

Maisy knew Braddock's kind, and she didn't like them. "No, there's no problem here, but there's going to be, if you don't go away and let this girl get on with trying to sell us something for my sister's birthday."

Braddock backed away. "Yes, of course. I'm terribly sorry for the intrusion. I'll just go and leave you to Miss Killoy."

"Thank you. What was your name again?"

The short fellow fidgeted with his tie. "Braddock. Thaddeus Braddock, the floor manager."

Maisy turned to Cole. "Write that down, will you, Milo? Just in case I want to complain to somebody about being interrupted while I'm trying to buy a birthday present for my sister."

Cole made a show of retrieving a pen and something to write on from an inside coat pocket. "Yes, Miss Malone."

Braddock paled. "Oh, my!" Then he vanished from sight.

"Maisy, that was naughty of you."

An impish grin spread Maisy's lips. "Yes, Milo, but it was fun. Why does every little twerp with a little authority have to act like he's Napoleon?" She turned to the salesgirl. "We'd better make a show of this, Lizzie, or Mr. Braddock just might get wise to what I just did to him. So why don't you show us some nice dresses for a girl who's soon to turn twelve years old? We can talk more while you do."

"Right this way, Maisy."

As Lizzie made a display of showing Maisy dresses for pre-teen girls, Cole excused himself and wandered over to the toy department to have a look around.

"You really don't want to buy a dress, do you, Maisy?"

"No, but I will if it's the only way I can keep you out of trouble with your boss. Now pretend to show me a dress, and tell me how your brother Jack is doing with his carpenter's apprenticeship."

"Oh, he's doing swell, especially since he moved out a few weeks back. Ma doesn't know it, but I think he's got himself a girlfriend and he doesn't want Ma to know about her just yet."

"Really? And what makes you think he's got a girlfriend?"

"He let part of her name slip last Sunday when he came home for dinner. She must be Dutch because he said her name was Miss Van something. He didn't say her whole surname. Only Miss Van, and then he quickly changed the subject. Of course, Ma didn't hear him, but I did. I tried to ask him more about this mysterious Miss Van later on, but he wouldn't tell me nothing and made we swear not to tell Ma about her."

"And you haven't told her, have you?"

"Not a word. Although, maybe I should. Jack ain't old enough to be thinking about just one girl and having thoughts of settling down and all. Besides, he still ain't got nothing he can call his own yet. He was a fool to move out when he did. He was living free with us, and now he has to pay for his own room, wherever it is."

"You don't know where he lives?"

"He says he doesn't want us to know because he doesn't want Ma or me coming over and snooping around. And he's only right, you know. That's exactly what either of the two of us would do. Ma would want to clean up the place for him, but I don't know why she would want to do that. Jack has always been the neat and clean one in the family." She snickered. "I've teased him many times about how he's going to make some girl a fine *househusband* one day."

The two of them giggled at the notion for a few seconds before Maisy asked another question. "Why would *you* want to know where he lives?"

"Me? I'd want to see if he's got room for me the next time Ma and me get to shouting at each other over nothing."

Maisy caught a glimpse of Braddock on the other side of the store, and he was looking straight at them. "I see that fussbudget boss of yours looking this way, so I'd better buy a dress. I'll take this one."

"Oh, no, Maisy, you don't have to buy it for no good reason than to keep me out of trouble."

"Lizzie, it's okay. I've got a lot of sisters, not to mention even more nieces and cousins who would love this dress. So ring it up. Okay?"

* * *

Hortencia answered the door when Browning rang the bell. "May I help you?" She tried to make her voice sound as pleasant as possible, although she knew in advance that the detective and his stenographer were coming to the boardinghouse to request a visit with Vivian Vanover.

The policeman displayed his badge for the housekeeper's benefit. "I am Detective Sergeant Ed Browning of the Los Angeles Police Department, ma'am, and this is Miss Nellie Sharpe, a stenographer for the department. We are here to see Miss Vivian Vanover. Is she at home this afternoon?"

"*Sí, Señor*, she is, but *Señorita* Vivian is not feeling well and is not receiving visitors today." Hortencia backed away from the door as if she intended to close it. "I will tell her you came by to see her, *Señor.*"

Browning stuck his foot between the door and the threshold. "Then perhaps you can help me, *Señora*. May we come inside and talk to you?"

Noting his aggressive manner put fear into the Mexican woman's eyes. "Yes, of course, *Señor. ¿Como se llama a ver, por favor?*"

The detective had only picked up a smattering of Spanish since removing from Georgia to California ten years earlier, but he recognized her question. "Browning, ma'am. Detective Sergeant Ed Browning. *¿Y Usted?*" He stepped back to allow Nellie Sharpe to enter the house ahead of him. Then he removed his bowler and went inside a polite distance behind her.

"*Señora Hortencia Ramos*. I am the housekeeper here." She closed the door behind them. "We can go into the parlor, *Señor.*" She waved a hand at the arched doorway to the left and followed the two visitors into the living room. "Please sit down, *Señor, Señorita.*"

They took up places at opposite ends of the sofa, while Hortencia sat on an upholstered straightback chair, her hands folded primly on her lap.

Browning went right to work. "You said Miss Vanover is not feeling well. Is that correct, Mrs. Ramos?"

"Yes, sir, that is correct."

"What's ailing Miss Vanover that she's feeling so poorly that she doesn't want any visitors?"

Hortencia glanced up at the ceiling as if the answer to his question was carved in the plaster, betraying the fact that she was trying to remember the exact words Maisy had told her to tell Browning when he came by to see Vivian. "*Señorita* Vivian has a broken heart because the man she loved died two days ago."

"The man she loved died two days ago?"

"Yes, *Señor* Browning. That is correct."

"Do you mean Mr. Leslie Clover, the actor?"

Hortencia nodded rapidly. "Yes, he is the one, *Señor*. He died Thursday morning in his home."

"Yes, I know, Mrs. Ramos. Mr. Clover's death is exactly why I am here to speak with Miss Vanover. But since she is in mourning for him, I will not intrude on her privacy at this time. So perhaps you could answer a few more questions for me."

"Yes, of course, *Señor*."

"Very good, ma'am. Do you recall whether Miss Vanover went to work Thursday morning?"

Hortencia thought for a moment before responding. "Yes, she went to work that morning."

"And do you recall what time she came home from work that day?"

"She came home in the middle of the afternoon that day. I remember because she was crying and she went straight to her room. She has not left her room since then."

"Did you speak to her then or since then?"

"Oh, yes, I have spoken to her."

"And she told you she was weeping because the man she loved had died?"

"Oh, no, *Señor* Browning, she has never said that. Her friend, *Señorita* Phoebe, told that to me when—"

Browning interrupted. "*Señorita* Phoebe? Do you mean Miss Phoebe Alden from two houses down the street?"

"Yes, she is the one. She came by that evening to tell *Señorita* Vivian about *Señor* Clover's death, and when I tell her *Señorita* Vivian is not feeling well, she said she just wanted to tell her that *Señor* Clover had died that day."

"Can you recall Miss Alden's exact words when she told you about Mr. Clover's death?"

"She only said *Señor* Clover had died that morning and it was too bad because *Señorita* Vivian loved him so much. Then she left and went to her own home down the street. Maybe you should go talk to *Señorita* Phoebe about what she said to *Señorita* Vivian the other day."

"Thank you, Mrs. Ramos. I just might do that." Browning stood up. "Well, I guess that finishes things here, Miss Sharpe. Shall we go?"

Nellie closed her notebook and put it and her pencil in her purse. She stood up beside Browning and smiled at Hortencia. "It was a pleasure to meet you, Mrs. Ramos."

Browning nodded at the housekeeper. "Yes, it was a pleasure to meet you, Mrs. Ramos. Thank you so much for your co-operation. No need for you to show us out. We can find our way." He donned his hat and tipped it to Hortencia. "Wait. There is one more thing. If Miss Vanover should begin feeling better, would you please call me at the Central Police Station and let me know." He handed a business card to her.

112

"Yes, of course, *Señor*."

"Good day, ma'am." He followed Miss Sharpe to the front door, and they left.

Browning stopped at the edge of the street where the Ford Model T waited for them. "Miss Sharpe, would you please type up the interviews with Miss Alden and the one with Mrs. Ramos as soon as we return to the station. I want to go over them and see if I missed asking them something that just might determine whether or not Miss Vanover needs to be put under arrest for the murder of Mr. Leslie Clover."

Nellie gasped. "Do you really think she did it?"

"She does seem like the prime suspect right now, don't you think? So far, she's the only person without an alibi for the time of the murder."

"But Mrs. Ramos said she went to work that morning."

"Yes, but we don't have anything to corroborate her statement just yet. Therefore, I will have to go to the Universal Motion Picture Studio in Hollywood first thing Monday morning and make further inquiries about her work status there this past Thursday." He looked at the two uniformed officers in the front seat of the car. "In the meantime, Barney, I want you and Fitzgerald to stay here and watch this place to make certain Miss Vanover doesn't suddenly decide she needs to take a little vacation in the desert or somewhere back east. One of you watch the front and the other go around to the back. And you don't have to hide. You're police officers. You can stand around in plain sight because it's nobody's business why you're here. When I get back to the station, I'll have other officers sent over to relieve you. Until then, keep a keen eye on this place. Understood, gentlemen?"

"Yes, sir, but if she does try to leave? What do we do then?"

"You arrest her and bring her in for questioning."

"On what charge, sir?"

"Murder, Officer Barney. You arrest her for the murder of Mr. Leslie Clover."

After waiting nearly an hour since Detective Browning and Miss Sharpe departed, Phoebe Alden peeked through the curtains of the front window of her second floor apartment to see if the car with the other policemen had left yet. It had. She was relieved and delighted. Finally, she could go over and see her friend Vivian Vanover. Hurrying the short distance from her apartment building to Vivian's boardinghouse, Phoebe failed to take notice of Officer Fitzgerald standing in the shade of a California live oak across the street.

However, Fitzgerald spotted Phoebe immediately, and having seen her exit her residence and scurry to the home of a suspected murderess, he deduced correctly that she was the person Detective Browning had interviewed prior to calling on Miss Vanover. Quickly, he moved behind the trunk of the large tree, hiding himself from the view of anyone who might be looking through a window or the front door at 222 South Beaudry Avenue.

Phoebe rang the doorbell at the boardinghouse, and Hortencia appeared shortly. "*Señorita* Phoebe, how nice to see you?"

"Is Vivian feeling better? I must see her immediately."

"She is still in mourning for *Señor* Leslie and does not wish to be disturbed."

"She can't go on like this forever. I really must see her, Hortencia. I'm afraid I've done a wrong thing by her. Please tell her I must see her right now, Hortencia."

The housekeeper shook her head. "No, that is not possible, *Señorita* Phoebe. She does not wish to be disturbed."

Without saying another word, Phoebe brushed by Hortencia and raced up the stairs to the second floor and down the hall to Vivian's room.

Shocked by the sudden invasion, Hortencia stood at the door holding it open for several seconds. "*Señorita* Phoebe, you must not disturb her!" Sensing she was wasting her breath, the housekeeper closed the door and followed Phoebe up the stairs.

Phoebe banged on Vivian's door. "Vivian, it's Phoebe. You must let me in to talk to you. I've done something terrible, and I must tell you about it before it's too late. Please open the door." She struck it again, and then tried to open it with no success. The door was locked. Frustrated all the more, she turned to see the housekeeper coming toward her. "Hortencia, she's locked herself inside. You must get a key and let me in to see her."

Other residents who were at home that afternoon poked their heads into the corridor to see what all the ruckus was about.

"*Señorita* Phoebe, you cannot behave this way. You are disturbing our other lodgers. Now come away with me, *por favor.*" She took the actress by the arm and tugged on it.

Phoebe jerked her arm away, her voice verging on the precipice of hysteria. "No, I must see Vivian right now before it's too late."

An older man grouched at the disruption of his afternoon. "Hey, will you knock it off, girlie? I'm trying to take a nap in here. Now pipe down, will you?"

"Go back into your room, *Señor* Pickering, *por favor.* This is not your business."

"It is when she's making all that racket. Now pipe down, will you, girlie? Please?"

Phoebe shrieked. "Why won't you let me see Vivian? I must see Vivian, and right now, Hortencia. Do you hear me? Right now." She turned to pound on the door again.

The housekeeper grabbed her by both arms and put her mouth close to the frantic woman's ear. "*Señorita* Vivian is not here."

Phoebe gasped. "What do mean, she's not here?"

"Oh, for Pete's sake! Will you please pipe down?"

Hortencia leaned closer to Phoebe and whispered to her. "If you will come downstairs with me quietly, I will tell you everything. So come with me, *por favor.*" She pulled the actress toward the stairway, and this time Phoebe went with her.

"Vivian really isn't here?"

Hortencia shook her head. "Come with me downstairs, and we will talk some more."

* * *

After leaving The Broadway, Cole invited Maisy to dine with him at the Hotel Clarendon next to the department store.

"So where do we go from here, Maisy?"

"I was hoping you would show me which Red Car I need to take to get back to the Hollywood Hotel."

"No, silly! I mean where do we go from here with finding out who killed Leslie?"

"Oh, *that* where. Well, with that where, there is no *we* going anywhere together this evening. Well, at least nowhere for the moment because right now I would like to go back to your apartment building and see if Jack Shannon is at home."

"Why do you want to see Jack?"

"I really haven't had much of a chance to talk to him yet."

"You don't think he had anything to do with Leslie's murder, do you, Maisy?"

She sighed. "Milo, if you hadn't been with me all morning the other day, I'd suspect you of killing your pal just as much as anybody else."

"Thanks a bunch, Maisy."

"Don't let it bother you. I was only joking."

Cole shook his head. "I don't see the humor in it. No, I do *not* see the humor in it. Not at all."

"Then what are you doing working at a studio that only makes comedies, and not just any kind of comedies, but farcical comedies with more pratfalls than a boarding school for teenage boys going through their growth spurts. Catch up, Milo, before it's too late."

"Okay, we'll go to my place and see if Jack is home this evening."

* * *

Although he had seen Phoebe Alden barge into the boardinghouse where Vivian Vanover resided and heard the commotion within the building, patrolman Fitzgerald followed his orders and maintained his post under the spreading branches of the California live oak across the street. He did this in spite of the virulent urge to investigate the domestic disturbance. Then he wondered if Orville Barney had remained at his station in the woods behind the house. Or had his fellow officer gone inside to intervene and had succeeded? Maybe Barney —? No, if Barney had gone inside and something truly bad had happened to him, Fitzgerald would have heard—heard what? gunshots? more screaming and yelling? cries for help?

All of the racket had ceased, and now nearly a half hour later Phoebe Alden came out of the boardinghouse as calmly as you please with Hortencia bidding her a pleasant farewell, waving and saying, "*¡Hasta luego!*"

Fitzgerald scratched the ash brown hair on the back of his head, wondering why there had been such a drastic change in the actress from the time he had seen her come from her building and enter the residence of Vivian Vanover until this moment. His curiosity nagged at him to cross Beaudry and do some instinctive detective work, but his good sense advised him to continue following the explicit order Browning had given him. Badly wishing to become a detective himself, a failure to obey a superior officer would delay or even prevent him from achieving that goal. He chose the latter course over the former and stood his ground until relieved.

* * *

From his place of concealment in the rear of the boardinghouse, Orville

Barney heard all the same sounds as Fitzgerald had, but he had no idea that Phoebe Alden had taken any part in them. As much as he wanted to rush into the building and quell the trouble inside, he held his ground exactly as his counterpart standing watch on the east side of Beaudry had done. He saw no good reason to expand the orders Browning had given them, especially since no shots had been fired and nobody inside had called out for help from outside. Although anxious to intercede, he stayed the course by observing and waiting for his relief, which finally arrived in the form of Officer John Fitzgerald.

"What are you doing back here, Fitz?"

"Browning sent me here to tell you we can go back to the station now. We're done for the day."

"But I thought we were supposed to watch this place and make sure the Vanover woman doesn't leave."

The wily twinkle danced in Fitzgerald's brown eyes, accenting his leprechaun looks. "Apparently, she already left. Browning got a phone call from the woman who lives up the street from here, and she said the Vanover woman had fled the premises before we even got here to see her. He just verified that with the Mexican housekeeper."

The brown-haired Barney chuckled. "I'll bet Browning's really riled up over that."

"You better believe it, so we'd better get moving. He's waiting for us out front."

The two policemen walked between the boardinghouse and the house north of it to Beaudry Avenue where Browning waited for them in the Department's Ford Model T.

"I'm sorry for making you boys stand around out here all this time watching the place."

"Fitz just told me the Vanover woman was gone before we even got here, Sarge. Is that right?"

"Yes, it is. She was tipped off that we were coming to talk to her. The Mexican woman wouldn't tell me who it was, but I've got a sneaking suspicion I already know who it was. So climb in, boys. We're taking a little ride out to Hollywood."

* * *

Jack Shannon returned to the three-story Belvedere apartment building on 3rd Street late that afternoon to get ready for his date that evening. He was near the conclusion of those preparations when Cole knocked on the door of his one-room flat on the second story.

"Is that you, Milo?"

"Yes, Jack, it's me."

"Come on in, pal."

Cole turned the doorknob and opened the door a few inches. "Are you decent, Jack? I've got someone with me."

"Yes, Milo, I'm dressed. Just combing my hair. Who's with you?"

Cole opened the door all the way to allow Maisy to precede him into the apartment. "Miss Malone is with me, Jack."

Shannon turned away from the full-length wall mirror to greet them. "What a surprise seeing you, Miss Malone, and with Milo. You two going out on the town?"

Maisy shook her head. "No, we're not."

"We've already had dinner, Jack. At the Clarendon Hotel restaurant next to that giant department store, The Broadway. Maisy just wanted to see where we lived, and I thought I'd bring her by to see if you were up to anything this evening. Maybe the three of us could take in a movie this evening."

Shannon wiggled his eyebrows as he slipped on his coat. "Not me. I'm going out with Vivian Vanover. I'd like to take her to the Palm Court at the Alexandria Hotel for dinner and dancing, but I can't afford that kind of luxury. So, I'm taking her to the Hotel Ramona on the other side of Bunker Hill at 3rd and Spring."

"Now I know why you were so anxious to pick up Vivian this morning. Trying to impress her with a ride in a taxi. And at my expense."

"You can afford it, Milo, with what you make running around for Mr. Sennett and Miss Normand all the time."

"I'd rather be acting. I'm never going to be a lead, if I don't get more bit roles."

Maisy patted Cole on the shoulder. "Don't trouble yourself over it, Milo. With your pal out of the way now, you should move up the ladder at the studio a lot faster."

"That's a terrible thing to say. Don't you agree, Jack?"

Suddenly pale, Shannon swallowed hard. "Yes … yes, it is."

"I'm surprised at you, Maisy, saying something like that."

"Don't get all emotional about it, Milo. I know he was your friend and—"

Shannon interrupted. "He was my friend, too. And I agree with Milo. That was a terrible thing to say, even if it might be true. It's still a bad thing to say."

Maisy tilted her head to one side and studied Shannon for a moment. "You know, now that I think about it, that applies to you, too, Jack. You stand to move up that ladder a little faster now that your friend is out of the way."

"Maisy, you're being absolutely insensitive about poor Leslie's passing."

"Passing? Passing implies he died a natural death. Poor Leslie was murdered, and he was murdered by someone who knew him fairly well." She pinpointed a stare on Shannon. "So what did you tell Detective Browning when he asked you where you were Thursday morning when your friend was murdered?"

"Tell who what?"

"Detective Browning. When he questioned you this morning, what did you tell him when he asked you where you were Thursday morning when your friend Leslie was murdered?"

A shudder ran through Shannon. "I ... I ... I didn't ... I didn't tell him anything. He didn't ask me that question."

Maisy forced her face to appear incredulous. "Oh, come on now, Jack. Surely he asked you where you were that morning. He's a police detective. I'm sure he asked everybody he interviewed this morning where they were the other morning. Why wouldn't he ask you the same question?"

Shannon was visibly shaken. "How should I know why he didn't ask me that question?" He paused only a heartbeat. "And how do you know he asked everybody that question? Were you there when he was questioning everybody?"

Seeing how the exchange between Shannon and Maisy was becoming a little heated, Cole stepped in. "All right, you two, I believe this has gone far enough. Let's be on our way, Maisy, so Jack can be on his."

"Yes, that's right. I do have an engagement to keep with Miss Vanover. So if you don't mind, I'll have to ask you to be on your way, so I can be on mine."

"Fair enough. We'll be on our way. Come on, Milo. Show me where I can catch the Red Car back to the Hollywood Hotel."

Shannon followed them out of his apartment and then out of the building. Once outside, they walked west along 3rd Street to Figueroa. At the corner, Maisy and Milo stopped to wait for the Red Car that would take them north to Sunset Boulevard, and Jack continued across Figueroa toward Beaudry Avenue.

Feeling the moment called for civility, Maisy called out to Shannon. "Have a pleasant evening with Miss Vanover, Jack. See you at the studio on Monday."

"Yes, Jack, have a nice evening with Vivian. And kindly give her my regards, won't you please?"

Shannon glanced over his shoulder. "Thank you, Milo, I will."

Maisy tipped her head toward Cole without taking her eyes off Shannon. "Gee, I wonder why he didn't say good-bye to me."

"Oh, I don't know. Could it be because you tweaked his nose a bit too hard back in his apartment?"

"Tweaked his nose? Now how did I do that?"

"You know perfectly well how you did that. In fact, it rather hurt me a bit as well, although I know what you said was only the truth. With Leslie gone now, there will be more room for me to move up the ladder at Keystone. For Jack, too. In fact, I believe he's already up a rung or two on me. I heard he's being considered to replace Leslie in a film that's scheduled to be produced the week after next. Something called *The Double Wedding* where he'll be playing a groom opposite Fred Mace as the bride."

"Fred Mace as the bride? Isn't that going too far?"

"Don't ask me. I'm not doing the casting for it."

Maisy shook her head. "The more I learn about this moving picture business, the more I miss Vaudeville."

Cole stared after Shannon. "You don't think we wronged him by not telling him that Vivian won't be home when he gets there, do you?"

"Like I said before, Milo, we can't tell anybody what we know about all this and who we know it from. If we tell anybody besides Mabel about what we learned today, your friend's killer might up and run off before the police can do anything about it." She looked south along Figueroa. "Is that my Red Car coming?"

"Yes, it is. I'll ride with you up to Sunset Boulevard and wait with you until the car going to Hollywood comes along. How would that be?"

"Milo, you're a real gentleman, but I hope you're not too much of a gentleman that you won't be able to go through with our plans for tomorrow night."

"If breaking the law is what it takes to prove the guilt of Leslie's killer, then I guess I can stop being a gentleman for one night."

* * *

The Red Car stopped at the intersection of Highland Avenue and Hollywood Boulevard. Maisy stepped down to the street and walked the short distance to the Hollywood Hotel entrance, where she was surprised to be greeted by the regular doorman.

"Good evening, Miss Malone."

"Good evening, Mr. Wilson."

"Miss Malone, a word of caution, if I may?"

Maisy stopped. She had learned long ago to heed people in Wilson's position. "Yes, Mr. Wilson?"

"There are three police officers inside waiting for you, Miss Malone." He nodded toward the Ford Model T. "They arrived here about an hour ago and have been inside all this time."

Maisy dug into her clutch purse and pulled out a quarter for the man. "Thank you, Mr. Wilson. It's probably Detective Browning and a couple of his officers."

"You were expecting them, Miss Malone?"

Maisy grinned. "Don't tell them that, will you, Mr. Wilson? I want that copper to keep on thinking he's smarter than me."

Wilson removed his hat and brushed back his hair. "I'm not sure what that means, Miss Malone, but I believe I like the sound of it."

She tapped him gently on his forearm. "Don't worry, Mr. Wilson. I'll let you in on what's going on as soon as I get the whole thing figured out. In the meantime, would you mind keeping this little talk of ours under your hat?"

"Certainly, Miss Malone. Mum's the word."

Maisy gave him a coy wink. "Thank you."

Wilson opened the door, and Maisy entered the hotel's lobby where she immediately saw Browning sitting on a lounge sofa, holding his bowler in his hands and flanked by officers Barney and Fitzgerald standing at each end of the divan. She strode straight across the room toward the policemen.

"Detective Browning, how nice to see you! And you brought some friends with you. Just for me?"

Browning rose gracefully, still holding his hat. "Good evening, Miss Malone. I need to talk to you right now."

"Of course, you do. Would you like to talk here? Or would you prefer the privacy of my room? Your officers can join us, if you wish to have them along."

"Miss Malone, your attitude is a bit too snippy for me. I have a mind to take you to jail right here and now."

"But you won't, will you?"

The sound of Mabel Normand's voice coming from his left actually startled Browning. He turned toward her instantly and recognized her in the next second.

"Miss Normand, I do not believe this matter concerns you."

"I beg to differ, sir."

"And so do I." Ford Sterling appeared behind Mabel.

"I don't know what we're talking about," said Fred Mace, two steps beyond Sterling, "but I'm with them, whatever the problem might be."

Browning surveyed the three actors as they came to a halt on Maisy's right. "Miss Normand ... gentlemen ... I repeat ... this matter does not concern you."

"And I said I beg to differ, Detective Browning. Miss Malone is an actress in our company, and whatever involves her also involves us. Am I correct in that assumption, Mr. Sterling?"

"Yes, you are, Miss Normand."

"And what say you, Mr. Mace?"

"Oh, yes, Miss Normand, I am in concurrence. Yes, absolutely in concurrence."

Attempting to bluff Detective Sergeant Edward Browning of the Los Angeles Police Department was a fool's errand. "Then I shall call for more officers and arrest the lot of you moving picture people."

Mack Sennett joined his actors. "On what charge, sir?"

"Ah, Mr. Sennett. How nice to see you again."

"I repeat, Detective Browning, on what charge?"

"On the charge of interfering with an official police investigation."

Maisy stepped forward, spun around, and faced the director-general of Keystone Moving Pictures. "Mr. Sennett, I certainly appreciate the moral support all of you are giving me here, but I can handle this all by myself. Detective Browning only wants to ask me what I was doing at Vivian Vanover's boardinghouse this afternoon, and once I tell him he'll toddle off to the police station with these other fine representatives of the Los Angeles Police Department. So you folks can go about your business. I'll be just fine. I promise."

"Are you sure, Maisy?" asked Sennett.

"Trust her, Mack," said Mabel. "She's sure."

Maisy smiled at the lead actress. "Thank you, Mabel."

Sennett returned his attention to the policemen. "All right, Detective Browning, we'll go, but I want to be kept informed about what's going on with your investigation. Is that clear?"

"You can read about it in the newspapers, Mr. Sennett. Now move along, while I speak with Miss Malone."

Sennett glared at Browning, but kept his words to himself.

Mabel took the boss by an arm. "Come on, Mack. We're hungry, aren't we, boys?"

Sterling elbowed Sennett gently. "That's right. Let's go eat."

"Just one question before you leave, Mr. Sennett."

"And what's that?"

"Have you arranged a wake and a funeral for the deceased yet?"

"You can read about it in the newspapers, Detective." And with that Sennett led his people away to the hotel dining room.

"All right, Miss Malone, you know exactly why I am here. So tell me exactly what you were doing at Miss Vanover's boardinghouse this afternoon."

"I was investigating the murder of Leslie Clover, just like you were when you went there to talk to Miss Vanover."

"How do you know I went to see her?"

"Why else would you be here, if you hadn't gone there and talked to her and she told you I was there ahead of you?"

Browning appeared abashed. "I didn't see, Miss Vanover. The housekeeper told me she was too ill to accept visitors. So I did the courteous thing and left the poor woman alone and questioned the housekeeper instead."

"So Hortencia told you I was there ahead of you?"

"No, she didn't tell me either. I figured it out on my own after Miss Alden called the station to tell me Miss Vanover had left the boardinghouse before I arrived there."

"Miss Alden? Phoebe Alden the tall, red-headed actress from Keystone?"

"You know her?"

"We did a couple of scenes together yesterday. Interesting gal. Good actress but not very funny. So you went by her place this afternoon?"

"Yes, she lives down the street from Miss Vanover's boardinghouse. I went there to ask her where Miss Vanover lived."

"Fair enough. So everybody you talked to today had an alibi for Thursday morning?"

"Yes, everybody I talked to had an alibi. Everybody except Miss Vanover, which is why I went to see her. So what did Miss Vanover tell you, Miss Malone? More importantly, what did you tell her?"

"Nothing."

"Nothing? What do you mean nothing?"

"Exactly that. She didn't tell me a thing, and I didn't tell her anything because I didn't get to speak with her. Just like you, I paid her the courtesy of not disturbing her, but not because she was ill. I respected her right to a little privacy while she was mourning the death of her lover."

Browning's mouth went agape with astonishment before he could utter a response. "Leslie Clover was her lover?"

"Surprised, Detective?"

"Something tells me I should** arrest you right now, Miss Malone."

"Why? What did I do to merit being arrested, Detective?"

"I don't know exactly how yet, Miss Malone, but I just know you are interfering in my investigation of Leslie Clover's death."

Maisy shook her head. "I'm not interfering in *your* investigation, Detective Browning. I'm simply conducting *my own* investigation into *his murder*. Nothing more, nothing less."

"Is that right, Miss Malone?"

"Have I broken any laws, Detective?"

Browning tilted his head back. "None that I know of … yet. But if you have, I guarantee you I will find out. And when I do, I promise you a trip to jail and a day in court to prove your innocence."

A mischievous grin curled Maisy's lips as she leaned close to him to nudge him with a gentle elbow. "No, Eddie, this is America. Here *you* have to prove me guilty. I'm innocent until you do."

Browning turned to Officer Barney. "Orville, you and John go start the car. I'll join you in a minute. I want a private word with Miss Malone first, if you don't mind."

"Sure, Sarge."

Barney and Fitzgerald left the hotel as ordered.

"So what's on your mind, Eddie?"

"You haven't told anybody about our little wager, have you?"

"The only two people other than you and me who know about our wager are Miss Normand and Milo Cole. As far as I know, neither one of them has told another soul."

"Good. I want it kept that way."

"Oh, so do I, Eddie. I'd really hate it if word got out that we had a bet and *I* lost."

"I feel the same way, Miss Malone. By the way, have you learned anything new that you would care to share with me."

Maisy studied Browning for a few seconds. "If I let you in on something,

124

will you return the favor?"

The policeman's head bobbled a bit. "I suppose that would only be fair. After all, we both want the same thing."

"And what would that be?"

"Why, to catch the perpetrator of this heinous crime, Miss Malone, of course."

"Oh, yes, that, too."

"What else would it be?"

"Winning our bet, of course."

"Miss Malone—"

She nudged him again to interrupt. "We're alone now, Eddie. You can call me Maisy. Okay?"

"Miss Malone—"

"Maisy!"

"All right then, Maisy." He stopped, stared up at the ceiling for a second, shook his head, and then refocused on Maisy. "Now you've made me forget what I was going to say."

"You were going to lecture me on how much more important it is that we catch this killer than our silly little bet is. Am I right, Eddie?"

Browning lifted his hat to her in a gentlemanly manner. "Have a good evening, Miss Malone." Without further ado, he departed, leaving Maisy to chortle as she watched him exit the building.

* * *

"Well, I'm certainly glad to see you weren't arrested, Maisy," said Sennett as soon as Maisy joined him and the three lead actors for Keystone at their table in the hotel restaurant.

"I told you before, Mack. Maisy can handle herself quite nicely." Mabel patted Maisy's forearm. "I'm proud of you, dear."

"So what did you tell him, Maisy?" asked Sterling.

"Yes, Maisy," said Sennett, "why did you go see this … what was her name again?"

"Miss Vanover. Miss Vivian Vanover."

"Oh, yes," said Mabel. "I remember her. She's one of our extras, isn't she?"

"Not anymore," said Maisy. "She's gone back to Polyscope as I understand it."

Sennett appeared insulted as well as completely oblivious as to why anybody would want to leave his studio for another, especially one that wasn't making comedies. "Really? Why would she do that?"

"That was something I was going to ask her as well, Mr. Sennett, but I didn't get to talk to her when I went by to see her this afternoon."

"Maisy, we're not at the studio now, and we're not around the other people at the studio. You can call me Mack now."

Mabel giggled. "Call him, Mr. Bossy Pants. I do."

"I'd better not ever hear you call me that."

"It's true, Mack," said Sterling. "You are Mr. Bossy Pants."

"That will be enough—"

Mace interrupted. "Will you two save that for the studio? Right now I want to hear Maisy. Go ahead, Maisy. Tell us why you didn't get to talk to this Vivian this afternoon."

"Fred's right, Maisy," said Mabel. "Go ahead and tell us about it."

"Well, there's not much to tell. She was too sick to receive visitors, so I spoke to the housekeeper for a few minutes, and then Milo and I left."

"Milo was with you?" queried Sennett. "Our Milo?"

"Yes, Mack, our Milo. He was showing me around Los Angeles a little bit this afternoon. We went to the Broadway Department Store on Broadway and 4th Street so I could buy an alarm clock like ..." She looked at Sterling. "May I call you George now?"

The actor smiled at her. "Of course. Please do."

"I bought the alarm clock like you advised me to do, George." She turned back to Sennett. "Milo and I ran into Katy Killoy coming out of the store as we were going in. She told me about her daughter working in the girls' department on the third floor. We stopped by there to meet Lizzie and to buy a dress for one of my sisters."

"One of your sisters?" asked Mabel. "How many sisters do you have?"

"Just five."

"Just five?"

Maisy nodded rapidly. "Yes, that's right."

"Do you have any brothers?"

"Well, my mother gave birth to two sons before I came along, but neither of them lived long. The first died before his second birthday, and the second died before his first."

"Oh, that is sad."

Mace leaned closer to her. "No one to carry on your family name. Your father must have been real heartbroken to lose both of his sons like that."

"Mama said it made him take to drink."

"I'm so sorry to hear that, Maisy," said Mace very sincerely.

"Thank you ..." She gave him a quizzical look. "Do I get to call you Fred or Freddie now?"

"Whichever one strikes you at the moment, Maisy."

"Fair enough."

* * *

As soon as they finished eating, Maisy took Mabel to a dark corner of the hotel lounge for some serious conspiracy talk. She had a plan, and it included her new friend helping with it.

"You want to do what? Maisy, you're talking about committing a serious crime. Are you crazy?"

Maisy feigned wistfulness as she peered into the distant darkness of the night. "I wish I had a dollar for every time I've been asked that. Then I'd be a regular John D. Rockefeller." She sighed heavily, intentionally dramatizing the moment. Just as quickly, she turned serious again. "Okay, I might be a little off my nut, but I need to see those payroll records in McHatton's office."

"Why? What's so important about the payroll records?"

"One of them just might be the piece of evidence I need to prove who murdered Leslie Clover."

Mabel's brow furrowed with perplexity. "How can a payroll record prove who murdered Leslie Clover? I don't get it."

"If my suspicion is correct, it will show that somebody wasn't where they said they were on the morning Clover was murdered."

"I still don't get it."

A little exasperation crept into Maisy's voice. "Look, Mabel. Eddie told me—"

"Eddie? Who's Eddie?"

"Detective Browning?"

"Oh, yes, of course. That Eddie."

Maisy wanted to say something sarcastic like "Try to keep up, will you?" but she chose to be polite to Mabel. "Anyway, Eddie told me everybody he talked to today had an alibi for where they were Thursday morning when Clover was murdered. I have a hunch somebody was lying to him, and I'm hoping the payroll records will tell us who that person was. Do you get it now?"

"I think so. But why do we have to break into the studio in the middle of the night to look at the payroll records? Why can't we just wait until Monday morning and ask Mr. McHatton to show them to us?"

"Why can't we ask Mr. McHatton? Simple. First thing he'll ask us back is, 'Why do you need to see them?' Then he'll ask why I'm so interested in Clover's murder."

"So lie to him."

Maisy shook her head. "Oh, no, can't do that."

"Why? Because it would be a sin to lie?"

"Religion has nothing to do with it."

"Then what does?"

"My integrity. Lying would be sacrificing the one thing nobody can take away from you. I was taught early on by my daddy that my integrity is the one thing nobody can take away from me. That's why I don't lie, and I don't steal, and I don't cheat … at anything."

"Okay, but don't you think breaking into the studio is stealing?"

"How is it stealing?"

Mabel shrugged. "Okay, maybe it's not stealing, but it certainly is cheating."

"How do you figure that?"

"You're breaking into—"

Maisy put her hands on Mabel's shoulders to stop her from going any further. "Mabel, let me explain something to you. There is no crime unless there is a victim. There is no injury to anybody if there is no monetary loss. Do you get that? Before a law can be broken, somebody has to be hurt, either physically, emotionally, mentally, or monetarily. Do you get that? These new laws about speeding down a street in an automobile are just a lot of horse manure. Nobody is hurt when you drive fast. It just annoys people."

"But what if you hit somebody with your automobile?"

"That's a horse of a different color, but let's not get into all that right now. Are you with me on this or not?"

Mabel thought about her answer for a few seconds. "And you say Milo is going to help us?"

"Milo has thrown his hat in the ring on this. He wants Clover's killer caught and punished, and he said he'll do whatever it takes to catch the fiend. So what about it? Are you in or out?"

The actress bit her lip as she continued to mull over her decision. Finally, she heaved a sigh and spoke with great reluctance. "Okay, I'm in. So when do we do this?"

"Tomorrow night."

"Tomorrow night? I don't know, Maisy. I might change my mind by then. Why not do it tonight while Mack is staying here and while I still have the courage to do it?"

Maisy smiled. "Two good points in one sentence." She threw her arms around Mabel. "I knew I could count on you."

Mabel reciprocated with a gentle hug. "Don't be so sure about that. We're not there yet."

"Another good point." Maisy backed away, holding Mabel's shoulders at arm's length. "Let's call Milo right now and tell him to meet us at the Red Car stop on Sunset and Allesandro."

"Whatever you say, Maisy. You're as crazy as a loon, but I'm with you. I guess."

* * *

Although he lived on the premises for the time being, Mack Sennett still employed sixty-year-old Arthur Verring as the night watchman at the studio. Old Artie was a relic, leftover from the days when Fred Balshofer was the director-general of Bison Pictures. He was an extra in the westerns Bison made in and around Edendale until Tom Ince moved the company's operations to the hills between Santa Monica and Malibu. Not wishing to make the long, daily commute to and from his boardinghouse room in Los Angeles to Bison studio, Verring stayed on in Edendale as the caretaker for the old ranch where he had worked long before it became a motion picture studio. Needing someone to guard the place at night, Sennett retained Artie when the Keystone comedy group came out from New York.

Verring started work at sundown every evening of the work week and left every morning except Sunday at sunrise. In between sundown and first light the next day, he mostly slept in the old barn that he knew so well. He had a bedroll on a cot in the equipment room. However, since this was Saturday night and Sennett was off the property enjoying some personal time until the following day, the night guard spread his blankets and pillow on the porch of the bungalow and set his alarm clock to wake him at midnight for his next inspection round of the lot. Before settling down for his first nap of the night, he focused on the eight-foot high picket-fence gate protecting the only easy way in or out of the studio lot. The hard way was climbing over the eight-foot wooden fence that surrounded the premises. Satisfied that all was well, he hunkered down for forty winks.

Knowing this much about Verring and the layout of the studio, Mabel informed Maisy they would have to surmount the linear obstacle in order to get inside. "We'll need a ladder to get over the fence."

"We don't need a ladder. We've got Milo."

"We do?"

Cole held up a hand. "Wa-a-ait a minute now. What are you planning for me to do?"

Maisy nudged him. "Relax, Milo. All you have to do is climb up on top of the fence, then help me up and lower me down on the other side. Then you can get down, and we can go into the studio and get into McHatton's office and find the payroll records, and as soon as I find what I want, we're out of there and back over the fence here. See? Easy as pie."

"And what do I do?" asked Mabel.

"You distract the night watchman if he hears us."

"How do I do that?"

Maisy jostled Mabel's arm. "Use your feminine wiles on him."

Mabel shook her head. "Sorry, no can do. Fresh out of feminine wiles. Besides, Artie is older than those hills behind us. I don't think the fanciest of feminine wiles would work on him."

"Then just talk to him. That's the least you can do, can't you?"

"Talk to him?" Mabel sighed. "Okay, I'll give it a shot. But give me a minute to get in place, will you?"

"Sure, go ahead."

Mabel went around the corner of the fence and walked down Allesandro to the studio's gate, which was closed and locked for the night, not to be opened until Monday morning, unless Sennett came back and ordered it opened sooner, which wasn't likely to happen because he hadn't done so yet since moving into the place.

"Okay, Milo, boost me up."

Cole seemed unsure of himself. He took Maisy by the waist with both hands and lifted her a few feet off the ground.

"Put me down, you dope."

He obeyed without hesitation.

"Now interlock your fingers like this." She demonstrated the maneuver for him. "And hold them tight together out in front of you like this." Again, she showed him how to do it.

"I know how to do it, Maisy. It's not like I've never helped anybody over a fence or something before."

"Well, you sure don't act like it."

"None of them were girls."

"Well, forget I'm a girl and boost me up there."

Cole complied, locking his fingers together tightly, holding them in front of him, and bending over slightly so Maisy wouldn't have to step so high.

She put her foot in his hands and her hands on his shoulders. "On the count of three you lift me up. Ready?"

"Sure, let's do this thing."

"One, two, three, up!"

Cole straightened up and lifted at the same time, practically throwing Maisy on top of the fence. She was able to brace herself with her hands, her arms straight down in front of her.

"Now grab my feet and push me up a little more."

He did and she was quickly sitting atop the fence.

"Good. Now climb up here and help me down on the other side."

"Maisy, I don't think I can do that."

"Sure, you can." She extended her right arm. "Come on. I'll pull you up. Take my hand."

"I don't think that will work. I'll probably only pull you back down on this side. So why don't you get down on the other side, and look around for a ladder or something. The carpenters have wood stacked just about everywhere. Maybe you can find something like a ladder. Go ahead. I'll wait right here."

"Okay. Wait there. I'll be back as soon as I find a ladder."

Maisy disappeared on the other side of the fence, and Cole began pacing and mumbling to himself. "Here it is almost midnight, and I'm trying to break into the place where I work with the lead actress and crazy Maisy Malone. Well, I must be crazy, too, because here I am. I just know I'm headed for jail. Or Hell. Or both." He shook his head. "And now I'm talking to myself. I never talked to myself before, not until I met this crazy girl from who-knows-where. I must be nuts, as nuts as she is anyway."

Just that second he heard a thud against the fence. A few seconds later

Maisy appeared at the top of it.

"I found a ladder close by here. I'll pull it up and lower it down to you." Less than a minute passed before the ladder came down to Cole. "Now climb up here." He did exactly that. "Now pull the ladder up here and put it back down on this side. Then you climb down first, while I hold the ladder in place. Then I'll be right after you, while you hold the ladder for me." He lowered the ladder inside the compound and climbed down. Maisy followed a few seconds later. "Stop looking up my dress, Milo."

"It wouldn't do me any good to look up your dress, even if I was. It's too dark to see anything worth looking at."

Maisy reached the ground again. "Why don't I believe you?"

"I'm a gentleman, and—"

"Skip it, Milo. Let's go see if the barn is locked."

They slinked across the open ground to the door on the north side of the building. Maisy found the knob and turned it. The door creaked open.

"I don't recall it making that sound in the daytime. Do you?"

Cole shuddered. "Can't say that I have, and that gives me the creeps. It sounds like a crypt door opening up."

"A crypt door? You aren't afraid of ghosts, are you, Milo?"

"Never mind that, crazy girl. Let's just get inside and find those payroll records and get the heck out of here before Old Artie wakes up and finds us here."

* * *

Verring's alarm clock clanged him awake promptly at midnight. He rolled out of his kip to shut it off. Slowly, he stood up and stretched his aging muscles.

Mabel heard the ringing of the hammer on the two bells atop the clock from her vantage point just outside the studio gate. Behind her the last Red Car of the night from Los Angeles crawled up the hill toward its end-of-the-line destination in Glendale, reminding her of the urgency the trio of trespassers were facing. She knew the last train from Los Angeles to Hollywood and the last one from Hollywood to Los Angeles would be at the Sunset and Allesandro stop in little over an hour from now. She and Maisy had to catch the former or walk the few miles back to the hotel, and Milo had to do the same with the latter or walk the few miles back to the Belvedere.

Peeking through the pickets of the gate, Mabel saw Verring sit down in the only chair on the porch to pull on his boots. She continued to watch as he stood up again. From what she could recognize in the dark, he then cinched up his belt. Then by the shape of his silhouette she realized he had donned the slightly tattered, old derby, his personal trademark, that he had brought with him from England when he was a youth. Because the night was a little on the chilly side, he put on the long frock coat he said made him look and feel like the famous lawman Wyatt Earp.

While waiting outside the gate, Mabel had devised a plan for what she would say to Verring should she have to distract him long enough to allow Maisy and Milo to find the evidence Maisy hoped would be in the studio's payroll records. Seeing him coming down the porch steps, she cleared her throat and took up the cause.

"Oh, Mr. Verring, I am so glad to see you."

Her voice startled the watchman. He reacted by turning sideways, pulling back the right side of his coat, and dropping into a semi-crouch. "Who's there?"

"It's only me, Mr. Verring. Mabel Normand."

"Miss Normand?"

"Yes, that's right."

Verring held his ground for the moment. "What are you doing here this late at night, Miss Normand?"

"Well, I came to see if my earrings are in the dressing room."

"Your earrings?"

"Yes, my earrings. You see they were a gift from my mother on my fifteenth birthday, so they're kind of special to me. I didn't realize that I had left them here until I went to take them off in my room at the hotel this evening. It was then that I realized I might have left them in the dressing room. I wanted to make sure they were safe, so I came here tonight hoping you would let me in so I can go to the dressing room and get them. You wouldn't mind, would you? Letting me in, I mean, so I can get them from the dressing room."

The watchman straightened up and ambled to the gate. "No, of course, I don't mind, Miss Normand. Just give me a second to unlock the gate, and we'll go get your earrings together. Wouldn't do to have you wandering around here in the dark all by yourself, now would it? What would Mr. Sennett say … or do, if anything should happen to you? Why, he might even discharge me. We can't have that now, can we?"

"No, we certainly can't have that."

* * *

The interior of the barn was dimly lit by a single bulb suspended from the center rafter of the roof. It gave off just enough light for Maisy and Milo to see their way around without stumbling into anything.

The door to McHatton's office was locked.

"So now what do we do, crazy girl?"

"We pick the lock."

"*We* pick the lock? How do *we* pick the lock? Do you have a mouse in your pocket? Because if you don't—"

"Milo, will you just shut up? I can pick the lock."

"How do you know how to pick the lock?"

"Doesn't everybody know how to pick a simple door lock?"

"Not everybody. I certainly don't know how to do it."

132

Maisy shook her head with chagrin. "Then you should have read Houdini's book *Handcuff Secrets*. I did during the crossing to England in O-nine. I haven't been locked out of anyplace since then."

"That figures."

"Now hush and let me pick this lock." She removed a hair pin from her coiffure and stuck it in the lock. In a few seconds, she had the door open. "Find the light, and then let's find the payroll records."

Cole found the light switch next to the door and pushed the upper button. The overhead light came on, and the two of them started to search the cabinets and drawers of the desk, neither of them noticing the window high up on the east side wall.

* * *

Artie Verring saw the light shining through the window of McHatton's office the second he and Mabel Normand rounded the corner of the studio. He reacted instantly, grabbing the actress by the right arm with his left hand to stop her from going any farther. Simultaneously, he used his right hand to pull back the lower right part of his frock coat. In the wink of an eye, he drew out the Colt's .45 Peacemaker from the holster of his gun belt.

"What's—?"

The watchman jerked on her arm to silence her. At the same time, he whispered sharply. "Hush, Miss Normand! There's someone in Mr. McHatton's office."

Seeing how he was looking up at the illuminated window, Mabel whispered back at him. "How can you be sure of that, Mr. Verring? Perhaps Mr. McHatton left the light on when he left this afternoon."

"No, ma'am, he didn't. That light was not on two hours ago when I made my last round. Someone's inside there."

Mabel finally spied the six-shooter in Verring's hand. She gasped. "You've got a gun!"

"I sure do, and I know how to use it, too. You stay here, ma'am. I'm going in there to deal with whoever it is who's trying to rob this place."

Against the night watchman's orders, Mabel followed Verring to the main entrance of the studio.

"I told you to stay back, Miss Normand. We don't know who we're dealing with here yet. They could be cold-blooded killers for all we know. Now stay back please, while I go inside and see what they're up to."

The watchman turned the doorknob and pushed the door open slowly. He stopped when the hinges started creaking. After considering what to do to prevent the noise which seemed loud to him, he continued opening the door a little faster. It didn't help. More creaking every inch of the way.

"Dang it all to heck! I sure hope they didn't hear that."

Mabel wished for just the opposite.

Verring poked his head inside for a look around before proceeding toward the bookkeeper's office. Assured nobody was wandering around the main part of the building, he stepped through the doorway, leaving the door open behind him. With great stealth he tiptoed toward McHatton's private domain.

Even more covertly, Mabel slinked inside right behind the unwary watchman, still wishing Maisy and Milo had heard the squeaky door and were in the midst of hiding somewhere so secretive that Verring wouldn't find them. More than that, she prayed silently that the night guard wouldn't shoot them first and ask questions later. After all, Old Artie had been a cowboy on the ranges of Texas long before he moved to California and took up a more peaceful line of work in the oilfields. Weren't Texans notorious for plugging bad *hombres* on sight? That's how it played out in the movies, anyway.

Verring stopped inches from the door to McHatton's office because he heard muffled voices inside. He cocked an ear to get a better bead on what they were saying.

"Why do there have to be so many extras in the motion picture business? Can you tell me that, Mr. Expert?"

"Quit bellyaching, crazy girl. Just find the one you want so we can get the heck out of here. Okay?"

Positive he had heard a woman and then a man, Verring felt secure enough to break in on them. He took the knob in his left hand and threw the door open.

"Hold it right there, you two!"

Cole was sitting in the extra chair in the room, leaning it back away from the desk by using his right leg like a piston. The unexpected invasion put the frights in him, causing his leg to involuntarily straighten out more than he intended and sending him flailing backward and crashing onto the floor behind him.

Maisy simply looked up at Verring from the desk where she was examining the payroll records and glared at him for a second before resuming her search for the one account she needed as proof of who might have killed Leslie Clover.

"Be careful with that Colt's, old-timer. You might hurt someone with it."

"I said for you to stop what you're doing."

"No, you didn't. You said to hold it right there. As you see, I'm still right where I was when you walked in. Now put that gun away before it goes off and poor Milo here gets shot."

Verring squinted at Milo. "Mr. Cole? Is that you?"

The actor stayed put on the floor, his eyes wide with fear. "Yes, it's me, Artie."

"What are you doing here, Mr. Cole? And who's this with you?"

Mabel stepped up beside the night guard. "She's our new feature actress, Mr. Verring. Maisy, I'd like you to meet our night watchman, Mr. Arthur Verring."

Maisy looked up. "Nice to meet you, Mr. Verring." And she immediately resumed her search.

"Mr. Verring, allow me to introduce Miss Maisy Malone."

"I still want to know what you people are doing here. Now somebody better start talking before lead starts flying."

Maisy glanced up again. "Oh, come on. Mr. Verring. What kind of dime novel chatter is that? Before the lead starts flying?" She giggled. "Where'd you find this old geezer?"

"Maisy, there's no reason to be rude."

"You're right, Mabel. My apologies, Mr. Verring. Please forgive me for being so flippant. You see, I'm kind of busy here and I'd like to get this done so Mabel and I can all go back to our hotel and Milo can go back to his place in the city. So would you please put that gun away and leave me alone to finish this business?"

"You still ain't told me what you're doing here."

"Tell him, Mabel. I'm busy."

"Maisy is trying to find a payroll record that might be a clue to the identity of the person who murdered Leslie Clover."

"Is that right? You think someone from the studio killed him?"

"Pretty sure," said Maisy without looking up.

"Well, if that's what you're doing, how can I help?"

"Why would you want to help, Mr. Verring?" asked Mabel.

"Leslie Clover was from England, wasn't he?"

"Yes, that's right."

"Well, so am I. So what can I do to help?"

* * *

Maisy, Mabel, and Milo stood at the Red Car stop at the intersection of Sunset Boulevard and Allesandro Street a few minutes after one o'clock, hoping they weren't too late to catch last train of the night. Cole faced the two girls as they looked east along Sunset.

"I can't believe you won't tell us what you found in those payroll records, Maisy. We risked getting shot to help you, and you won't tell us a thing. Don't you trust us?"

"Sure, I trust you … a little."

"A little? I can't believe this."

"No, Milo, she's right. We only met Maisy two days ago. She hasn't known us long enough to trust us completely. If I were in her shoes, I'd feel the same way, and you should, too. She's doing us a favor by not telling us."

"How do you figure that, Miss Normand?"

Mabel patted him on the arm. "Come on, Milo. We're not at the studio now. You can call me Mabel."

He shrugged. "Okay, Mabel, but you didn't answer my question. How do you figure Maisy is doing us a favor?"

Maisy interceded. "Milo, would you like the burden of having to keep a secret for the next several days?"

"What are you talking about, crazy girl?"

"Look at it this way. Suppose I did tell you what I learned tonight, and like me, you drew a conclusion about who murdered your friend Leslie Clover. What would you do with that knowledge?"

"I'd go straight to Detective Browning and tell him who did it."

"That's what you'd do? For sure?"

"For sure."

"And what if the conclusion turned out to be wrong? Then what?"

"Well, that would be Detective Browning's problem, not mine."

"Would it? It wouldn't be a problem for the person he would arrest on your word who turned out to be innocent?"

Cole considered her words for a few seconds. "I get that, but what if they were guilty, then what?"

Mabel took a turn at interceding. "You aren't getting it, Milo. Maisy is saying she now has a pretty good idea who did it, but she can't prove it completely yet. Am I right, dear?"

"That's pretty much it, Mabel. I can't go to Eddie just yet because I don't have all the evidence he needs to make an arrest that will stick. There still might be a couple of pieces missing from this puzzle, if you get my drift."

"I get it, dear. How about you, Milo?"

Cole nodded reluctantly. "Yes, I think I get it now. You want to make sure you have all your ducks in a row before you go to Detective Browning with your evidence. But can't you at least tell us who it is you suspect of killing Leslie?"

Maisy shook her head. "If I did that, you might let it slip to that person."

"I wouldn't tell a soul. I promise."

"Oh, I believe that much, Milo. You wouldn't tell them knowingly, but you would act differently around them, which might give it away that you know they're the perpetrator of this crime."

"Yes, you're probably right about that."

"It's bad enough that I suspect this person and have to watch everything I say and do in their presence. Just think how difficult it would be for all three of us to be on our toes with this person."

"You keep saying person. Why won't you at least tell us whether it's a man or a woman? I mean, does it make that much of a difference?"

"It could. I don't know for certain. I don't want to take any chances of letting this person know we're on to him or her."

"Okay, Maisy, I'll go along with you for now, but I hope we get to learn this person's identity soon or I'm going to have a stroke thinking about it so much."

* * *

Mabel couldn't wait to get Maisy alone on the Red Car back to their hotel in Hollywood. She had one very important question for her.

"Okay, Milo's gone. So how about telling me what you found out back in McHatton's office?"

Maisy squinted at Mabel, astounded that she would ask her that. "I can't do that."

"Why not? I thought we were friends."

"We are, but I'm also friends with Milo. If I tell you after telling him no, that would be a betrayal of my friendship with him. And if he asked me the same thing, I'd tell him exactly what I'm telling you now. No."

"But we're a different kind of friends. We're—"

Maisy shook her head and interrupted. "Yes, Mabel, we are a different kind of friends. We're both girls. But that's the only difference. Friendship is a back-and-forth deal. We have to build trust in each other. Would you want me to tell Milo and not you? Of course, you wouldn't. And that's why I'm not telling you anymore than I'm telling Milo. When I'm ready to tell you about it, I'll tell both of you at the same time. Okay?"

Mabel's lips quivered into a pout. "Okay, I suppose so. But can't you tell me what you plan to do next?"

"I could … if I actually knew what I was going to do next."

* * *

Bad news waited for Mabel and Maisy in the lobby of the Hollywood Hotel in the form of Mack Sennett.

"Where have you two been?"

Mabel hesitated to answer.

Not so Maisy. She recognized the look on Sennett's face. Just like with her own father when he caught her doing something she should not have been doing, she had only one course here.

"We were at the studio."

Slightly disappointed that he received such a straight answer from her, his head bobbled in acknowledgement. "How did you get into the studio at this time of night?"

"Milo and I went over the fence in back, and Mabel came through the front gate."

"Artie let you in?"

Mabel looked sheepish. "Kind of."

"What does that mean? He either let you in or he didn't. Now which is it?"

"Okay, he let me in. Don't fire him for it, Mack. He's such a nice old man, and he has a gun, you know?"

"Yes, I know about the gun, but I'm not worried about it. He's not going to go nuts and shoot me like that Japanese gardener who murdered Frank Boggs last year." Sennett turned back to Maisy. "So you roped Milo into helping you, is that right?"

"Yes, it is. I needed Milo to help me get over the fence."

Her honesty was refreshing on the one hand and a bit exasperating on the other. Sennett searched for places to go with his interrogation and the lecture he had been planning to give them. "So why did you feel the need to break into my studio at this time of night?"

Maisy smiled at him because he so reminded her of her father back home. She patted his arm. "For goodness sakes, Mack, will you please stop pussyfooting around here? It's obvious Old Artie called you and told you about us being there and what we did … or at least what I did. What you really want to know is why I'm snooping into all this murder business, isn't it?"

"I already know the answer to that one, Maisy. You're a female, and all women are naturally nosy. You can't help it. It's part of being female. You all snoop around where you shouldn't be snooping at all."

Maisy put both hands up to her face, her fingers over her mouth, which she had forced into a mock gape. She pulled them down and turned her head toward her co-conspirator. "Mabel dear, can you believe it? Here is a man who understands women. What a catch he'll make for some lucky lady!"

"Okay, Miss Wiseacre, anymore talk like that will get you fired."

"Oh, don't let that scare you, Maisy. He's fired me four times in the past two years, and I'm still here making the funniest comedies in the moving picture business, aren't I, Mack?" She cozied up to him as coyly as she could.

"You want to make it five, Mabel? And this time it'll be for good. Maisy here can take your place, if I don't fire her, too."

Maisy followed Mabel's lead and moved closer to Sennett, rubbing her cheek on his shoulder. "Oh, Mack, you wouldn't fire me, would you? Not after all the money you've invested me without getting a cent of it back yet, you wouldn't fire me."

"She's right, Mack. You have too much money tied up in Maisy to fire her now. You really should wait until you've at least recouped some of Mr. Kessel's and Mr. Baumann's for them."

"Stop it! Both of you! People are staring."

Maisy gave him the *coup de grace*. "All the more reason not to fire us, Mack."

"All right, enough already. I won't fire either of you … for now."

The girls backed away from him, looked at each other, and giggled.

Sennett's head bobbled at Maisy. "I knew you were a smart cookie when I met you in Chicago, but don't let it get in the way of business. We're here to make moving pictures, not snoop into matters that should only concern the police. Is that understood?"

Maisy tried to appear properly chastised. "Whatever you say, Mack."

"Yes, Mack, whatever you say."

"Good. Now go to bed. You'll need your rest. We have a big week ahead of us. Taking time out for Clover's funeral on Tuesday means we'll have to work faster and longer, including next Saturday afternoon to make up for Tuesday. So get some sleep while you can."

Mabel curtsied to him. "Yes, Mack. Come on, Maisy. I'm bushed. How about you?"

Maisy followed her lead again. "Me, too."

They moved away from Sennett, shoulder to shoulder, whispering and giggling all the way to the stairway to the second floor.

Sennett watched them, scratching his head and wondering what they were conspiring to do now to make his life a bit more challenging than it already was.

* * *

Before going to bed, Maisy placed a telephone call to the Los Angeles Police Department's Central Station.

"Sergeant Toolen speaking."

"Sergeant, my name is Maisy Malone. I am in acquaintance with Detective Sergeant Edward Browning. He wouldn't happen to be there at this time of night, would he?"

"No, Miss Malone, he's not here. Is there something I can do for you?"

"Yes, would you take a message for Detective Browning please? I have some information for him that might help him with his investigation into the murder of the actor Leslie Clover."

"Yes, I can do that, Miss Malone. What would you like him to know?"

"Well, actually, I would like him to meet me at the Hollywood Hotel tomorrow afternoon, if he has the time. If you can contact him and ask him that, would you also ask him to call the hotel before he comes out here and leave me a message about when he plans to be here? That way I can meet him in the lobby."

"Yes, Miss Malone, I can do that, but it would be more helpful if you gave me a little more information to relate to Detective Browning."

"Sure, I can do that. Tell him I think I know how he can find Vivian Vanover and how he can find the evidence he needs to make an arrest in the case."

"Would you repeat that name please, Miss Malone?"

"Vivian ... Vanover. It's spelled just like it sounds. Van ... over."

"Yes, I have it. Thank you."

The call ended.

Maisy smiled to herself.

* * *

When he returned home, Cole saw a light shining through the window of Jack Shannon's apartment on the second floor of the Belvedere and wondered why his fellow actor was up so late. He made a mental note to ask Shannon about it the next day. Tonight, all Cole wanted was a lot of sleep. He crept up the stairs, hoping he hadn't disturbed any of the other lodgers. Luck was not his side.

"Hey, Milo, where have you been?"

Almost to the door of his place, Cole turned around to see Shannon at the top of the stairs he had just ascended. "On a wild goose chase. You just getting in, too?"

Shannon finished his ascent to the third floor hall. "No, I've been home for hours."

"Really? So how was your evening with Vivian?"

"Oh, I think you already know the answer to that, Milo."

"What does that mean, Jack?"

"Why don't we go inside your apartment and talk about it?"

"Can't it wait until tomorrow? I'm really bushed, and I'd—"

"No, it can't wait. I want to talk about it now."

Cole shrugged and heaved a big sigh. "Sure, why not?" He unlocked the door and let Shannon enter ahead of him. He closed the door behind them. "Have a seat, Jack, and tell me what this is all about."

Shannon remained standing. "Hortencia told me you were by the boardinghouse to see Vivian earlier today, Milo."

Cole had expected this but not until the next day. "Okay, I was by the boardinghouse this afternoon. So what?"

"So what were you doing there, Milo?"

Cole burped a laugh. "Good gosh, Jack, you're jealous."

"Why didn't you tell me you were by her boardinghouse when you and Maisy Malone stopped by to see me? Was she with you when you went to see Vivian?"

"Sure, she was. I took her over there just to meet Vivian. I wanted to see how Vivian was doing since she and Leslie were close once."

"Then you got to see Vivian?"

"No, we didn't. Hortencia said she was nursing a broken heart, and we figured it was over Leslie. So we talked to Hortencia for a while, and then we left to go shopping at The Broadway."

"Hortencia said you were asking questions about Vivian and Leslie. Why would you do that, Milo?"

"I told Detective Browning that I'd talk to some of the people who knew Leslie. Since Vivian had left Keystone and had gone back to Polyscope, I figured Browning hadn't talked to her yet, and since I was there, I thought I'd ask Hortencia what she knew about Vivian and Leslie. Hortencia being Mexican and all, I figured she would be more likely to talk to me than to Browning."

"So what did she tell you about them?"

"Nothing that I didn't know before. Vivian was kind of stuck on Leslie, and he jilted her just like he jilted just about every other girl he took out more than once. You know how Leslie was."

"Maybe I don't know how Leslie was, Milo. Why don't you tell me?"

"Leslie considered himself to some kind of *bon vivant* and Don Juan. He used women and then threw them aside. I can't say that I approve of that, but nearly every woman I've known who went out with him confessed she knew what kind of man he was before she went out with him. And every last one of them said she went out with him because he was so irresistible. Face it, Jack. Leslie was a real charmer."

"Yes, I suppose he was."

"A fellow like Leslie is hard to compete with, my friend. And now that he's dead, he'll be even harder to match in the eyes and hearts of any woman who was smitten by him."

"You mean Vivian, don't you?"

"Yes, Jack, I mean Vivian."

Shannon's aspect melted until he looked so forlorn that Cole thought he might begin crying any second. "Do you think I should give up on her, Milo?"

"That's hard to say at this point, Jack. She might get over Leslie tomorrow or the next day or maybe not for a month or a year. She might never get over him. You just don't know. Her heart *might* heal in time. The question you have to ask yourself is, do you want to wait around to find out?"

"Yes, I suppose that is the question, isn't it?" Shannon's demeanor changed suddenly. "Damn him! Damn Leslie Clover. Damn him for what he did to Vivian! Damn him all to Hell! I'm glad I—" He stopped himself in mid-sentence and regained his composure. "I'm sorry, Milo, for ranting like that."

Cole patted him on the shoulder. "It's all right, Jack. I understand what you must be going through. You have feelings for Vivian, don't you? Deep feelings, I'll bet."

"Yes, Milo, I do. I'd do anything for her."

"Anything, Jack?"

"Yes, anything."

"Even murder someone for her?"

"Murder?" Shannon backed away from Cole. "Say, what are you getting at, Milo? You don't think I had anything to do with Leslie's death, now do you?"

"Well, if I was Detective Browning, you'd be on my list of suspects. You had a reason for wanting him dead, now didn't you?"

"No, I didn't. Not until now, at least. I knew he had gone out with Vivian a few times, and all the other ..."

"And you knew about how he was with the ladies, and you knew he might have been that way with Vivian, didn't you?"

"No, I didn't know. Not for sure, anyway. And even if he had been that way with her, I wouldn't have held it against her."

"But you would have held it against *him*, isn't that so?"

Shannon stared at Cole with a fiery hate. "I see what you're trying to do, Milo. You're trying to make me confess to something I didn't do."

"Why would I do that, Jack? You're my friend."

"Am I, Milo? Am I your friend? Am I your friend like Leslie was your friend?"

"Friendships come in different weights and measures, Jack. My friendship with you isn't the same as the one I had with Leslie. In the first place, you're much younger than Leslie was. In the second, you're Irish and he was English."

"And you're Bohemian. What has all that got to do with being friends?"

"Nothing, Jack. That's the point. You two were different, and I'm still your friend as well as I was his. But in a different way. Do you see what I'm getting at, Jack?"

"Yes, I believe so, Milo."

"Good. Now why don't you toddle off to your place and try to get some sleep. Don't you have to get up early to go to mass with your family?"

Shannon stared at him again. "I don't have any family here in Los Angeles, Milo."

"Really? I thought you did. I must be thinking of someone else." He scratched his head deliberately. "Just the same, it's time you went to bed and got some sleep."

"Yes, you're right. Good night, Milo."

Shannon left.

Cole collapsed in a chair, feeling like he had just missed being run over by a Red Car.

Sergeant John Toolen of the Los Angeles Police Department's Central Station gave Maisy's message to his relief in the morning. Sergeant Charles Johnson didn't call Detective Browning to tell him about it until noon.

"That's all she said, Charley?"

"That's what Johnny wrote down here, Ed. Miss Maisy Malone would like you to call on her at the Hollywood Hotel this afternoon, but first she wants you to call the hotel and leave a message for her about when you'll be going out there. She wants to tell you something about the Leslie Clover murder. That's it, Ed."

"Thanks, Charley."

"Will you need any officers to go with you, Ed?"

"No, I don't think so. If I do, I'll call the Hollywood division for help. Thanks again, Charley."

Browning and his wife Nealy lived at 915 East 6th Street. Red Car tracks ran right past their house. They had plans to take in a matinee at one of the downtown theatres that afternoon, but Maisy's message changed that for them.

"I have an idea, Mrs. Browning. Why don't you come with me out to Hollywood? We can take in a moving picture show after I'm done chatting with Miss Malone. If we're lucky, we might see some of her fellow moving picture friends who are presently staying at the Hollywood Hotel. I might even entice Miss Malone to introduce you to them."

"You know, Edward, that's a wonderful idea."

Browning called the hotel and left a message for Maisy that he would be arriving at the hotel to meet with her at two o'clock.

* * *

Maisy awakened only a few minutes before the bellboy delivered the message from Browning to her room. She tipped him a dime and read the words on the note. "Detective Browning called to say he would meet you in the lobby at 2 pm."

"Fair enough. Gives me time to get cleaned up and have lunch with

Mabel before he gets here."

She picked up the telephone and clicked the receiver hook twice. "Switchboard," said the hotel operator. "How may I help you?" "Could you connect me to Miss Normand's room please?" "One moment please. I'll ring Miss Normand's room for you, Miss Malone."

Maisy smiled to herself. She really liked the respect she was receiving in this place and at the studio. Miss Malone. The sound of it gave her goose bumps.

"Hello?"

"Mabel, this is Maisy. Are you up yet?"

"I am now. What time is it?"

"It's past noon already. I just received a message from Eddie that he's coming to the hotel this afternoon to talk to me. He said he would be here at two o'clock. Are you hungry?"

"Ravenous."

"Good. Why don't we meet in the hotel restaurant at one? I want to talk to you about something."

"Does it have anything to do with Leslie Clover's murder?"

"What else?"

"I'll be there with bells on. See you soon, dear."

* * *

Mabel wasn't kidding. About the bells? Just an expression. But the implication of that popular phrase was for real. She already had a table when Maisy showed up in the restaurant.

"So what's up, dear? Are you going to tell Eddie everything you know? Or are you going to send him on another wild goose chase?"

"I haven't sent him anywhere yet. He's on his own with where he goes and who he talks to."

"Darn! I was hoping you were going to do that."

"Well, I'm not. I am going to suggest he should check with the Polyscope studio to see if Vivian Vanover was there the morning of the murder. He might have already thought of that, but I'm going to suggest it to him anyway."

"Why would you do that?"

"Because the only other way for me to get that information is to break into the business office at Polyscope tonight and go through their payroll records just like we did at Keystone last night."

"Oh, that sounds exciting."

"Exciting, yes, but too risky and unlawful. I don't know my way around Polyscope, and neither do you. Milo probably does because he worked there before coming over to Keystone, but I can't ask him to commit burglary again. Besides all that, I don't think Mr. William Selig and his night watchman will be as co-operative and as forgiving as Mack and Old Artie were."

"No, I don't think they will either. I see your point, dear. Suggesting Eddie go there tomorrow and check the payroll record for Vivian Vanover to see if she has an alibi is the safe thing to do. Is that what you wanted to talk to me about? About telling Eddie to go to Polyscope and check their records tomorrow, I mean."

"No, that's not it. I was going to ask you about your relationship with Leslie Clover."

Mabel was aghast. "My relationship with Leslie Clover? What on earth are you talking about?"

"Relationship is the wrong word, Mabel. I'm sorry. I didn't mean to imply that there was anything between you and Clover. I'm curious about your professional relationship with him. I mean, the top dog at Keystone is Mack. And then come Henry, George, and Fred among the men. Then there's you and Mother Davenport at the top of the women here."

"Oh, I see where you're going with this. Mother is the old bitch in the Keystone kennel, and I'm the young bitch. Is that it, Maisy?"

"Okay, referring to Mack as the top dog was a bad metaphor. He's not top dog. He's the leader of the pack, so to speak."

"As in wolf pack? Still implies Mother and I are bitches."

"I don't mean to imply that at all, Mabel."

The studio's lead actress burst out laughing and reached across the table to pat Maisy's hand. "Oh, I know you don't mean that, dear. I'm only teasing you. I know you only want to know what I know about Leslie Clover, and you're trying to find a delicate way of asking me without offending me. Isn't that right?"

"Well, yes, it is."

"Maisy, we're friends. Just come right out and ask me anything. If I don't want to answer the question, I'll say so. Or I'll ask you why you want to know something. We're friends, Maisy. Friends are honest and straightforward with each other."

"Good, I'm glad you see it that way."

"I do. Now ask your questions."

"When Milo brought me into the office the first day, you, Mother, Fred, Henry, and George were all there with Mack. Milo said the six of you have lunch up there every day like that. He didn't say so, but I gathered that's when the six of you discuss what goes on around the studio."

"Yes, that's right. We talk about the film we're shooting at the time, the next film that's in the works, storylines, who will play which roles, and who can we bring into the company in the future when we start shooting more than one picture at a time. We started this routine back in New York. We were already talking about bringing in another male lead and another female lead before we got on the train for Chicago. That's when Mack got the idea of asking Eddie Foy to come out here and make pictures with us. Mack thought adding his name to the company stationery would be great for business."

"So when Eddie said no, you settled for me."

"Oh, no, Maisy, that's not how we saw it. We saw you, and right off, Mack thought Fate had brought us to see you by making us think we were after Eddie. Mack and I are both convinced you have what it takes to be a star in this business. Now that the others have seen you and talked with you, they think so, too. George can't wait to play a scene with you. Pathé says you're—"

Maisy interrupted. "Pathé? Who's that?"

"Oh, that's right. You don't know that we call Henry Pathé. When Henry first came to America, he went to the Biograph studio where we all worked and said he had worked as a cameraman for the Pathé brothers back in Paris. So D.W. gave him a job. We knew the day he started that he didn't know a thing about working a camera or making moving pictures. But Mack kept him on because anybody who could put one over on sour old D.W. Griffith was okay in his book."

"I see."

"Well, anyway, Pathé says you're a handful to direct, but all the great ones are, according to him."

"I'm flattered, Mabel, but let's get back to the subject at hand, meaning Leslie Clover."

"Yes, of course, Leslie Clover. We saw Leslie on stage back in New York last winter before we came out here. He was part of the Fred Karno troupe from England. We thought he was truly animated with his comedy, which is what you need to be for moving pictures. We liked another fellow in that company as well. His name is Charles Chaplin. Mack wanted to recruit him, but he went back to England in April. At the same time, Leslie came out here to do comedies at Imp. Bad luck for him that Carl Laemmle was making mostly westerns at the time. He worked as an extra at Imp, and then he tried Polyscope up the road from our studio in Edendale. Mack got a letter from him while we were still back in New York. He said nobody out here was making comedies and the field would be wide open for him. That's when Mack got together with Kessel and Baumann. He partnered up with them to create Keystone just like they did with Fred Balshofer when they started up Bison Pictures to make westerns out here. Mack wrote back to Leslie that we were moving out here, and as soon as we got here, he wanted Leslie to join the company as a bit player. Leslie showed up at the studio the first morning we were here. Mack explained to Leslie that Kessel and Baumann were pretty tight with their money, so he had to produce several pictures for them before he could add any more regulars to the company. Leslie said he'd been working as an extra and a bit player for four months already, and if had to do it another four months at Keystone, then he was okay with that because at least he would be working in comedies instead of westerns. Mack appreciated Leslie's loyalty and patience. He gave Leslie a bit part in every one of these first few pictures we've made out here so far. Remember that scene we shot the other day where Fred chases me past the store one way and then chases me back the other way with a cop chasing the both of us?"

"Sure. How could I forget my first bit part?"

"Well, Leslie was supposed to play the part of the cop instead of Hank Mann. This was going to be his first featured role. His next one was going to be opposite Fred in *Double Wedding*. Leslie was supposed to be the groom, and Freddie is the bride. Now that Leslie is gone Mack is considering Jack Shannon for the part. Leslie was perfect for the part because he looks great in black face. Shannon is still learning this business. He was okay with you and that other girl—what was her name again?"

"Alma McComb."

"Yes, that's right. I have to remember to tell Mack about her. I'm sure Henry has already said something to him about her, but it won't hurt for me to put my two cents into the pot for her. She doesn't seem to have lead quality, but she could be another Alice Davenport. Mother isn't making big money, but at least she works steady. That's more than a lot of girls can say in this business. I can only hope that I can last half as long as Mother has in the entertainment business."

"Didn't she start out as a kid right after the War Between the States?"

Mabel stared at Maisy. "War Between the States? Do you mean the Civil War?"

"Yes, of course, you Yankees call it that, don't you?"

Mabel giggled. "We Yankees? Are you from the South?"

"My grandfather was conscripted into the Confederate army in Arkansas near the end of the war. Fortunately, for him he never saw any action. He had barely learned to fire a cannon by the time Lee surrendered to Grant."

"My father was too young to fight in the Civil War. My grandfather was French-Canadian from Quebec. He didn't fight in the war either. I don't know about my mother's father. She's never said whether he did or not. All I know about him is he was from Rhode Island, and my grandmother was from Ireland." At that moment Mabel realized what Maisy was getting at with this line of questioning. "It just occurred to me that you think someone wanted Leslie out of the way so he could get a place in the company, and that someone is Jack Shannon. Is that right, Maisy? You think Jack Shannon did it, don't you?"

* * *

"Miss Malone, allow me to introduce my wife."

"How do you do, Mrs. Browning?"

Nealy Browning held out her hand cordially to Maisy. "How do you do, Miss Malone? Edward tells me you are an actress in the moving picture business?"

Maisy accepted the handshake politely. "Yes, ma'am, I'm trying to be one."

"Have you been in that … *profession* for very long?"

The way she said profession—as if she meant the profession most single women found most lucrative—raised the hackles on Maisy's neck, but the actress maintained her calm and responded with a courteous smile. "No, ma'am, I haven't. I only arrived in Los Angeles this past Thursday morning and began work immediately that afternoon."

"Really?"

"Yes, I was in Vaudeville before coming here, and Mr. Sennett offered me a job in his company out here. So here I am, trying to become a moving picture lead performer."

Nealy looked beyond Maisy. "Is that Mabel Normand over there?"

Maisy knew Mabel was behind her, watching her interact with the Brownings. She glanced over her shoulder, and then returned her attention to Nealy. "Yes, that's Miss Normand. Would you like to meet her?"

"Oh, could I? She is such a funny lady in the moving pictures I've seen her in."

"I'll invite her over." Maisy turned and signaled Mabel to join them with a wave of her left hand. As soon as she made their trio into a quartet, Maisy made the introductions.

"I am so thrilled to meet you, Miss Normand. Edward told me he had the pleasure of making your acquaintance the other day, and I must admit I was green with envy."

"I'm quite flattered, Mrs. Browning. Detective Browning didn't mention he had such a charming wife. Shame on you, sir."

Browning blushed.

"Oh, Edward. She's only teasing you, aren't you, Miss Normand?"

"Of course, I am. Is he always this serious?"

"No, thank heaven. He'd be a terrible bore if he was."

Browning indulged his wife. "My dear, I don't mean to be rude, but if you wouldn't mind waiting over there," he indicated the divan against the wall opposite the front desk, "I'd like to get on with the business I have with Miss Malone. As soon as I am finished, we can be on our way to enjoy the rest of this fine day."

"Yes, of course, Dear. It was a pleasure to meet you, Miss Normand, Miss Malone. I hope we meet again under more sociable circumstances."

Maisy nodded. "The pleasure was all mine, Mrs. Browning."

"Would you mind if I waited with you, Mrs. Browning, seeing as how I have to wait for Miss Malone?"

"Oh, that would be wonderful."

As soon as Mabel and his wife had left them, Browning turned his full attention on Maisy. "Shall we go out on the patio where we can speak more privately, Miss Malone?"

"The patio? What's that?"

"The courtyard. Through those glass doors there."

"Fair enough." She headed in the direction of the patio.

Browning held the door for her.

"Your wife is a real southern lady, Eddie."

He closed the door behind them. "Thank you, Maisy. I'm sure you made a good impression on her as well."

"How long have you been married?"

They wandered over to a table with a large umbrella shading it.

"Nine years." He pulled out a chair for Maisy.

"Any children?" She sat down.

"We have not been so blessed yet." Browning sat across from her.

"That's too bad. I think you and your wife would make wonderful parents."

Browning nodded at Maisy. "Thank you for that, Maisy. Now tell me why you wanted to meet with me this afternoon."

"Well, first off, did you canvass the neighborhood to see if any of the neighbors saw anything that morning?"

"My men went to every house on the block and asked everybody who was home that morning if they saw any strangers in the neighborhood or if they saw anybody go into or leave Leslie Clover's bungalow. Nobody saw anything. As you know, I'm sure, not every house on that block is presently occupied."

"I kind of thought that when Mabel and I went to his house that evening and very few places had any lights on." Maisy paused for thought. "Darn! I was kind of hoping you might have turned up something there. At least then we'd know whether a man or a woman was there that morning, and we might have a description of the person as well. "

"Having a witness like that would be very helpful, yes. So what else did you have for me? Do you have some word on the whereabouts of Miss Vanover?"

"Sorry, I don't. But I do have an idea on how you can find out where she was Thursday morning when Leslie Clover was murdered."

"Go ahead. I'm listening."

"Miss Vanover left Keystone after only a few days of working there, and she went back to the Polyscope studio to find work as an extra."

"The Polyscope studio? I was informed she went to the Universal studio in Hollywood."

"Who told you that?"

"It would be unethical for me to reveal my sources, Maisy."

"Unethical? Or do you only want to keep that to yourself because we have a bet on who will solve this crime first? I just gave you a tip on how you can find out where Miss Vanover was when Leslie Clover was murdered. The least you can do is tell me who told you she went over to Universal instead."

The detective heaved a sigh. "Oh, all right. I suppose that would only be the fair thing to do. Miss Alden told me."

"Phoebe Alden?"

"Yes."

"Well, if that don't beat all."

"Why are you so surprised by this?"

"I hadn't really considered Miss Alden to be one of your suspects … until now."

"One of my suspects? The only person I suspect of murdering Mr. Clover is Miss Vanover. Everybody else I interviewed has an alibi for the time of his death."

"Everybody?"

"Yes, everybody. Why? Do you think one of them might be lying?"

Maisy chortled. "One of them? How about nearly all of them? Eddie, did you do anything to corroborate their alibis?"

Browning's aspect turned sheepish. "Not all of them."

"Well, I did, and I can tell you this much. Several people who work at Keystone were unaccounted for Thursday morning."

"Several? Are you sure?"

"Pretty darn."

"How do you know this, Maisy?"

"I checked the payroll records at the studio."

"How did you do that?"

Maisy related her adventure of the previous night. "And I discovered several people didn't work that morning. Now whether they weren't there or not, I can't say, but I suggest you go over the records there as well to see who worked and who didn't."

Browning grinned at her. "Why don't you just give me a list of their names and save me the trouble?"

"Hey, I'm already helping you here. Do I have to do everything to solve this murder for you?"

"Maisy, you're being obtuse."

She threw up her hands. "Well, that's gratitude for you. I call you to give you a tip to point you in the right direction, and you call me obtuse."

"All right, I apologize for that remark."

"That's better. Now back to the payroll records. When you find out who didn't work that morning, you can have them verify their alibis with some kind of corroboration. Anybody who can't do that should go to the top of your list of suspects."

"I believe you're right, Maisy, but why are you helping me like this?"

"I want to see how long it will take you to figure out who killed Leslie Clover."

"How long it will take me to do it? What does that mean?"

A coy smile brightened Maisy's face as she winked at him. "It means I just might already know who did it, Detective Browning."

* * *

Mabel joined Maisy on the patio after the Brownings left. "So did you tell him about Jack Shannon?"

"I don't think he even knows Jack Shannon exists."

"What makes you think that?"

"He's never mentioned him, and each time I mentioned Browning to Jack, he hems and haws a whole bunch before he can come with the right words to say to me."

"Really?"

"Really. But never mind that now. Have you got your cat burglar shoes ready?"

"Cat burglar shoes? Oh, no, Maisy, you're not thinking about breaking into the studio again, are you?"

"Not the studio. Another place."

"Another place? Where?"

"Come on. Let's take the Red Car into the city and round up Milo to go with us."

"Not until you answer me. What other place?"

Maisy demurred. "Leslie Clover's bungalow."

"Are you serious?"

"Absolutely."

"But why?"

"We need to search the place more thoroughly. I've got a hunch something is missing that we missed."

"Okay. So why do we need Milo?"

"Milo can verify what's missing. At least, I hope he can."

"What's missing? What do you mean by that?"

"I mean somebody cleaned up the place a bit, and I think they took something with them when they left."

"Like what?"

"Like, I don't know. And that's why we need Milo to come with us. Now get your coat and let's go get him."

By the time they arrived at the Belvedere, Maisy and Mabel learned from the apartment building manager that they had missed Milo by mere minutes. As usual on Sunday evenings, he had gone to Ye Bull Pen Inn on South Hope Street for dinner. Not really hungry but anxious to find Cole, the two actresses caught a Red Car on Figueroa and rode it down to Seventh Street, where they walked the two blocks east to Hope and went around the corner to the busy dining hall. A waiter met them at the door.

"Would you like a booth or a table, ladies?"

Mabel indulged him with a sweet smile. "Actually, we're looking for a gentleman friend of ours. We were told he dines here regularly on Sunday evenings."

The twentyish server studied her for a moment as if he recognized her face but couldn't quite recall where he had seen her. "Does your friend have a name?"

"Mr. Milo Cole."

"Oh, yes, Mr. Cole. Come this way, ladies."

Maisy gazed curiously at the design of the dining hall. It had no ceiling; only exposed roof rafters between which hung chandeliers for lighting the place. Pictures of bulls' heads adorned the walls. Down the center and along the exterior walls to each side were booths for two people only. Between those were double rows of tables set at forty-five degree angles, each of them intended for two people. If a party had more than two in it, the tables could be easily turned to be end-to-end and then returned to their original position when the diners departed. Every table was covered with a white tablecloth. The chairs had wrought iron backs, which made them become very uncomfortable after sitting on them more than fifteen minutes; the point being customers were less inclined to linger after eating. A good eighty percent of the seating was presently filled, giving rise to a cacophony of chatter and laughter.

The somewhat churlish waiter led the pair of young women down the aisle between the tables and booths along the right wall. As they passed them, several patrons glanced at the attractive duo with some doing double-takes when they spotted Mabel. Halfway down the row the server stopped at the booth occupied by Milo.

"Mr. Cole, these ladies were asking for you."

Having had his back to them as they approached, a perplexed Milo turned and looked up to see Maisy standing next to the waiter. A smile of delight spread over his face. "What are you doing here?" Then he saw Mabel, and his joy vanished. "Oh, no. What are you two up to now?"

"Are you about done eating?" asked Maisy.

"I will be as soon as I finish my apple pie."

"Fair enough. We'll wait for you up front."

The waiter frowned. "You ladies don't wish to be seated?"

"No, we're not eating," said Maisy.

"Wait a minute, dear. I'm a little hungry now, and that pie does look so delicious."

"It is," said Milo.

Maisy shrugged on shoulder. "Sure, why not? I could go for a piece of pie myself." She turned to the server. "Can you get a chair for me? Miss Normand will sit in the booth. All right with you, Mabel?"

The waiter's sour aspect changed to a friendlier expression. "Miss Normand? Miss Mabel Normand the moving picture actress?"

No sooner had the man said her name than the diners immediately around them ceased their conversations and swiveled their focus to the two female newcomers.

A wee bit embarrassed by the sudden attention on the one hand and yet quite pleased on the other Mabel tilted her head slightly and smiled nervously. "Yes."

More people in their vicinity became quiet for the moment, making the trio of Keystone players slightly uneasy.

The waiter effervesced with elation. "Gee, Miss Normand, I've seen all your pictures. You're really fun to watch. In your pictures, I mean."

"Thank you. That's very kind of you to say."

As if cued, all of the patrons who had gone silent burst into muffled chatter that was too soft to be coherent to anyone except someone very close to the speaker. In general, they whispered Mabel's name with giddy glee, some nodding toward her, others pointing rudely.

An older waiter came up to them. "What's the problem here, Jake?"

"Oh, nothing, Mr. Rader. I was just seating these two ladies. This is Miss Mabel Normand, the moving picture actress."

"Then get them seated. You've got other customers waiting to be served."

"Yes, sir." Jake pulled out the chair opposite Cole to allow Mabel to sit down. Then quickly, he grabbed a chair from a table where another man was eating alone and placed it at the corner of Cole's table on Mabel's side.

Maisy sat down, putting her French purse on the table in front of her. "I'm only having pie and a glass of milk. How about you, Mabel?"

"Yes, the same for me except I want mine a la mode."

"What kind of pie would you ladies like to have?"

"Apple is fine with me," said Maisy.

"Yes, the same for me," said Mabel.

Jake wrote their orders on a slip. "I'll be back in a jiff." He scurried off toward the rear of the hall.

"Okay, so what's going on? Why are you two here? And how did you find me?"

Maisy spoke before Mabel could. "Your building manager told us where we could find you. He said you eat here every Sunday evening."

"So what if I do?"

"Don't get your drawers in a bunch, Milo. We're all creatures of one habit or another. I used to go to the same pub in London for lunch almost every single day I was there. The food was good and cheap, and the owner kept the sports away from me. I loved that place."

"So why are you here?"

Maisy and Mabel exchanged devious glances before Maisy leaned toward him and said her reply as softly as possible and yet loud enough for him to hear her on the first try. "We need you to help us break into Leslie Clover's bungalow."

Shock froze Cole's face for an instant before he could get a word from his mouth. "You want—"

Both girls expected this reaction, and each of them reached across the table and grabbed an arm to hush him. They pinpointed their eyes on his as he looked back and forth from one to the other repeatedly for a several seconds.

Mabel took up the gauntlet. "Milo dear, you know we wouldn't be asking, if we didn't really need your help."

"Yes, I know, but why do you want to do this?"

Maisy's turn. "I think we missed something when we were there the first two times."

"We missed something? You're the snoop, not me."

"Okay, I missed something. Well, I need to go back there and look around again, and I need you to help because you knew Leslie Clover probably better than anyone."

"I still don't get why you need my help."

"*I* missed something the first times because what *I* missed probably wasn't there. You knew him. You would know what was missing."

"But I didn't notice anything was missing when we were there the last two times."

"That's because, like me, you weren't looking for something that was missing. If we can figure out what's missing from his place, it might lead us to the person who"—she lowered her voice even more—"... murdered him."

At that second, Jake returned with their pie and milk and set the plates and glasses appropriately in front of each actress. He smiled at Mabel. "Is there anything else I can get you, Miss Normand?"

"No, this is fine."

Maisy felt invisible. "I could use a fork. Or do I have to eat my pie by hand?"

"What?"

Mabel giggled. "My friend needs a fork to eat her pie, Jake."

"Oh, sure, Miss Normand."

Maisy made an addition to the request. "And a napkin would be a nice touch as well."

The waiter disappeared again.

"I'll bet you a three-cent nickel he comes back with just a fork and puts it down in front of Mabel. Any takers?"

Cole shook his head. "Never mind that, Maisy. When do you want to go to Leslie's place?"

"Sundown."

"Sundown? Why then?"

"Most people are distracted by the setting sun, if they're outside. If they're inside, they're usually busy preparing for the final hours before they go to bed or getting something ready for tomorrow. We're less likely to be seen entering his house at that time."

"Okay, if you say so. But won't the neighbors notice the lights on inside while we're there?"

"Not if we pull all the shades as soon as we go inside."

"What if the place is locked?"

"Really, Milo?"

"Oh, I forgot. You know how to pick locks."

Jake returned with only a fork, and just like Maisy predicted, he placed it in front of Mabel. "Miss Normand, if it's not too great an imposition, could I get your autograph?" He held out an order pad and pencil to her.

"Certainly, but only if you get my friend a napkin first."

"Oh, sure." He disappeared again.

Mabel took the pad and pencil and wrote a few words and signed them for their server.

"What did you write, Mabel?" asked Maisy.

"To Jake, what a wonderful waiter, Mabel Normand."

"A wonderful waiter? You've got to be kidding."

"He's a member of the moving picture public, Maisy. This little gesture is worth dozens of more sold tickets at the local theatres. Just wait until someone asks for your autograph. You'll understand how important it is then. They think we're special, and it's our duty to our craft to cultivate that adoration they have for us. Remember, they buy tickets to the moving picture shows, and part of that dime nickel they spend filters down to you and me. The more tickets that sell, the more pennies find their way to us."

Jake returned with Maisy's napkin and offered it to Mabel initially. Then realizing his mistake he handed it to Maisy without looking at her.

Mabel returned the pad and pencil to the waiter. "Have you seen my newest film *The Water Nymph*?"

"No, not yet, Miss Normand, but you can bet I will on my next day off from work." The waiter handed the bill to Milo. "Nice seeing you, Miss Normand."

Mabel winked at him. "Thank you, Jake."

"See you next Sunday, Mr. Cole."

Milo waved abjectly at Jake.

The server started to ask another question, but seeing the head waiter coming his way out of the corner of his eye canceled that idea. He simply walked away from the table.

Maisy picked up her fork. "Let's eat up, and get out of here before anybody else wants Mabel's autograph."

* * *

Maisy, Mable, and Cole disembarked the Red Car at Sunset Boulevard and Normandie Avenue as the sun dropped below the crest of the Santa Monica Hills west of Hollywood, giving the range a deep purple hue against the white gold line of the horizon. They had to walk two blocks back to Alexandria Avenue and half a block from there to Leslie Clover's bungalow. The first stars appeared in the east as they turned up the walkway to the dead man's house.

Cole nervously scanned the neighborhood for any prying eyes as they mounted the porch steps. Much to his relief, he saw none.

Maisy opened the screen door and tried to turn the knob on the inside door only to discover it was locked. Just as she had done the night before at the studio, she picked the lock to gain them entry to the crime scene.

"Make sure we pull all the shades before we turn on any lights. Milo, you take this room. Mabel you get the dining room and extra bedroom. I'll take the kitchen and back bedroom."

As each of them went about pulling the shades and drawing the curtains closed, the house became darker and darker. Satisfied that they had secured their privacy, Maisy turned on the kitchen light first. She went back into the dining room, turned on the light there, and put her purse on the table. Looking around she saw Cole about to turn on the living room light.

"No, Milo, don't turn it on. This is enough light for us to see what we need to see in just about the whole house. If the police happen to be in the area and come by here, they shouldn't be able to see any light in any of the windows this way." She moved to the living room. "Let's start in here. Milo, look around and see if you notice anything out of the ordinary, you know, that might be missing or something that's here that wasn't here before."

"Okay." Cole began his inspection of the room.

"Take your time, Milo. There's no hurry here."

Mabel shook her head. "Leslie was certainly a very messy man, wasn't he? All this clutter and the ashtrays full of cigarette butts." She shuttered. "I can't stand dirty ashtrays."

"Neither can I," said Milo, "which is why I didn't like staying here. Leslie smoked like a chimney."

Maisy nodded in agreement. "And that's what I believe led to his death." In the next instant, her whole demeanor changed as an epiphany struck her. She snapped her fingers to emphasize the sudden adjustment in her thinking. "Cigarettes. I didn't see any cigarettes when we were here before. Did either of you see any? Look around in here, and I'll go look in the kitchen and his bedroom." She charged through the dining room to the rear rooms. In a few minutes, she was back in the dining room. "Did you find any?"

Milo shook his head. "Not me."

Mabel's head also moved in the negative. "I didn't either."

"That makes three of us. I didn't even find any matches."

"Leslie didn't use matches. He had this German lighter he received as a going-away present when he left England to come to America. Expensive little thing. The case was Sterling silver, and it was engraved with some very ornate designs. That lighter was really special to him."

Maisy's head bobbled as she thought back to Thursday morning. "If the last thing he did was light up a cigarette, his lighter should have been in the bedroom with him. Come on. Let's go look for it."

They went to Clover's bedroom.

Maisy pushed the top button on the light switch. "Nothing in plain sight. Milo, you look in the bathroom for it. Mabel, check the closet. Feel any clothes hanging in it to see if it's in some coat pocket or trousers pocket. I'll look through the drawers of his dressing table."

They searched diligently for several minutes, but none of them found the lighter or any cigarettes or matches.

Mabel gasped. "You don't think Leslie was murdered for his lighter, do you?"

Maisy shrugged. "People have killed for stranger reasons. I heard about a man in London who was stabbed to death for a handful of copper half-pennies. And just this past summer in Chicago a newsboy was pushed under the wheels of a streetcar by a man who wanted his last copy of the latest edition of the local German paper and didn't have the three cents to pay for it. A woman murdered her husband with a frying pan because he criticized her cooking. So I suppose somebody could have killed him just for the lighter. Milo, do you know of anybody who envied Leslie Clover for his expensive lighter?"

"Besides me?"

Maisy rolled her eyes. "Yes, besides you."

"I know Jack Shannon said he'd like to have a lighter like Leslie's so he could impress the girls with it. And I remember Fritz Schade saying something about it once when we were all sitting on the extras bench outside the barn one day last week."

"All? Do you mean you and the other extras?"

"No, Leslie was there, too."

"Was this before or after Fritz and Leslie had butted heads over Leslie flirting with Fritz's wife?"

"Oh, before. After that, Fritz wanted nothing to do with Leslie. Every time Leslie came near him after that incident old Fritz's face would get the nastiest scowl on it that he could muster. He was one jealous little man, that Fritz."

"He's that way because he's short. All men below average height are like that. They're angry with God for making them diminutive, but since they can't take their anger out on God, they take it out on the rest of the world, especially on men who are taller than they are. My father always said, 'The shorter the man, the better the lawyer.' He said short men become lawyers because then they can beat up taller men with the law."

Mabel nodded. "So you think Fritz might have murdered Leslie?"

"It's possible, but it's not very likely. He was too jealous to make up with Leslie. Besides, what would he have to gain by killing Mr. Clover? Unless more happened between Mr. Clover and Fritz's wife than any of us know about." She held a finger to her lip for a second as she mulled over that thought. "You know, that might be the answer. Maybe there was more between Betty Schade and Leslie Clover than any of the rest of us know. It certainly deserves checking into, don't you think?"

Cole shook his head. "No, Maisy, I don't think Fritz had anything to do with Leslie's death. Leslie would never have allowed Fritz to take one single step in here. Betty, yes, but never Fritz. And I don't think he would have been involved with Betty either."

"Why not?"

"She was married. Leslie didn't fool around with married women. He always said, 'Why chase a woman with a husband when there are so many who don't have husbands?' Certainly made sense to me."

"It would."

Mabel had to ask. "So you're crossing Fritz off your list of suspects?"

"Not entirely. But never mind that now. I'm tired, and we have to get up early tomorrow, don't we?"

"We certainly do."

"Milo, would you turn out the lights as we leave?"

"Sure. You two go ahead. I'll be right behind you."

Maisy and Mabel headed for the front door to wait for Cole as he turned off all the lights in the house. When he joined them at the exit, he reached for the light switch, then hesitated.

"Should we pull up the shades before we leave?"

Maisy shook her head. "Why bother? I don't think anybody will even notice that they're down, and if they do, who will they complain to? Detective Browning? And what would he do about it? Put a guard on the place? That's his business. So let's get out of here."

Cole pushed the button, and the living room went dark.

Maisy opened the door and allowed Mabel to go first. She followed, and Cole closed the door behind them.

"Aren't you going to lock it up again, Maisy?"

"I don't have a key, Milo."

"You didn't have a key to get us in."

"That was to *unlock* the door. Nobody ever taught me how to *lock* a door with a hairpin. Come on. Let's get out of here."

They were halfway down the block when Maisy remembered she had left her purse on the dining room table. "Wait here, and I'll be right back."

Cole offered to do the gentlemanly thing. "I'll get it for you."

"No, Milo, it's mine, and I should get it."

"Then I'll go with you."

"No, you stay with Mabel. She's a lot more lady than I am and should never be left unattended. Besides, if anything happened to me, who would miss me? The world of moving pictures would never be the same again if anything happened to Mabel."

Mabel squeezed Maisy's hand. "Oh, Maisy, you are too kind."

"Thank you. Now wait here."

Maisy bustled up the street to Clover's bungalow and double-timed up the porch steps to the front door. She stopped to catch a breath before quietly opening the screen door and then the inside door. After entering, she closed the door just as silently as she had opened it. Turning around she headed for the dining room, but before she could get there she noticed an eerie glow coming from Clover's bedroom. Her initial thought about it startled her. She gasped lightly, put a hand to her lips to stifle the reaction, and whispered to herself. "Omigosh! It's his ghost."

* * *

"Milo, I don't feel good about Maisy going back to that place by herself. Why don't you after her just to make certain she's all right?"

"She said I was to stay here with you."

"That's nonsense, and you know it. Now go on."

Cole shook his head. "She said to stay here."

"Milo, I've got a premonition that something is wrong in that house. If you won't go back by yourself, then I'm going."

Before Mabel could take two steps, Cole grabbed her by an elbow. "Okay, I'll go."

"We'll both go."

* * *

Maisy crept through the dining room and into the kitchen. Not one floorboard creaked. She continued to the doorway to Clover's bedroom. Still, she made nary a sound. She stopped just inches short of the opening to peek around the corner to determine the source of the creepy glow. The second she did the light within evaporated. She reached around the doorjamb to feel for the light switch on the wall, only to be disappointed that the hinges were on that side and the switch was on the other. Withdrawing her hand, she took one more step to bring her closer to other side of the doorway. At that instant, a shadowy figure lunged at her. She tried to elude her attacker but failed as the two of them crashed onto the kitchen floor.

Startled but not stunned and assuming the attacker was a man, Maisy fought back physically and verbally. "Get off me!" She made a pair of fists and began pummeling her assailant on whatever part of his body presented itself as a target. "Get off me, you bastard!" She found his head and struck one side then the other. "Get off, bastard!" Her next two blows whiffed the air. Sensing the aggressor was attempting to regain his feet, she raised both knees as hard as she could, hoping to strike some vital part of his anatomy. Lucky for him, her knees landed too high on his backside, completely missing his male organs. Fortunately for her, the contact propelled him forward and sent him over her head and sprawled him headlong on the floor in front of the sink and cabinets.

Instantly, Maisy recognized the opportunity to escape. Nimbly, she rolled onto her hands and knees and sprang upright. In the next heartbeat, she determined whether to stand and fight or retreat to the living room and flee through the front door. She chose the latter alternative.

* * *

Mabel turned onto the walkway leading up to Clover's house, took two steps, then stopped suddenly. "Did you hear that?"

Cole stopped beside her. "Sounded like it came from inside the bungalow."

"There it is again."

"Maisy's in trouble. Wait here."

Cole bounded up the porch steps, crossed it in a single stride, wrenched the screed door open so hard that he nearly tore it from its hinges, grabbed the doorknob of the inside door, gave it a violent turn, and threw his shoulder against the door, bursting into the darkened house.

"Mais—"

She banged into Cole before he could take a third step into the living room. Ricocheting off him to his left, she folded over the back of the sofa, catching herself from going all the way over and popping back erect.

"Mais—?"

"Milo, he's going out the back door. Get him!"

Cole hesitated for a single heartbeat before racing through the house toward the rear entrance. He heard it open and saw the shadowy intruder straight ahead a few feet. One more step and he grabbed the fleeing villain from behind, wrapping both arms around him. In the next instant, he realized his hands were clutching breasts.

"*¡Pinche carón!*"

Shocked that he had a woman in his grasp, Cole released her for a second before grabbing her again, this time by her arms.

"*¡Libérame!*"

Hearing the Spanish words being spoken angrily, Maisy recognized the voice in the dark as that belonging to Hortencia Ramos. "Milo, hold on to her."

Hortencia struggled to free herself, but Cole was too strong.

Maisy found the light switch in the dining room and pushed the top button. "Bring her in her, Milo. *Vamos, Señora.*"

"Tell him to let me go."

"Let her go, Milo, but don't let her get away."

Cole released Hortencia completely, but he made sure to keep himself between her and the back door.

Maisy entered the kitchen and turned on the light there. "Hortencia, what are you doing here?"

"*Señorita* Maisy, I could ask you the same thing."

The housekeeper's mild belligerence surprised Maisy and Cole. They exchanged questioning glances before Maisy responded.

"Okay, we'll play it your way. We came here looking for another clue as to who murdered Leslie Clover. Now it's your turn."

"I was doing the same thing."

Maisy shook her head. "Sorry, Hortencia, I'm not buying that. Why were you in his bedroom?"

"I told you already. I was looking for a clue to who murdered him, just like you were doing."

"Milo, go look in the bedroom and see if anything is different."

Cole went to the bedroom doorway, reached inside, and pushed the light switch. He made a quick survey of the room without stepping inside.

"Looks the same to me, Maisy."

Mabel entered the kitchen. "What's going on here, Maisy? Who's this woman?"

Maisy related everything she could about Hortencia from the moment she and Cole first met her right up to his pronouncement of nothing new in the bedroom. "I was just about to ask her again why she's here when you walked in."

"Then you don't believe she's here looking for clues?"

"No, I don't. Hortencia, I wish you would just tell us the truth. If you're doing something to protect Vivian Vanover, just tell us. Maybe we can help."

Hortencia studied Maisy's face for a moment. "All right, I tell you the whole truth."

F irst thing **Monday morning after** arriving early at the Los Angeles
Police Department's Central Station Detective Ed Browning read
the morning edition of the *Los Angeles Herald.* He turned to the obituary page
and learned the viewing for the late Leslie Clover would be that evening from
six to eight at Pierce Brothers Funeral Parlor on South Flower. A special
advertisement invited mourners to continue the wake around the corner at
the Abbotsford Inn on the southwest corner of Eighth Street and Hope.
Food and beverages would be available. The funeral would be held the next
day at 11:00 a.m. with burial at Forest Lawn Cemetery in Glendale.

As soon as he finished reading the newspaper, Browning took the
Red Car out to Hollywood to make an inquiry about Vivian Vanover's
employment with the Universal Film Manufacturing Company studio on the
southeast corner of Gower Street and Sunset Boulevard. He took only ten
minutes to learn that Vivian Vanover had not worked at Universal since its
inception in June of that same year. Now that he had confirmation that
Phoebe Alden had lied to him Browning took another Red Car to Edendale
to make the same inquiry at the Polyscope studio.

The payroll manager at Selig's studio confirmed Vivian's presence on the
lot the two weeks before the last week and on Monday and Tuesday of the
previous week. She did not show up the day Leslie Clover was murdered or
the day before or the following two days. Now that he had learned these facts
Browning wanted to find Vivian more than ever, convinced she either
murdered Clover or she possessed some piece evidence that would lead him
to the killer.

After concluding his business at Polyscope, Browning walked down the
hill to the Keystone studio. He knew exactly where he had to go.

"Good morning, Mr. McHatton. How are you today?"

"It's Monday. Do I need to say more?"

"No, nothing more is necessary, sir."

"So what brings you here today, Detective Browning? Do you need to question more of our employees or something?"

"I wish to inspect your payroll records, Mr. McHatton. I have reason to believe that not all the people who said they were here working this past Thursday morning were actually here. I would like to inspect your records to verify who was telling me the truth and who wasn't."

"I can't let you do that, Detective Browning, without an okay from Mr. Sennett. If you don't mind waiting outside a few minutes, I'll go speak to him and ask him if it's okay."

"Not at all, Mr. McHatton."

Browning followed McHatton out of the office and was surprised that the bookkeeper locked the door behind them.

"I'll be back in a jiff, Detective. I know exactly where he is."

McHatton left the building and went straight to the set where Sennett was directing a beach scene with Mabel Normand, Ford Sterling, Fred Mace, Alice Davenport, Jack Shannon, Milo Cole, and Maisy Malone. Mabel wore the same bathing suit she had worn in *The Water Nymph*, the last film Keystone produced before leaving New York for California. The four men were attired in suits, while Alice and Maisy wore dresses and large sun hats. Several extras stood in the background.

Sennett cupped his hands to bark out his orders. "Extras, I want you to walk through the set and casually look around while you talk to each other. But I don't want any of you staring at Miss Normand. That's for the actors to do. Gentlemen, I want you all to look shocked at Miss Normand, while Miss Davenport and Miss Malone laugh and share a crude comment with each other. Now let's rehearse this scene and see if you can get it right the first time so we don't have to waste any more time before shooting. I don't want to lose the light."

The director turned around to walk back to his chair and immediately spotted McHatton standing beside it. "What are doing here, Hugh?"

"It's that police detective, Mr. Sennett. He says he wants to inspect our payroll records."

"What for?"

"He wants to compare them to the notes from his interviews with our employees. He wants to see who was telling him the truth about being here last Thursday morning and who was lying to him."

Sennett frowned. "Tell him to kiss off. Our payroll records are private property, and he doesn't get to see them."

Maisy overheard their conversation and wasted no time intervening. "Mr. Sennett, may I have a word with you?"

The director-general of the studio rolled his eyes heavenward. "Why certainly, Miss Malone. Why not? I'm only trying to make a moving picture here. We've got all day to do it. So come hither, young lady, and speak to me."

As she passed Mabel, Maisy whispered to her. "Is he always this touchy?"

"Only when he's awake, dear."

Maisy approached Sennett, getting close enough to him so only he could hear her soft words. "Mack, you might as well let Browning see the records now. If I know him, he'll come back with a warrant and a whole bunch of officers who will make us stop filming until he's finished going over the books. Why not have Mr. McHatton co-operate with Browning so we can get on with shooting this film?"

"Do you really think he'll disrupt everything?"

"He's a cop. He'll want to show you who's really the boss."

"Yes, I see your point." He turned to McHatton. "Come here, Hugh." He waited the two seconds it took McHugh to get close to him. "You go tell that flatfoot he can look at the payroll records and you stay with him the whole time he's doing it. If he needs anything else, just give it to him. I want him to finish whatever it is he has to do and get off my lot as soon as possible. Understand?"

"Yes, sir."

"Good. Now go do what I said." He turned back to Maisy. "Thanks, Maisy. Now get back to your place."

McHatton returned to his office. "Detective Browning, Mr. Sennett says I'm to let you look at the payroll records as long as you want."

"Good, good, Mr. McHatton. But before I get started with them, is there a telephone I can use? I need to call the Central Station."

"Certainly, Detective. There's one in my office." McHatton unlocked the door, and they went inside. "I'll step outside while you use the telephone, Detective."

"That won't necessary, Mr. McHatton. You can stay." Browning picked up the telephone, lifted the receiver from the hook on the transmitter, and clicked the hook twice until an operator answered. "Yes, ma'am, would you please connect me to the Los Angeles Police Department's Central Station?"

"One moment please."

Browning waited. In a very few seconds, he heard the dulled ringing at the other end.

"Police Department, Sergeant Johnson speaking."

"Charley, it's Ed Browning."

"Oh, hello, Ed. Thought I saw you leave here early this morning. What's up?"

"I need Nellie Sharpe to come out here to Edendale, Charley. Tell her to bring me a list of all the people I questioned the other day, and tell her I need it as soon as possible. Put her in a car and have someone drive her out here to the Keystone moving picture studio on Allesandro. She knows where it is. Can you do that for me, Charley?"

"Sure can, Ed. You wanted Nellie Sharpe to make a list of all the people you questioned the other day and you want her to bring it to you as soon as possible at the Keystone studio in Edendale. I'll get on it right away. Orville Barney is hanging here with nothing to do. I'll have him drive her out there."

"That's swell, Charley. Thanks. I'll see you back at the station this afternoon." Browning rang off and returned his attention to the bookkeeper. "Miss Sharpe won't be here for at least a half hour, Mr. McHatton. Would it be all right if I wandered around the studio and maybe watched them do some filming?"

McHatton remembered his orders from Sennett. "I can do better than that, Detective. I'll take you around the place personally."

Browning gave him a toothy smile. "That would be most gracious of you, sir."

* * *

By the time McHatton led Browning to the set where scenes from *Mabel's Lovers* were being shot, Sennett had just given the cast and filming crew a ten-minute break. Maisy was the first to approach the policeman.

"Glad to see you took my advice, Detective Browning."

"How do you know why I'm here, Miss Malone?"

"Word travels fast around here, or so I'm told."

Mabel joined them. "Good morning, Detective Browning. Have you come back to question us some more about Leslie Clover's death?"

"Not you, Miss Normand, but possibly some of the other people here. I really don't know yet."

Sennett came over. "I hope you catch Clover's killer soon, Detective Browning. I'm getting tired of these interruptions by you."

"I hope to have the killer in jail by tomorrow, Mr. Sennett."

"Really?"

Maisy injected a thought of her own. "Perhaps you shouldn't count your chicks before they hatch, Detective."

"Are you trying to tell me not to be so sure of myself, Miss Malone? Because if you are, then I assure you I never boast idly."

"Oh, I didn't think you were boasting at all. I simply thought you might be too sure of yourself this early in your investigation."

"This early, Miss Malone? Mr. Clover was murdered four days ago. I hardly think I am premature in my determination of the perpetrator of this heinous crime."

Sennett had a question. "Really? Who do you have in mind as the guilty party, Detective? One of my people, I presume."

"You know, Mr. Sennett, I have seen you on the screen several times portraying the fictional detective Sherlock Holmes. Your parodies of him were quite entertaining to say the least."

"Thank you, Detective, but you still didn't answer my question. Who do you have in mind as the culprit for Clover's murder?"

"I'm sorry, Mr. Sennett, but I can't divulge that information at this time. However, I assure you, you will be among the first to know when I do make the killer's identity known."

Maisy drifted over to Mabel. "Is Mack still knocking off at three this afternoon?"

"Why? Do you have plans?"

"You don't think we could get out of here a little earlier than that do you?"

"Depends on how much earlier." Mabel peered quizzically at her friend. "Maisy, what are you scheming to do now?"

"I'll tell you about it later."

* * *

Browning and McHatton waited at the studio gate for Miss Sharpe to arrive with Officer Barney. Much to their delight, they didn't have to wait very long.

"Thank you, Orville. You don't need to wait around. Miss Sharpe and I will take a streetcar back to the station when we're finished here." He turned to the stenographer. "We'll be working in Mr. McHatton's office again, Miss Sharpe. So if you'll come along now, we'll get started immediately, and if we are still working at lunch time, I'll send out for some food for both of us."

McHatton led them back to his office, where he presented Browning with the Keystone payroll records. "They're in alphabetical order, Detective, which should make them easier for you to ..." He paused. "Exactly what is it you're hoping to learn from the records, Detective?"

"As I said earlier, I believe some of your employees lied to me about their presence here on the morning of Mr. Clover's death. I believe your records will verify who was telling me the truth and who wasn't." He sat at the bookkeeper's desk. "Miss Sharpe, I will be going through the records alphabetically because that is the way Mr. McHatton has them."

"That would be fine, Detective Browning. My list of the people you questioned Saturday morning is also in alphabetical order of their surnames. I thought it would be helpful to index the interviews for future reference."

McHatton smiled at the stenographer. "You're very well organized, Miss Sharpe. I must admit I am impressed by such orderliness."

"Thank you, Mr. McHatton."

"Yes, thank you, Mr. McHatton. Now if you will excuse us, we have work to do."

"Yes, of course, sir. And I have to make my rounds of the studio to see if any additional extras were used this morning."

* * *

McHatton returned to his office fifty minutes later to inform Browning that the actors and crew were going on their lunch break. "If you like, I can go down to the corner grocery and get you and Miss Sharpe a sandwich and soda pop each. Mr. Sennett says I am to pay for it out of petty cash, if that's acceptable to you."

"That's very kind of Mr. Sennett *and* you, Mr. McHatton. What do you think, Miss Sharpe? Should we accept their gracious offer of lunch?"

"I think it would be rude of us to refuse, sir."

"Very well then. We accept."

McHatton recited the choices of sandwiches and soft drinks that were available at the corner market, and then wrote down their requests. "I'll return shortly with your food and beverages."

Browning waited for McHatton to leave before speaking to Miss Sharpe. "Nellie, do you think Mr. Sennett and Mr. McHatton are being a little too courteous to us?"

"Why do you ask me that, sir?"

"Well, it seems to me they might be hiding something."

"Something to do with Mr. Clover's murder?"

"Possibly, but I can't imagine what it would be except they might be trying to protect someone who is employed here."

"That would be the obvious reason, don't you think, sir?"

"Yes. Too obvious, and that is what concerns me. They are so obvious about it that I believe they might be hiding something else."

"Such as what, sir?"

"I really don't have an inkling what it could be. Perhaps it's just in my nature to be suspicious of people." He shrugged. "I am like that, you know. My wife says so, and she's never wrong."

* * *

Sennett washed down a bite of sandwich with a swallow of Vernor's ginger ale. "Anybody here got any ideas about who Browning thinks is guilty of Clover's murder?"

"My money's on one of the girls he jilted," said Sterling.

"Mine, too," said Mace.

"Why does it have to be a woman who killed him?" asked Alice. "Maybe it was a jealous lover of one of the girls who did it."

"Like who?" asked Sennett.

"How should I know? I don't keep track of the girls he jilted, and I don't keep track of who's seeing who in this place."

"What do you think, Maisy? You seem to be chummy with Browning. Has he said anything to you about who he suspects of killing Clover?"

"No, Mack, he hasn't, but I do know he's trying to find Vivian Vanover in connection with Mr. Clover's death."

Sennett screwed up his face with perplexity. "Vivian who?"

Everybody else except Mabel and Milo leaned forward to hear Maisy's reply. "Vivian Vanover. She was an extra here for a few days, and then she went back to Polyscope because you weren't using her here, I guess."

"I don't' remember her. Any of the rest of you remember her?"

Lehrman searched his memory bank. "I recall an extra by the name of Miss Vanover. I used her several days in a row and was thinking about giving her a chance at playing bit roles. I was going to speak to her about it, but she never showed up that day or any day after that. I wondered what happened to her. And you say she went back to Polyscope?"

"That's what I heard from a couple of extras."

Sennett's head tilted down and to the right. "Really? Who?"

"Gloria Newman told me Miss Vanover was working at Universal and was doing well before she came here. Then she left Keystone and went up the hill to Polyscope because, as Gloria told it, she learned Mr. Clover would be a regular here."

"And who else told you about her?"

"Alma McComb mentioned her once."

Sennett set his eye on Cole. "What about you, Milo? What do you know about this Vivian Vanover?"

Cole had a mouthful of ham and mild cheddar on white bread and had to wash it down with Coca-Cola before he could answer. "Well, I don't know much more than what Maisy just told you. Vivian was doing just fine at Universal before she came over here, and then she left to go to Polyscope when she learned Leslie was a regular here and moving up the ladder. I didn't realize she was doing so well here before she left."

Mabel jumped into the conversation. "You know, I'm with Mother on this. Why does it have to be one of the girls he jilted who did him in? Why can't it have been a man? Just think about it. Leslie Clover was a man, and he was trying on a corset to make him look thinner for the camera. Would he really do that in front of a woman? You have to be naked or at least in your undies to do that. How many men would be comfortable putting on a corset in front of a woman?"

Sterling burped a chuckle. "How many men would be comfortable putting on a corset in front of another man? Unless, of course, he was on the queer side and liked doing that sort of thing."

Cole came to Clover's defense. "I can safely say Leslie preferred women just as much as any man in this room."

Sennett snickered. "What are you trying to say, Milo? That we're all queer here?"

"No, sir, just the opposite."

While everybody else chortled at Cole's defensive response, Maisy shook her head in dismay. "For goodness sake, Milo! When are you going to grow a sense of humor? Don't you know a joke when you hear one?"

Cole blushed with embarrassment and anger, but he retained control of his emotions and said nothing in return.

Mabel felt a little sorry for Milo and thought to draw attention away from him. "Back to what I was getting at. I think he could have been killed by a man as well as by a woman."

Sterling took the bait. "Okay, who did you have in mind for the guilty party?"

"Well, we know Milo didn't do it because he was with Maisy that morning, and so was Willie James. And we know none of you men in here did it because you were all on the set with me and Mother that morning. Except for you Henry. I can't vouch for you."

"I was on another set. You know that, Mabel."

"Okay, I'll take your word for it."

Sterling egged her on. "So who else were you thinking of Mabel?"

"It could have been any of the male extras, but the question is, which of them had a reason for wanting Clover out of the way?" She focused on Sennett. "Now that Clover is gone, who's next in line to get the parts he had been playing? Jack Shannon, right?"

Sennett was quite visibly taken aback. "You don't think he did it, do you, Mabel?"

"He could have done it. Does anybody know if he was on the lot that morning? I can't recall seeing him here, but then again, I couldn't say for sure whether Henry was here either. I'm not in the habit of keeping track of everybody's comings and goings around here."

"No, none of us do that," said Sennett, "but Hugh McHatton does."

"Precisely, Mack, which is why Detective Browning is going over the payroll records right this very minute. I'll bet he's going to find out Shannon wasn't here that morning."

"I'll take that bet," said Sterling.

Maisy smiled coyly. "I've got an idea. Why don't we all bet on who we think did it?"

Alice gasped. "That's rather morbid, don't you think? Betting on who the killer might be, I mean."

"It's no different than taking out a life insurance policy on someone else," said Mace.

Maisy sought to clarify her idea. "Actually, I was thinking maybe we should bet on *who* Detective Browning will arrest for the murder. If he arrests someone none of us bet on, then we all get our money back. If more than two people bet on the same person, then they will divide the pot. How does that sound to everybody?"

"How much do we have to put in the pot?" asked Mace.

A cunning smile spread over Maisy's face. "Let's really make it interesting, Fred. How about ten bucks each?"

Sennett responded first. "I'm in."

All the others followed until Alice spoke up again. "Tell me again what happens if we're all wrong and he arrests someone that nobody bet on. What do we do with the money?"

"We get our money back," said Mace.

Mabel giggled. "Why don't we take the money and have a night on the town at the Alexandria Hotel?"

Sterling seconded her idea. "I say the winner should take the rest of us to dinner at the Alexandria anyway."

"I'm for that," said Sennett. "Mother, how about you holding the pot for us?"

"I can do that."

Maisy had another idea. "Now we want to keep this secret among ourselves. So each of us should write down who we think Browning will arrest and we sign our names with our guesses. Then fold the paper several times so nobody can read it without unfolding it completely. Then we put those slips in the pot with the money. After Browning makes his arrest, we'll convene here again and open the slips and see who won. Fair enough?"

They all put their money and their slips into a brown paper sack that Alice Davenport held out to them. The pot was right.

* * *

Detective Browning and Miss Sharpe completed their work on the payroll records at the same time the Keystone director-general finished his lunch. With McHatton right behind them, the detective and the stenographer met Sennett at the bottom of the stairs to his office.

"Mr. Sennett, here is a list of your employees that I would like to question some more about where they were this past Thursday morning."

Sennett took the sheet of stenographic notebook paper from Browning and read it quickly. "Why is there a line under Jack Shannon's name and not under any of the others?"

"It seems that Mr. Shannon was here Saturday when I was questioning your employees. Yet, he somehow eluded me, which is why I want to talk to Mrs. Killoy again, and I want to speak to her first."

"Katy is the head of our costume department." Sennett pointed to the appropriate door. "Right through there. She should be back from lunch by now. As for the rest of these people, Mr. McHatton can round them up for you as you need them and if they're available. They work first and ask your questions second, Detective."

"I have all afternoon, Mr. Sennett."

"Well, you just might need it." And with that, the director returned to the set.

"Come along, Miss Sharpe."

The detective, his stenographer, and Keystone's bookkeeper crossed the open space to the costumed department and went inside without knocking on the door. They found Katy Killoy sitting at her mending table, cutting the stitches on a seam of a skirt to let it out another inch.

"Detective Browning, what brings you around this afternoon?"

"I have a couple more questions for you, Mrs. Killoy."

"More questions for me? What on earth can I tell you, Detective?"

"Well, you can start by telling me why you didn't bring Jack Shannon to me Saturday morning so I could question him about Leslie Clover's murder."

"Are you sure I didn't bring Jackie to you?"

"According to his payroll record, he was here Saturday morning, acting in a film Mr. Lehrman was directing. And according to Miss Sharpe's transcriptions of all the interviews I did here that day, no one by the name of Jack Shannon, Jackie Shannon or John Shannon was interviewed. So I'll ask you again, Mrs. Killoy. Why didn't you bring him to me to be questioned?"

Katy shrugged. "I can only say that I overlooked him, Detective Browning. After all, there are a lot of people working here. Actors, extras, directors, filming crews, prop men, laboratory men, carpenters, painters, electricians, and the night watchman. Now I know I didn't bring Old Artie to see you because he wasn't here for me to fetch him. He's only here at night, and he was already gone home by the time you arrived here. And I didn't bother the workmen who make the sets and do the wiring around here because you only asked for the folks who make the films, which I took to mean the actors, directors, and filming crews. So I don't know why I missed Jackie. All I remember is I was picking folks as I saw them when they were free for the few minutes you were asking them your questions. And somehow I missed Jackie in all that. You ain't thinking I missed him on purpose, are you, Detective Browning?"

"I don't know. You tell me."

"I told already you, sir. There are a lot of people working here, and I don't know why I missed bringing Jackie to you."

Browning nodded his head. "Okay, Mrs. Killoy, I'll take what you just said under consideration." He turned to face McHatton. "Would you mind finding Mr. Shannon for me, sir? And would you please bring him to your office so I may question him there?"

"Certainly, sir."

As soon as McHatton was gone from the costume department, Browning turned back to Katy. "Mrs. Killoy, would you mind telling me again where you were this past Thursday morning at the time of Leslie Clover's murder?"

"Like I told you the other day, Detective Browning, I was right here in this department like I am every day I come to work."

"And was there anyone working with you that morning?"

"As a matter of fact, there was. I asked Mr. McHatton if I could use one of the extra girls to help me for a while, and he said I could. So I asked Alma McComb to help me. Why is that so important, Detective?"

"I just wanted to verify that Miss McComb was here with you is all, Mrs.

Killoy. Nothing more." Browning tipped his bowler to Katy. "Thank you, Mrs. Killoy. You've been very helpful again. Good day, ma'am." He turned for the exit. "Come along, Miss Sharpe. We shouldn't be late to question Mr. Shannon."

"Tell me, Mr. Shannon, how** is it that you avoided being questioned by me the other day when I was here?"

Shannon shrugged. "I don't know, sir. I was here. Mr. Lehrman can vouch for me on that score. I acted in a few scenes he directed that day."

"Yes, I know you were here, sir. Your payroll record verifies that much." Browning shot a glance at the little man in the corner. "I have full faith in Mr. McHatton's bookkeeping competence."

"Thank you, Detective. I give it my best."

"I'm sure you do, sir." Browning looked at the transcription of the interview with Katy Killoy, but he wasn't really reading it. He only wanted to make Shannon think he was reading it and that it contained some damning information about him. "When I questioned Mrs. Killoy about how you managed to avoid being interviewed by me, she had no definitive answer for me. She told me to ask you why you avoided her all morning when she was bringing others to me for questioning. So I'm asking, Mr. Shannon. Why did you avoid her Saturday morning?"

Sweat became quite visible on Shannon's forehead. "I didn't avoid her, sir. I was on the set the whole morning either in a scene or waiting to be in a scene. You can ask Mr. Lehrman. He'll tell you I was there. It's not my fault she didn't bring me in here to talk to you, Detective. I was more than available for your questions."

"How do you know I was questioning people in this office, sir?"

"Word about who you are, where you were, and what you were asking spread around the studio in minutes, Detective. Nobody can keep a secret in a place like this. We all talk to each other constantly, especially when we've got a subject like a murder investigation to speculate about."

"All right, Mr. Shannon, let's get down to business here. State your full name for the record please."

"John Michael Shannon."

"And your address, sir?"

"One hundred Green Street in Pasadena."

"Pasadena?"

Shannon blanched and swallowed hard. "Did I say Pasadena? I meant Los Angeles. I live on the second floor of the Belvedere rooming house on West Third Street in Los Angeles. Milo Cole lives on the floor above mine."

"But why did you say Pasadena before, Mr. Shannon?"

"I lived there for a while in a boardinghouse before moving to my current place in Los Angeles. Mr. and Mrs. Whitney owned the house and rented rooms to mostly single people."

Browning nodded as he studied Shannon for a moment before leaning close to the stenographer to whisper to her. "I believe Mrs. Killoy lives in Pasadena. Could you check her address in the transcription of her interview when we return to the station?"

"No need, sir. I have it right here." Miss Sharpe flipped a few pages in her notebook. "She lives at Twenty-six South Pasadena Avenue."

Browning made a mental note to check out both addresses at the first opportunity. He straightened up and faced Shannon again. "How long have you been with Keystone?"

"About four weeks now."

"How well did you know Leslie Clover?"

"Not as well as Milo Cole did, but I'd say I knew him fairly well. I stayed at his bungalow several times until I found my own place. Leslie was very generous to me. He knew I had a long ride on the Red Car from Pasadena, so he let me sleep in his spare bedroom on weeknights when he wasn't entertaining a lady there."

"Did Mr. Clover entertain many ladies over the time you were staying with him?"

"Only two and both of them were on Saturday nights when I was staying at my room in Pasadena." Shannon held up a finger. "Oh, wait there was one time … no, two times… yes, two times during the week when he had a lady over to the bungalow."

"And where did you stay at those times?"

"Milo let me stay with him instead of me going all the way back to Pasadena or renting a hotel room for the night. I don't make that much money here yet to afford paying for a decent hotel room even for one night. So sleeping on the floor at Milo's was the preferable alternative."

"So would you say you and Mr. Cole are close friends?"

"We're getting that way, I suppose. Before this tragedy happened to Leslie, I'd say the three of us were becoming real chums with each other."

"You, Mr. Clover, and Mr. Cole. I see." Browning leaned close to Miss Sharpe to whisper to her again. "Remind me when we get back to the station to look up the transcription of my interview with Mr. Cole when he came into the station on Friday. I want to go over the list of people he told me about in that interview."

"Yes, sir."

Browning resumed his line of questioning of Shannon. "I know it's only four days since your friend's passing, but has anything changed between you and Mr. Cole?"

"Well, we did have a bit of a tiff the other night. Saturday night I mean. I thought I had an engagement with a lady, but when I went to her home, she was unavailable because she wasn't feeling well. I learned from the housekeeper that Mr. Cole and Miss Malone had been by to see Miss Vanover earlier in—"

"Did you say Vanover? Miss Vivian Vanover? Who lives on Beaudry Avenue?"

"The very same, sir."

"How do you know Miss Vanover?"

"We met when she was working here at Keystone a few weeks back. She rode the same Red Car to and from work that I did. We talked some on the ride to and from Edendale, even after she left Keystone and went to work at Polyscope again. Tuesday, I asked her if she would care to accompany me to dinner and a moving picture downtown, and she agreed to go with me. I went to her home early Saturday evening to escort her to dinner, but like I said before, the housekeeper told me Vivian wasn't feeling well and asked that she be excused from our engagement this time. After a little more conversation, Hortencia, that's the housekeeper, she told me Milo and Miss Malone had been by to see Vivian earlier in the afternoon. That night when Milo returned to our rooming house, I confronted him about it. That's when we had our tiff. Actually, now that I've had more time to think about it, the tiff was more from me than it was Milo. I thought he was seeing Vivian or at least trying to see Vivian, but he explained that he had no romantic interest in her whatsoever. We talked some more about women and things, and then I left and went back to my own apartment for the night."

Browning nodded. "Well, enough about you and Mr. Cole. I'd like to know more about you and Miss Vanover. Do you know her present whereabouts?"

Shannon shrugged. "I assume she's either at her home or she's at work, if she's still grieving over Leslie."

"Are you sure of that, Mr. Shannon?"

"Well, no. As I said, she's either …" His voice drifted off for a few seconds. "Wait a minute. You aren't trying to tell me Miss Vanover is missing, are you?"

"I'm not trying to tell you anything, Mr. Shannon. The fact is, Miss Vanover is not at her residence, and she failed to arrive at the Polyscope studio this morning. Putting it simply, she is missing, and we don't have a clue as to her whereabouts. Do you know where she might be?"

Shannon shook his head. "No, I don't. I don't know her that well. You might ask Miss Phoebe Alden, Miss Alma McComb or Miss Gloria Newman.

Of all the people around here, I think they knew her best."

"What about Mrs. Killoy? How well does she know Miss Vanover?"

"I can't really say. I don't know Mrs. Killoy that well. I get my costumes from her when I'm called on to act. We chat a bit, but that's the extent of our relationship." A memory popped to the front of Shannon's thought processes. "She did say once that I reminded her of her late husband. Then she touched my cheek and wished me good luck on the set that day." He snorted a laugh. "Come to think of it, several ladies here have told me I remind them of somebody they've known and have patted my hand or squeezed it. Even Mother has done so."

"Mother? Who would that be?"

"Miss Davenport. We all call her Mother because she's been in the business such a long time, since the right after the Civil War, I've been told."

"Of the three ladies you mentioned who were close to Miss Vanover, which one would you say was the closest?"

"That would be Miss Alden. She lives up the street a few doors from Miss Vanover. We ride the same Red Car to work each day."

"Yes, I already know about Miss Alden. She's been very forthcoming in my investigation into Mr. Clover's death and with Miss Vanover's sudden disappearance."

"Disappearance? Is that what you're calling it?"

"What else should I call it? She's nowhere to be found. She left her home Saturday afternoon, and nobody has seen her since then. You don't know where she went. The housekeeper doesn't know where she went. Miss Alden doesn't know either. So I call that a disappearance. As far as we know, she's left the state."

"She wouldn't do that."

"What makes you say that, Mr. Shannon?"

The actor shrugged. "I don't know. I just don't think she would."

"Does she have family here in Los Angeles?"

"Not that I know of. You should ask Miss Alden about that. She probably knows Miss Vanover the best. Ask her."

"I intend to do just that. You can go now, Mr. Shannon. If I need you again, I know where to find you."

* * *

"Miss Alden, you told me Miss Vanover quit working here at Keystone last week, I mean the week before. And that she went back to working at the Universal studio in Hollywood. And then you said the last time you saw here was last Sunday. I've learned you lied to me, Miss Alden. Miss Vanover left here three weeks ago, and she went to work at the Polyscope studio up the hill from here, and she was there Monday, Tuesday, and Wednesday last week. You knew all that, Miss Alden, but you still lied to me about it. Now I want to know why you lied to me?"

178

"I was trying to protect Vivian."

"Protect her? From what?"

"Mostly from you, Detective Browning. Vivian is a gentle soul, and she does not handle confrontation very well. I was afraid she would suffer a breakdown if she had to answer your questions."

"A breakdown? Really?"

"Yes, a breakdown."

"So why did you tell me Saturday that Miss Vanover had left her residence, if you were trying to protect her?"

"From what Hortencia told me, I thought Vivian might be thinking of doing herself a hurt, and I thought you might be able to find her and prevent her from doing anything harmful to herself."

"She's still missing, Miss Alden. Do you have any idea where she might have gone?"

Phoebe shrugged. "I can't think of any place in particular. She could have gotten on a train and gone anywhere in Los Angeles County or even to San Bernadino or Riverside or Orange County. The Red Car goes all over this part of the state. She could also have taken a train to San Diego or San Francisco. She could be any place in the country by now."

"Do you know if she has any family in this area?"

"None that I know of. I do know Vivian came here from Illinois last winter. She worked as a waitress for a while before becoming an extra at Universal when it was still Imp."

"Imp?"

"That's what everybody called it. Actually, it stood for Independent Moving Pictures Company. A bunch of the independent filmmakers got together to start Universal back in June. They were making westerns there in Hollywood. A few other studios were making moving pictures there, too. Just across the street was the Nestor Company. They were the first studio to set up business in Hollywood."

"We're getting off the subject here, Miss Alden. We're talking about Vivian Vanover, not the moving picture business. So you don't know where she went when she left her boarding house residence on Saturday?"

"Yes, that's right, Detective, but if I had to guess, I'd say she's probably staying in a hotel somewhere in the city under a false name."

Browning frowned. "Thank you, Miss Alden. I've already figured that out for myself. You can go now. I don't have any more questions for you at this time."

* * *

Alma McComb came into McHatton's office next. "What's this all about, Detective Browning? Didn't you ask me enough questions on Saturday?"

"No, as a matter-of-fact, I did not, which is precisely why you are here again."

"Okay, ask away."

"Where were you the morning Leslie Clover was murdered?"

"I told you that before. I was right here at the studio. Ask McHatton. He'll tell you."

"But where were you *here* at the studio that morning?"

"I was helping Katy in wardrobe. She came and got me almost as soon as we started working that day. She said she had cleared it with McHatton for me to get paid like a bit player, so I went along with her because I needed the extra money. I was in wardrobe nearly the whole morning."

"Was anybody there with you to verify that?"

"Katy was there. Ask her. She'll tell you."

"I already have."

"So why are you asking me? Did you think she was lying to you?"

Browning ignored the question and asked another of his own. "Were you in the wardrobe department the whole morning?"

"You bet I was. Katy had me sewing up holes and tears in a whole bunch of costumes. My fingers hurt like hell by the time she came back and let me go to lunch."

"By the time she came back? What does that mean? Did Mrs. Killoy leave you alone in the wardrobe department?"

"Not the whole time I was there. She had errands to run, and she had to tend to some of the actors' costumes on the sets. I remember her saying something about Miss Davenport tearing her skirt, so she had to take her another dress. She was in and out most of the morning, just like she usually is."

"How do you know she is usually in and out of the wardrobe department?"

"Katy is one of a kind around here. Just like McHatton, she comes and goes everywhere on the lot all day long. Everybody knows that. Ask anybody. They'll all tell you the same thing."

Browning shook his head. "No, I don't think that will be necessary, Miss McComb. I'll take your word for it."

"Was there anything unusual about her comings and goings that morning? Anything out of the norm for Mrs. Killoy?"

"Well, just like I told Maisy Malone, Katy was complaining about a costume being missing. A man's costume. One that Slim Summerville usually wore."

"Slim Summerville?"

"Yes, Slim. You can't miss him. He's tall and gangly. Very funny, too."

"Oh, yes, now I remember him." Browning nodded. "Thank you, Miss McComb. That will be all for now."

* * *

Henry Lehrman accompanied Fritz and Betty Schade into McHatton's office to act as their interpreter once again. "They are Germans, Detective Browning. Germans fear the police. It comes from living under the Kaiser and his militarists."

"Yes, of course. Well, thank you then for coming in with them, Mr. Lehrman." Browning focused on Fritz. "Mr. Schade, you said the other day that you were here at the studio on the morning of Leslie Clover's murder, but the payroll records don't indicate that, sir. Can you tell me why?"

Schade shrugged. "I don't understand."

Lehrman explained it to him in German, listened to his reply, and then repeated it in English for Browning. "He says he didn't work that day, but he was here all morning."

"Can anybody corroborate his statement?"

"Corroborate? What does that mean, Detective?"

"Can anybody verify his statement? Can anybody else say he was here that morning?"

"Oh, I see. I will ask him."

Fritz listened to Lehrman's translation, then answered for himself. "My vife. She can say I was here."

Betty spoke up immediately. "Yes, that is right. He was here."

"Can anybody else support your statement, Mr. Schade?"

Schade paled for a few seconds, then became livid. "You say I lie? My vife lie?" He belched out a string of angry German words.

"I'm not sure what he said, Mr. Lehrman, but I know it wasn't good."

"He said he doesn't care if you are a policeman. You can't call him a liar."

Browning nodded sympathetically. "I'm not calling you a liar, Mr. Schade, but I do need you to find someone who can back up your statement. Do you understand?"

Lehrman explained the detective's meaning to Fritz and Betty who responded with affirmatives. "They understand now, Detective Browning. They will find someone to back up their statement."

"Very good, Mr. Lehrman. You may all go now. I have no more questions for you."

* * *

"According to your payroll record, Miss Newman, you didn't work the morning Leslie Clover was murdered. Is that correct?"

"Yes, that's right."

"But in our previous interview you said you were here at the studio that morning. Can anybody verify that you were here that morning?"

"Sure, lots of people. Ask any of the other extras. They'll tell you I was here that morning, same as they were."

"I've already done that, Miss Newman. Nobody seems able to recall whether they saw you here or not that morning. Now we know for certain you were here in the afternoon because you were paid for the afternoon. But your presence here in the morning is in doubt. Now can you think of anybody in particular who can verify your presence on the lot?"

"I'd have to think about that. Until we heard about Leslie's death after lunch, that Thursday was no different than any other day around here. Frankly, we were all sort of shocked by the news, so I'm surprised any of us remember what we were doing that morning … or who we saw … or talked to … or anything. Now that I think about it, I'm not even sure of who I talked to that afternoon or that night on the ride home. I know Milo Cole brought Maisy Malone to the studio that afternoon, but I didn't meet her until the next day. No, Detective, I'd have to think about that before I could tell you who could verify I was here that morning."

"Very well, Miss Newman. I'll be at the wake this evening. If you remember anything more, you can tell me then."

* * *

"So, Eddie, You must have found the same inconsistencies in the payroll records that I found."

"What makes you say that, Maisy?"

"Because you just finished questioning all the people I would have questioned again because of what I found in their records. Did any of them tell you anything you didn't know before?"

"I learned some new facts."

"Such as?"

Browning hesitated to reveal anything to Maisy. "I'm not really sure I should be sharing any information with you."

"Why not? I shared with you."

"Well, all right then. I think I can pretty much rule out everybody except Miss Vivian Vanover and Miss Newman as a suspect. She is the only person left who doesn't have an alibi of any kind. Mr. Shannon was here at the studio on the morning of the murder. Mrs. Schade says Mr. Schade was here. Mrs. Killoy verifies Miss McComb's presence on the lot. Miss Alden's payroll record indicates she was here working that morning as well."

"So you think Gloria Newman might be the person who murdered Leslie Clover?"

"No, I don't. Something tells me she was telling me the truth about being here. My top suspect is still Miss Vanover, but only because she has disappeared. What about you? Who do you suspect did it?"

"I can't say just yet, Eddie. Frankly, I'm not really sure at this point. For all I know, Hortencia Ramos could be the killer."

"Mrs. Ramos? The housekeeper at Miss Vanover's boardinghouse? Why would you think she could be the killer?"

"Because she's been the go-between for Miss Vanover. Did you get to speak to her? Miss Vanover, I mean."

"No."

"And neither did I, nor did Jack Shannon who was supposed to have a social engagement with her Saturday night. Don't you find that a little suspicious?"

"It could be, but I don't think Mrs. Ramos even knew where Leslie Clover lived."

"Are you sure? Did you ask her? Did you ask her where she was Thursday morning? You know how protective she's been with Miss Vanover. Maybe she was too protective of her."

"Anything is possible, I suppose."

"Yes, it is, Eddie. So maybe you should stop by the boardinghouse on your way home this afternoon and have a little chat with Hortencia. And don't let her buffalo you with that broken English of hers. She speaks our lingo better than she puts on."

* * *

"Come on, Mabel. We have to get Hollywood as fast as we can."

The lead actress held her ground. "Maisy, I'm not going all the way to the hotel and then back to the funeral parlor in the city."

"Who said anything about going to the hotel? I want to go to Leslie Clover's place as soon as possible."

"Leslie Clover's place again? We were just there last night. Did you forget something?"

Maisy toddled sheepishly. "Well, not his place exactly." She tugged on Mabel's arm. "Just come on. I'll tell you on the way."

A bit reluctantly Mabel allowed Maisy to pull her along. "Are we taking Milo with us?"

"We shouldn't need Milo this time. Besides, Willie will be there if we need a man's help."

"This better be important, Maisy."

"Believe me, it is."

* * *

Willie parked the Cadillac in front of the late Leslie Clover's bungalow. "Do you want me to come with you, Miss Normand?"

"Don't ask me, Willie. Maisy's directing this scene."

"No, Willie, I don't think you have to come with us. We're not going inside the house anyway."

"Well, I'll just be keeping an eye on you anyway, Miss Malone. Mr. Sennett would expect me to do that."

"Fair enough, Willie."

Mabel and Maisy exited the car and walked between Clover's place and the one next door to the north. Directly behind the bungalow on Mariposa Avenue a handful of workmen had another house under construction. The two women approached the back entrance, but before they could reach it, a burly, cigar-chomping, dour-faced man in a tattered black Homburg came out of the dark interior of the building, halting in the doorless opening to bark at them above the din of hammers pounding nails and saws cutting wood.

"Can I do something for you ladies?"

Maisy took the lead. "Good afternoon, sir. I was wondering if I might speak to you and your workers about what you were all doing this past Thursday morning."

"You don't have to speak to my men about that. I can tell you they were all right here doing their jobs."

"Yes, I thought they were, which is why we're here. My name is Maisy Malone, and this is—"

A big, tobacco-stained, toothy grin spread over the man's face as he interrupted her. "Miss Mabel Normand. I'd recognize you anywhere, Miss Normand. The family and I have seen a lot of your moving picture shows. You're a very funny lady."

Mabel blushed at the sudden attention. "Thank you, sir."

"Hogan. Dennis Hogan. I'm the builder of most of the houses in this neighborhood. And this is my crew." He turned his head into the house. "Hey, boys! Knock off for a minute and come here and meet Miss Mabel Normand."

Just that quick, the pounding and sawing ceased, and a few seconds later four strapping men ranging in age from mid-twenties to late-thirties appeared behind Hogan.

"Boys, this is Miss Mabel Normand from the moving pictures, and this other lady is ... I'm sorry, ma'am, I didn't catch your name."

"That's all right, Mr. Hogan. It's not important."

Mabel jumped to Maisy's defense. "Yes, it is important. This is Miss Maisy Malone, and she's going to be a lead actress at our studio soon. Remember her name, gentleman, because one day you'll be able to brag to the boys in the saloon that you met her when she was just starting out in the moving picture business."

Hogan doffed his hat. "I beg your pardon, Miss Malone. It's an honor to make your acquaintance." He replaced his Homburg. "So what can we do for you ladies?"

Maisy took control. "Gentlemen, are you aware that there was a murder committed in that house this past Thursday morning?"

"We heard about it," said Hogan.

"Did the police talk to you about it yet?"

"Nobody talked to me about it," said Hogan. "How about it, men? Anybody with a badge talk to you about it?"

To a man, they shook their heads or said no.

"Well then, would you mind if I asked you a few questions about it? You see, the victim was an actor at our studio, so we're kind of concerned about what happened to him."

Hogan shook his head. "I'm okay with that, Miss Malone. How about it, boys? You all willing to answer a few questions from Miss Malone here?"

Their heads bobbed collectively as they responded with something in the affirmative.

"Thank you, gentleman. Now the murder took place between eight and ten o'clock in the morning. I came by Mr. Clover's bungalow around ten-thirty or so. I was with another actor who was sent to pick up Mr. Clover in the studio's car. While I was here, I looked through the back door to his bungalow and noticed a couple of you gentlemen working on the roof over here. I didn't get a good enough look at either of you to remember your faces. So would you mind coming forward to talk to me?"

The youngest man in the bunch edged his way to the front. "I was up there that morning, Miss Malone."

"So was I." This man looked to be thirtyish. "Ed Moore is the name, Miss Malone."

"Oh, yes, and I'm Allen Kitchen."

"Nice to meet you both, Mr. Moore, Mr. Kitchen. Did either of you see anybody coming out of that bungalow between eight and ten o'clock last Thursday morning?" Maisy jabbed a thumb over her shoulder toward Clover's former residence.

Kitchen and Moore looked askance at each other.

"Go ahead, boys," said Hogan. "Answer the lady."

"I did," said Kitchen.

"So did I," said Moore.

"Was this person a man or a woman?"

The two workmen answered simultaneously.

Moore said, "A man."

Kitchen said, "A woman."

They stared at each other for a few seconds.

"She was a woman," said Kitchen.

Moore shook his head. "No, *he* was a man."

The two of them started to argue, and Hogan tried to intervene.

Mabel nudged Maisy. "Now what?"

"Now we give them a moment to blow off a little steam, and then we'll get to the bottom of this." Maisy turned back to the boss. "You said you built most of the houses in this neighborhood, Mr. Hogan. Did you build them for someone else or did you sell them as well as build them?"

"I built some of them under contract to the buyers, and some I built with the idea of selling them or renting them after they were done."

"How about Leslie Clover's house? Did you build it?"

"I certainly did, and then I rented it to him for a while before he bought it from me."

"When did he buy it?"

"Just a couple of weeks ago. He said he'd come into some money and could make the down payment on it. I require everybody to get a loan from a bank before I sell them a house. If they want me to carry their mortgage, then they have to make a down payment of twenty-five percent of the price. Mr. Clover came to me with the five hundred dollars about two or three weeks ago. I can look up the exact date, if you like."

"No, that won't be necessary."

Mabel peered curiously at Maisy. "Are you thinking what I'm thinking?"

"I believe I am, Mabel. I believe I am."

All but one employee of the Keystone Motion Picture Company and its director-general attended the open-casket viewing of Leslie Clover at Pierce Brothers Funeral Parlor on South Flower Street. Those Keystone people present were joined by more than two hundred other moving picture folks representing all the studios in southern California. Most were actors at all levels and extras who wanted to become actors. At least four directors and executives from each film company made a show of being there. They had come not so much to pay their respects to the deceased but to hobnob with their film industry counterparts and maybe talk a little business.

Ford Sterling, Fred Mace, Pathé Lehrman, and Mack Sennett each took a turn introducing Maisy around the gathering. With exaggerated pride, they pronounced her a salaried member of the Keystone ensemble who was bound to reach great motion picture heights. This was their way of saying she was off-limits to the other companies, especially Carl Laemmle's Universal Studio which was rumored to be developing its own comedy division.

Detective Ed Browning also came to the viewing. Instead of paying his respects to the guest of honor, he approached Sennett to let him know he was there. "Besides me, I've got several uniformed officers outside and a few in here in street clothes."

"Why so many men, Detective?"

"They're here just in case Miss Vivian Vanover shows up."

"Do you really think she will?"

Browning shrugged. "She's a woman, and they are an unpredictable lot, now aren't they, sir?"

"You got me there. But how will you know her if she does show up? To be honest, I don't think there's more than a half dozen people in this room who would know her on sight."

"Mrs. Killoy, Miss Alden, Mr. Shannon, and Mr. Cole have all volunteered to keep an eye out for her."

"Well, if she does show, try not to make a big fuss about arresting her, will you? These are moving picture folk here. Most of them are afraid of their own shadows, so you better believe seeing a bunch of cops making an arrest will scare the hell out of them."

"We'll be as discreet as we possibly can, Mr. Sennett."

* * *

Halfway through the evening, Sennett took Milo Cole aside in the viewing room. "I want you to stick around here with Pathé and Katy Killoy for another hour or so to meet and greet any latecomers. Then you can come over to the Abbotsford and join the party. Okay, Milo?"

"Yes, sir, Mr. Sennett."

"Milo, you can start calling me Mack. You've been with me long enough now." He winked at Cole. "And I want you learn more about this business than just acting. You might make a good director someday." He patted Milo on the shoulder as he left the funeral parlor for the banquet room at the Abbotsford Inn.

Maisy strolled up to Cole as soon as Sennett was out the door with Sterling and Mace. "I saw you talking to Eddie. What was that all about?"

"He wants me to keep an eye for Vivian Vanover along with Katy, Jack, and Phoebe. If she shows up, we're supposed to tip him off right away so he can move in and make the arrest. You don't think she'll show up here, do you?"

"You never know, Milo. You never know." She winked at him and moved away toward Browning.

"Good evening, Miss Malone."

"I see you've got the place surrounded, Eddie. You don't really think Vivian Vanover will show up here, do you?"

"Odd, but your boss asked me the very same question."

"And what did you tell him?"

"I told him she's a woman and you're all an unpredictable lot, now aren't you?"

Maisy patted his arm. "We have to be, Eddie, if we're going to keep fellas like you interested in us." She batted her eyes at him precociously.

"You've met my wife, Miss Malone."

"Yes, I have, haven't I? Is she as unpredictable as I am, Eddie?"

Browning twitched uncomfortably. "That's not a subject I wish to discuss with you, Miss Malone."

Maisy feigned a pout. "Spoilsport!" She huffed a sigh. "All right then, I'll stick to the business at hand. Why so many flatfoots casing the joint?"

"I have to take every precaution, Miss Malone. If Miss Vanover does show up here tonight, I want to be certain she has no way of escaping."

"You must be pretty confident she'll show up."

"What makes you say that?"

Maisy tilted her head toward a fortyish woman standing all alone near the entrance to the parlor. "You brought a police matron with you to accompany Miss Vanover to jail if you make the arrest."

"That is Mrs. Alice Wells, the department's very first female police officer."

"Right, a matron."

"No, Miss Malone, she is not a matron. She is a police officer with all the responsibilities and authority of any male police officer."

"Really? Do you mean she can arrest people?"

"She can."

Maisy nodded with approval. "Now that is progressive, Eddie. I'll bet you had something to do with her becoming a cop, didn't you?"

"As a matter of fact, I was asked whether it would be a good idea to have a female officer in the department, but then again, so were all the other ranking officers. Almost to a man we agreed with her that the department should have a female officer. She was a matron before attaining her present status, and as such, she frequently accompanied male officers when arresting female and juvenile lawbreakers. Now she can make arrests herself. She presently works with Officer Leo Marden, the department's first juvenile offender officer."

"I'd like to meet her, Eddie. Would you mind introducing me?"

Browning's brow furrowed. "Right now?"

"Sure. Why not?"

The detective grimaced and shook his head. "All right, I suppose it won't hurt anything. Come on. Let's get this over with." He took Maisy by an elbow and led her to the policewoman. "Officer Wells, I would like to introduce Miss Maisy Malone. She's an actress at the Keystone Moving Picture Company in Edendale. Miss Malone, Officer Alice Wells."

"How do you do, Officer Wells? It's a pleasure to make your acquaintance."

"How do you do, Miss Malone?"

"Miss Malone insisted on meeting the first female officer in the department. I hope you don't mind, Officer Wells."

"No, not at all, Sergeant Browning."

He turned to Maisy. "By the way, how did you know Officer Wells was one of us?"

Maisy nodded at Officer Barney and Officer Fitzgerald posted in front of the forest green curtained wall behind the bier. "Oh, not just her, Eddie, but those two men standing next to the potted plants in each corner from Leslie Clover's coffin are your men."

"But how do you know that?"

"I never forget a face, Eddie, and I remember those two being with you the other day at the studio. Besides that, they stand out in this crowd, just like Officer Wells here."

"And how do 'they stand out in this crowd,' Miss Malone?"

"Just look around, Eddie. Who else besides you and your people are taking this thing seriously? These are show business people, Eddie. We live in a different world from the rest of you. About the only thing we take seriously is our work. Or haven't you figured that out yet?"

"She's right, Sergeant. Everybody else here is chattering away about something besides the deceased. We do stand out."

"Yes, I see what you mean. But we have to remain serious about our job here, if we're to arrest a woman for murder."

"Are you really that sure Miss Vanover did it, Eddie?"

"Yes, I am." He studied her face. "Why? Do you think she's innocent?"

"Innocent? No. But she didn't kill Leslie Clover, not the man who broke her heart."

"That's precisely her motive for murdering him, Miss Malone. He broke her heart, and she wanted revenge. A woman scorned, Miss Malone. A woman scorned."

"Not that woman, Eddie. She doesn't have it in her to commit a cold-blooded murder."

"How can you be so sure of that?"

Maisy winked and gave him another precocious grin. "I'm a woman, Eddie. Or haven't you noticed?"

"Sadly, yes." He nodded at Maisy. "Now if you will excuse me, Miss Malone, I will get back to my purpose for being here." He walked away as casually as he could.

"You seemed to be very well acquainted with Sergeant Browning, Miss Malone."

"You bet, Officer Wells. Eddie and I go all the way back to … this past Thursday. We met at the deceased's home in Hollywood. I was with the man who discovered the late Leslie Clover in his present condition."

"Present condition?"

"Yes, dead."

"Oh, yes, of course."

Maisy felt a twinge of guilt. "I'm sorry for being so flippant, Officer Wells. I guess I'm a little uncomfortable being here with all these strangers and a dead man in a coffin. I meant no disrespect to you or to Detective Browning."

"No need to apologize to me, Miss Malone."

"Oh, please call me Maisy."

"I'm not sure that would be appropriate here, Miss Malone."

"Yes, of course, I know what you mean. But what about away from here? I would love to talk to you about how and why you became a policewoman and what you do at the police department."

"We could do that. Why don't you call me at the Central Station sometime and we can set up an appointment?"

"Thank you, I will."

Just about then, a woman dressed in mourning black entered the room. She walked slowly toward the casket in the rear of the parlor, her hands clutching a small purse in front of her. A heavy veil hung down from the brim of her large hat, hiding her entire head from onlookers. She halted at the head of the coffin to gaze on the powdered face of Leslie Clover.

Cole went to Browning and whispered to him. "I think that's her, Detective."

Browning answered in the same tone. "You think that's her? You're not certain?"

"She's about the right height and shape. It could be her."

Maisy joined them, also speaking conspiratorially. "What are two whispering about?"

"Mr. Cole seems to think that woman is Miss Vanover."

"Really, Milo?"

"I can't be certain, but she's the right height and shape for Vivian."

"Well, what you going to do, Eddie?"

"Until I'm certain it's her, I'm going to do nothing."

Maisy rolled her eyes heavenward. "He who hesitates is lost, Eddie. I guess I'll have to find out for you." Without another breath, she marched straight toward the woman in black.

"Miss Malone!"

"Don't bother, Detective. That girl is as crazy as a loon. Crazy Maisy Malone. What else can I say?"

Maisy stepped up behind her target and tapped her on the shoulder, causing the grieving lady to spin around suddenly. "Excuse me, but are you Vivian Vanover?"

She nodded.

Maisy glanced over her shoulder. "It's her, Eddie."

Browning motioned to his three officers to join him in surrounding Maisy and Vivian. The four of them closed in quickly; Browning and Wells blocking her path to the entrance and Barney and Fitzgerald coming at her from each side.

"Miss Vivian Vanover, you're under arrest for the murder of Leslie Clover. Take her into custody, Officer Wells."

Before the policewoman could act, Vivian pushed Maisy against Browning, effectively rocking him backward. She dropped to the floor to avoid the outstretched arms of Fitzgerald, Barney, and Wells who only succeeded in grabbing each other in an embarrassing free-for-all. Without a second of ado, Vivian rolled under the bier, crawled quickly to the wall, lifted the curtain, and scrambled beneath it into a dimly lit corridor beyond.

Browning released Maisy. "After her!"

Barney, Fitzgerald, and Wells untangled themselves, and each scanned the room for the fugitive who was nowhere to be seen.

Fitzgerald rotated three-sixty in a series of hops. "Which way did she go?"

"She went under the coffin," said Wells.

The three of them looked beneath the bier.

"She's not there," said Barney.

Browning noticed the drapes were moving slightly. "She's behind the curtain."

Maisy smiled joyfully as she watched the four members of the Los Angeles Police Department scurry around the casket to the green wall covering. Each of them frantically felt and prodded and probed the curtain in a vain search of their quarry until Browning realized the hanging cloth covered an open doorway. More poking and pulling and he finally found the ends of the two drapes and parted them to reveal the dimly lit hallway taken by Vivian as her escape route.

"Alice, go out the front door and alert the boys out there that she went out the back door. Orv, Fitz, come with me."

Wells followed orders, and Browning led the other two toward the rear of the building. At the end of the hall they came to a door that was still ajar.

"She must have gone outside," said Browning. He pushed through the exit with the pair of patrolmen right behind him. They halted there to allow their eyes to become accustomed to shadowy scene before them.

Street lamps and light from the windows of the Abbotsford Inn illuminated the alley that ran behind the buildings along Flower and Hope Streets from Eight Street to Ninth. Directly across the lane was the backyard of the only house left on Hope Street between Eight and Ninth. Browning squinted in that direction just in time to see the silhouette of a woman emerge from the darkness alongside the one-story structure and turn left in front of the Abbotsford.

Browning pointed straight ahead of them. "There she is, boys! She's on Hope Street, heading north!" He jabbed another finger up the alley toward Eighth. "Fitz, you go that way! Blow your whistle and alert the others. Orv, you come with me."

All three broke into a run; Browning and Barney toward Hope and Fitzgerald toward Eighth.

* * *

After bursting through the front entrance of the funeral parlor, Wells gathered several other officers around her and issued them orders that she felt quite certain Browning wanted her to relay, although he had told her nothing specific.

"The Vanover woman was inside. She escaped through the rear of the building. Sergeant Browning wants the block surrounded." She spotted

Speed Patrol Officer Thomas Kronschnable among the men. "Kronchie, get on your motorcycle and circle block."

"How will I recognize her?"

"She's wearing all black mourning clothes and a long veil that goes all the way around the brim of her hat. You can't miss her. Now get going!"

Kronschnable ran for his Indian bike, mounted up, and sped off to encircle the block in search of Vivian.

One by one, Wells gave an assignment to the other officers. She sent two to corner with Ninth; two to each side of the Pierce Brothers building and toward the alley behind; the last man was to go with to Eighth.

"And blow your whistles, boys. The sergeant wants every patrolman in hearing distance to join in on the search for this woman. Now let's get a move on!"

* * *

Browning and Barney rounded the corner of the Abbotsford Inn and found themselves confronted with several people strolling along the sidewalk, none of them appearing to be the woman in black.

"Orv, blow your whistle!"

Barney came to a halt beside Browning, dug into his pocket, and pulled out his whistle. He took one step forward and gave the instrument a long breath, filling the air with the shrill squeal of emergency.

Every pedestrian in front of them stopped and turned to face the policemen.

Still not seeing the woman in black, Browning patted Barney on the shoulder. "She's not here. Let's go."

They raced forward in their search.

* * *

Instead of chasing after the police officers, Maisy remained in the viewing room with Milo Cole who appeared to be a bit stupefied by what he had just witnessed.

"Come on, Milo. Let's go over to the Abbotsford now. We've seen all there is to see here tonight." She took his arm and pulled him through the doorway to the outer parlor.

Pathé Lehrman, Katy Killoy, and Jack Shannon hurried up to them.

"What's going on in there?" asked Lehrman.

"Why did that woman come running out of there and then go outside so quickly?" asked Katy.

"Didn't any of you see Vivian come through here?" asked Cole.

"Vivian came through here?" queried Shannon.

"That wasn't Vivian who ran out of here," said Katy. "That was some other woman."

"Yes, she came through here and into the viewing room. Didn't you see her? She was dressed mourning clothes with a veil."

"That wasn't Vivian," said Shannon.

"I saw a woman dressed like that," said Katy, "but I didn't think she was Vivian Vanover."

"Maisy asked her if she was Vivian, and she said she was. Isn't that right, Maisy?"

"Well, she didn't actually say anything, but she did nod her head when I asked her if she was Vivian Vanover."

"I tell you, that wasn't Vivian. I know Vivian, and that wasn't her."

Maisy patted him on the shoulder. "Don't get all excited, Jack. We all know how you feel about Vivian. You can believe it wasn't her, if you like. But she did nod yes when I asked her if she was Vivian. Now if she was lying to me, then who was she?"

"I don't know, but I do know that woman wasn't Vivian."

"Okay, we'll take your word for it." Maisy looked around the room. "Looks like we're all that's left here, so why don't we join the others at the Abbotsford now?"

Police whistles sounded outside.

"What's that all about?" asked Katy.

"That would be the police chasing after the woman who told me she was Vivian Vanover but who Jack doesn't think was Vivian."

"Okay, but who was the woman who rushed out of here?"

"Oh, *that* woman. That was Policewoman Alice Wells of the Los Angeles Police Department."

"Policewoman?"

"That's right, Katy. She's a policewoman working with Detective Browning. He and two other officers are chasing the woman who said she was Vivian out the back way right now."

"And all that commotion out front?" queried Katy.

Maisy grinned coyly. "That would be the rest of Detective Browning's men chasing after the same woman."

"This I have to see," said Lehrman.

"Let's all go," said Maisy.

* * *

Maisy and the others came around the corner of Eighth Street and Hope to see Browning and his gaggle of officers congregating in front of the Abbotsford's entrance. With Lehrman in the lead, they strolled up to the detective.

"Well, Detective Browning, have you caught your fugitive from justice yet?"

"Not yet, Mr. Lehrman."

"How could you lose a woman in mourning clothes?" asked Maisy. "She stands like a sore thumb."

"Yes, I agree, Miss Malone."

"So what happened? Did she simply vanish into thin air?"

"We were just discussing the possibility that she might have entered the Abbotsford."

"Well, we're going in there to join the rest of our Keystone party. Why don't join us?"

"No, thank you, Miss Malone. We have our duty out here."

"Fair enough, Detective. Good luck with your search."

"Step aside, men, and allow these people to enter."

The police officers parted to let Maisy and the others pass through them and up the steps of the hotel. As soon as they were inside, Browning resumed speaking to his unit.

"We'll surround the building first. I want four officers to each side. Officers Wells, Barney, and Fitzgerald and any others left over will accompany me inside to conduct a floor by floor search there. Officer Kronschnable will continue patrolling around the block." He pointed out four teams of four to take up posts outside before leading the others through the entrance.

In the lobby, the police officers were met by a sharp-nosed man with a bald pate fringed with graying auburn hair and a matching mustache that covered his upper lip from each corner of his mouth.

"I am Mr. Scireau, the manager." He spoke with a touch of a French accent. "May I help you officers?"

"Detective Sergeant Edward Browning, sir. We're in pursuit of a woman wearing mourning clothes. Has anyone matching that description entered this establishment in the past five minutes?"

"No one that I have seen, Detective, and I have been here in the lobby for the past quarter hour at least."

"Perhaps one of your staff has seen this woman?"

Scireau turned and clapped his hands to draw the attention of all his employees within earshot and sight of him. "Come here. All of you." In less than a minute they were assembled before the manager. "This is Detective Browning of the city police department. He has a question for you. You will give him your full cooperation. You may address them now, Detective Browning."

"Thank you, Mr. Scireau. As Mr. Scireau said, I am Detective Sergeant Browning of the Police Department. We are in pursuit of a female fugitive named Vivian Vanover who is wanted for the murder of the actor Leslie Clover. We believe she entered this hotel in the last five minutes or so and is now hiding within these premises. She was dressed in mourning clothes and wearing a long veil. Has anyone here seen a woman fitting that description?"

Every staff member shook his or head negatively.

"Are you certain?"

Not one positive response.

"Then we have no other alternative, Mr. Scireau, except to search this establishment immediately. If you don't mind, I would like two of your employees to accompany each of my teams as they conduct the search."

"Of course, Detective Browning. I and my staff are at your service."

"In the meantime, I will be joining the Keystone people. Could you direct me to them please?"

"Certainly, sir."

"Officer Wells, you will accompany me please."

Scireau showed Browning and Wells to the private banquet hall in the rear of the building. "If you need anything further, Detective, please do not hesitate to call on me."

"Thank you, Mr. Scireau."

The manager departed, while the detective and the policewoman approached the long table where Maisy, Lehr, and Cole had joined Mack Sennett, Ford Sterling, Fred Mace, Alice Davenport, and Mabel Normand.

Being the director-general of the studio, Sennett took it upon himself to ask the question everybody seated with him wanted to ask. "We heard all the police whistles a few minutes ago, Detective, and were wondering what all the ruckus was about. Then Mr. Lehrman and Miss Malone came in and told us you were chasing Vivian Vanover through the streets. Did you catch her?"

"No, we have not yet apprehended Miss Vanover, but I assure you, Mr. Sennett, we will have her in our custody before the night is over."

Mabel smiled sweetly at Browning. "Really?"

"I guarantee it, Miss Normand." Browning suddenly realized that he hadn't seen Mabel in the viewing room. "I'm sorry, Miss Normand, but have you been here the whole evening?"

"Well, no, not the whole evening. I only came in a few minutes before Maisy and Pathé and Milo did."

"Only a few minutes before your friends? Tell me, Miss Normand, when you came into the hotel, did you happen to see a woman dressed in mourning clothes and wearing a large black hat with a wide brim and a long veil that went all the way around the brim of the hat?"

"Mourning clothes? Do you mean she was dressed in black?" Mabel stood up to reveal she was wearing a black skirt. She took the black jacket from the back of her chair and slipped into it. "Like this?"

"Yes, yes, like that."

Mabel bent over and retrieved something from beneath the table. "And her hat? Was it like this one?" She placed a large black hat with a broad brim on her head.

"Yes, just like that one."

Mabel reached above the brim and lowered the veil the encircled it. "And was her veil like this one?"

"Yes, exactly like that one."

"No, Detective Browning, I haven't seen anyone dressed like that."

A roar of laughter from the rest of the people at the table finally lit the light of recognition in Browning's brain. He had been had.

Maisy and Browning stood in the lobby of the Abbotsford Inn. "Come on, Eddie, can't you take a joke?"

"You wasted my time, and you embarrassed me in front of my fellow police officers, Miss Malone."

"You need to laugh more, Eddie."

"Murder is no laughing matter."

"Okay, I will grant you that much, but nobody was hurt except your feelings. And I'll bet you a three-cent nickel that when you tell your wife about this little bit of fun we had tonight that she'll get a kick out of it, too. Nice lady, your wife. She has to have a sense of humor. She married you, didn't she?"

Browning knew Maisy was right, but he still didn't want to admit it. "I should run you and Miss Norman into jail for the night. And Mr. Cole as well. I'm sure he had hand in this prank of yours."

"No, Milo was just as much in the dark about our little joke as you were. In fact, nobody else knew about it except Mabel and me. It was my idea, and she pulled it off. Come on, Eddie. Admit it. If this had happened to any of your fellow officers, you'd think it was really funny, now wouldn't you?"

"Oh, all right, I will grant *you* that much."

"Okay, Eddie, that's more like it. Now tomorrow is the funeral. Something tells me Vivian Vanover will show up at the cemetery to pay her respects to Leslie Clover. You can nab her then."

"What makes you so sure she'll do that?"

"I'm a woman, Eddie, or hadn't you noticed? Besides if I were her, that's what I would do."

* * *

Since Leslie Clover was English, the Pierce Brothers funeral manager suggested the service should be held at Christ Episcopal Church on the southwest corner of Hope Street and west Twelfth. Mourners began gathering outside the church a quarter before eleven, the scheduled start of the memorial rite. Among the earliest attendees were Detective Browning, Maisy Malone, Mabel Normand, and Milo Cole who was scheduled to deliver the eulogy.

"I wouldn't do it, if Mack hadn't told me it was part of my job. I really hate getting up in front of crowds except on a stage."

Mabel patted Cole on the arm. "You'll do fine, Milo. Just read from the notes you made, and it will turn out all right."

"I'm glad *you* think so. I'm not so sure."

Maisy squeezed his other arm affectionately. "I think so, too, Milo. You'll do Leslie Clover proud. I'm sure of it." She turned to Browning. "You've got nothing to worry about, Milo. Eddie and his boys have the place surrounded just like they had the funeral parlor surrounded last night. Isn't that right, Eddie?"

"I do have men here just in case Miss Vanover shows up."

"I told you last night, Eddie, she won't show up to pay her respects until we're all at the cemetery. In fact, I wouldn't be surprised if she was already there waiting for the rest of us to show up."

Browning eyed Maisy with growing suspicion that she had actually been manipulating events ever since they made their wager the night that Leslie Clover was murder. "Something tells me you know more about this murder than you've been letting on, Miss Malone."

She smiled at him. "We'll see about that, won't we? Shall we go inside now?"

The four of them went into the church and took seats in the front row where the deceased's immediate family would usually sit. Joining them in the first pew were Mack Sennett, Henry Lehrman, Ford Sterling, Fred Mace, Alice Davenport, Hugh McHatton, Katy Killoy, and Jack Shannon. The second row was reserved for Ed Kennedy, George Jeske, Bobby Dunn, Hank Mann, Slim Summerville, and Chet Franklin who agreed to be Clover's pallbearers. Nearly all the women Clover had dated since arriving in Hollywood occupied the next row of pews. The one glaring absentee was Vivian Vanover, very much to Browning's disappointment.

At the assigned hour, the Pierce Brothers hearse arrived outside the church. The pallbearers removed the casket and the priest covered it with a pall. He nodded to the crucifer, a teenage youth in a sacramental robe, who took his place at the head of the procession. The priest fell in behind him, and the casket bearers came next. They entered the church and walked down the aisle to the altar where the casket was placed on the bier. The priest took his post at the pulpit. Because the departed had not been a member of this particular church and neither were any of the mourners in attendance, the clergyman decided to forego the usual practice of celebrating the Holy Eucharist and went straight into the recital of an Easter Liturgy. He followed up with a prayer for the friends of the deceased who had come to mourn his passing. A reading from the Bible came next. The priest then asked that all rise and sing the hymn, *Rock of Ages*. All in attendance stood, and the organist struck the tune. Those of various Protestant faiths sang with the man of the cloth. He bade them to be seated once they had concluded the hymn. When all were settled again, he offered a homily on living a practical life. He spoke one more prayer before stating the service would continue at the cemetery.

* * *

Maisy and Mabel made certain to stick close to Browning as the funeral for Leslie Clover resumed at Rosedale Cemetery on West Washington Street. The other mourners encircled the gravesite as soon as the coffin was placed over it.

Browning scanned the faces around him, searching for the one he wouldn't recognize but would assume was that of Vivian Vanover. He finally saw her standing beside Hortencia Ramos. Fearing she would attempt to escape in the crowd as soon as the service was concluded, he started toward her, but was held back by Maisy and Mabel, each taking him by an arm.

"Hold on, Eddie," whispered Maisy. "She's not going anywhere. Not now and not later. You'll have plenty of time to arrest her."

"Can't you see she's really grieving for this man?" said Mabel. "Let her be, Detective."

Browning knew they were both right. He held back while the priest conducted the internment rite.

The priest spoke the usual prayer about ashes to ashes and dust to dust and the Psalm about "the Lord is my shepherd" and not wanting. He concluded by committing Leslie Clover's mortal remains to the earth, sprinkling the coffin with sand in the shape of a cross as it was lowered into the grave.

A few of the women came forward and dropped a single rose or a lily on the casket. The last to do so was Vivian Vanover. Everybody else stood their ground, all waiting for Browning to make his move.

"Miss Vivian Vanover, I am placing you under arrest for the murder of Leslie Clover."

A stilted moment of silence followed as the crowd of mourners waited for Vivian's reaction. She remained absolutely stoic.

For Maisy Malone, the time had come for her to see that Clover received the justice he probably didn't really deserve all that much, considering how he had misused his short time in this world. She stepped forward, turned, and faced Browning.

"You got the wrong person, Eddie. She didn't kill Clover."

"I'm sorry, Miss Malone, but your opinion is not germane to the case. You are not a police officer; therefore, you have no say in this matter. Miss Vanover is under arrest, and that is all these is to it."

"Oh, come on, Eddie. Get off your high horse, and hear me out."

"No."

Mabel leaned against Browning. "Come on, Detective, let her have her say. She might be right, you know. And if she is, she'll be saving you a lot of trouble later on when you find out Vivian is innocent."

Browning's mouth twisted back and forth as he considered her thoughts on the business at hand. He heaved a sigh of disdain and frustration. "Oh, all right. Let's hear what you have to say, Miss Malone. What makes you think Miss Vanover is innocent?"

Everybody inched closer to listen.

"Well, in the first place, she's carrying Leslie Clover's child."

This brought a collective gasp from the crowd.

"How do you know that?" asked Browning. "Did she tell you?"

"No, she didn't. Hortencia told me."

All eyes shifted to the housekeeper, but Hortencia stood beside Vivian unfazed by all the attention.

"So when did she tell you this?" asked Browning, hoping to trap Maisy into incriminating herself with obstructing justice.

All eyes and ears returned to Maisy.

Now that she really had everybody's attention, Maisy took center stage. "She didn't actually tell me that. *She* didn't even know it until I asked her if Vivian might be expecting. You see, she had told me that Vivian had been sick for several mornings before Clover was murdered. I don't believe even Vivian knew she was pregnant until the day she went over to Clover's bungalow to tell him she was expecting their child."

"And when was this?" asked Browning.

"The morning Clover was murdered. You went there that morning, didn't you, Vivian? You went there to tell him you were with child and that the baby is his. Isn't that right?"

Vivian could only nod as she dabbed at her tears with a plain white handkerchief.

Browning smiled smugly. "So she was there that morning."

"Yes, she was, but she didn't get there until after Clover was murdered. She found him lying on the floor of his bedroom. Isn't that right, Vivian?"

Again, Vivian nodded.

"The shock of finding someone dead sometimes makes people do some very strange things. In Vivian's case, she cleaned up his bedroom for him. She tried to make it as neat as she would do, if she was his wife. Isn't that right, Vivian?"

Another dip of her head gave an affirmative answer.

"She would have cleaned up the rest of the house, but she was interrupted by Milo Cole knocking on the front door. She quickly grabbed the one thing that would remind her of Leslie Clover for the rest of her life, and she ran out the back door with it."

"What did she take from the house?" asked Browning.

"Show him, Vivian."

Vivian hesitated for a few seconds before reaching into her purse and removing Clover's cigarette lighter and holding it up for everybody to see, especially Browning.

"You're making my case for me, Miss Malone. That's very sporting of you."

"Don't be in such a hurry to judge, Eddie. I'm a long way from getting to the real killer."

"Well, I wish you would get on with it then."

"I figured out Vivian was expecting when Milo and I went by her boardinghouse Saturday afternoon. Right then and there, I figured she didn't kill Clover. How could she kill the father of her child? She couldn't, so it had to be someone else. I just didn't know who it was yet, so we … that is, Milo and Mabel and I … we kept digging into this murder. I had my suspicions about who could have done it and why. For example, I thought it might be Alma McComb."

Alma gasped. "What made you think it was me?"

"Well, Clover jilted you, for one thing. And when I saw you pick up some trash in the street when we had lunch together on Friday, I thought you were some kind of neatness nut. And since Clover's bedroom and bathroom were as neat as a pin, well, I naturally put you on the list of suspects. Of course, when I learned you were at the studio Thursday morning working in the wardrobe department for Katy Killoy, I knew you didn't do it.

"Since I've mentioned Katy, I might as well say it now that I had her on the top of my list for Clover's killer."

"Me? Why on earth would you think that, Maisy?"

"Well, for one thing, you're Irish and Clover was English. No love lost there, especially since your late husband was killed by an English soldier in a pub back in Ireland. And for a while, I thought you killed him because I thought Jack Shannon was really your son Jackie using a different last name so he could get work at the studio."

"Whatever gave you that notion?"

"When Jack first started working at the studio, his address was in Pasadena, not too far from where you live, Katy."

"How did you learn that?"

"It was on his payroll record. Or it was until he got his own place in the same building where Milo lives. The original address was crossed out on the record, but it was still legible. Jack is related to you, isn't he, Katy?"

Shannon spoke up. "Go ahead and tell her, Aunt Kate. It's time everybody knew the truth anyway."

"Jack's mother is my late husband's sister. We didn't have enough room for him at our house, so I got him a room in a boardinghouse around the corner from us when he came out here to California from New York this summer."

Shannon's face twisted with curiosity. "But why would you think Aunt Kate would kill Leslie?"

"To help you get ahead at the studio. With Clover dead, you'd get more roles to play and maybe even become a lead player someday. I even suspected you of killing him for the same reason, but your payroll record verified you were at the studio that morning. So you didn't do it."

"Then who did kill him?" asked Shannon.

Browning appeared more annoyed by Maisy's revelations than he was happy to listen to them. "Yes, Miss Malone, would you mind getting to the point? If it wasn't Miss Vanover or Miss McComb or Mrs. Killoy or Mr. Shannon, then who was it?"

"Quit being so impatient, Eddie. I'm getting there. So just hold your horses, will you?"

"Come on, Maisy," said Mabel, "you've got everybody on pins and needles now. Just tell them who did it?"

"Well, like I said, I thought Katy was the killer because her whereabouts on Thursday couldn't be completely verified. Alma told me, and I'm sure she told you as well, Eddie, that Katy was in and out of the wardrobe department all morning long and that she was gone for quite some time because she was trying to find a man's costume, one that fit Slim Summerville. Isn't that right, Alma?"

"That's right, Maisy."

"Now the only other person around the studio who matches Slim's description is Phoebe Alden."

A collective gasp hissed from the mourners.

"Look at her."

Everybody did.

"She's a near perfect match for slim. Put a suit of his clothes on her, and she could pass for a man, especially if someone was looking at her from a distance, say someone like Mr. Ed Moore, a carpenter who was working on the roof of the new house going up behind Leslie Clover's bungalow. He and Mr. Allen Kitchen were working on the roof together the morning Leslie Clover was murdered."

"How do you know this?" asked Browning.

"Unlike your officers, Eddie, I'm a lot more thorough when it comes to questioning the people in Clover's neighborhood. Besides, I remembered seeing them working there that morning when Milo and I were in Clover's house waiting for you to show up. Yesterday, Mabel and I went over there and talked to Mr. Hogan, the builder, and his workmen. Mr. Kitchen told us he saw a woman come out the back door of the bungalow just about the time Milo and I showed up there. That was Vivian leaving when she heard Milo at the front door. Isn't that right, Vivian?"

Vivian nodded.

"But it wasn't Mr. Kitchen saying he'd seen a woman leaving the house that interested me. It was Mr. Moore saying he saw a man leaving through the same back door a couple hours earlier."

"He saw a man leaving the bungalow?" queried Browning.

"That's what he said. He saw a man leaving the bungalow by the back door a couple of hours before Vivian left the same way."

"Is he certain it was a man?"

"That's what he says." Maisy focused on the tall redhead. "You know, Phoebe, I was suspicious of you right from the start. And when I heard about the man's costume that was missing, I was almost sure it was you who took it in order to disguise yourself on the morning Clover was murdered. But then Mr. Moore described the man he saw, and his description didn't fit you. In the first place, the man he saw was short." She pinpointed her stare on Jack Shannon.

All eyes followed hers to the Irish actor.

"But you already said you know it wasn't me who killed him."

Maisy snapped her fingers. "That's right, I did. No, Jack, it wasn't you. You're only guilty of bad acting." She shifted her view to Fritz Schade.

Again everybody looked where Maisy focused.

"So I thought of you, Mr. Schade."

"Me? *Nein, nein.* I kill nobody. *Ich ihn nicht toten.*"

"Easy there, Mr. Schade. I know it wasn't you. Mr. Moore didn't say the man was on the robust side. He said he was skinny as well as short."

Everybody searched the crowd looking for a short, skinny man. In seconds, all of them stared at Hugh McHatton.

"Why is everybody looking at me? I didn't kill him. I barely knew the man."

"No, but he knew enough about you, Mr. McHatton. Enough to blackmail you."

"I don't know what you're talking about, Miss Malone, and furthermore, I resent the implications of your remarks."

"Resent all you want, Hughie. I'm pretty sure I hit the nail on the head with you. Clover was blackmailing you, and you murdered him for it."

"That's absurd!"

"I would have agreed with you before I spoke to Mr. Hogan, the builder, yesterday. You see, he had been renting the bungalow to Clover up until two weeks ago when suddenly Clover came to him with five hundred dollars to make a down payment for buying the place from him."

This revelation stunned the crowd.

"Now where do you think Clover got that much money, Hughie?"

"I don't have the foggiest idea."

"Oh, sure you do, Hughie. He got it from you."

"That's preposterous. Where would I get that kind of money?"

"From the Keystone Moving Picture Company's payroll, and before that from your previous employer's payroll, which happens to be the same studio that employed Leslie Clover."

"I have never taken a dime from any of my employers, I'll have you know. You're being absurd, Miss Malone."

"I don't think so, Hughie. You see, when you paid me Saturday, you paid me for the half day I worked Thursday, the full day on Friday, and the half day on Saturday. But my payroll record says I was paid for a full week. When I saw that, I began wonder how many other people at the studio were being paid an amount not reflected on their payroll records." She turned to Sennett. "Mack, I think you've been paying for a lot of benchwarmers who haven't been seeing a lot of action in the game."

"That's a lie, Mr. Sennett. I've never taken a dime from the company."

"You don't have to believe me, Mack. Just ask everybody here to write down what they've been paid the last couple of weeks and then compare those numbers to the ones on their payroll records. I'll bet you a three-cent nickel everybody's records will indicate they were paid *more* than they actually were."

McHatton's head jerked back and forth as he searched for a way out of this trap. "All right. Maybe I was skimming a little off the top at the studio. So what? It doesn't mean I killed Clover. I was at the studio the whole morning. Everybody saw me there."

"I have an eyewitness in Mr. Moore who says he saw you come out of the bungalow that very morning, Hughie. Better fess up while you can."

Without another word, McHatton barged through the crowd and took off at a run through the cemetery toward the main entrance on Washington Street.

"Stop him, boys!" shouted Browning to his officers at the gate.

Seeing the policemen coming toward him, McHatton changed directions and weaved his way through the headstones.

Maisy shook her head. "Little guy sure is fast for a bookkeeper."

"He's not that fast," said Mabel. "I'll bet you one of those three-cent nickels of yours that I can catch him before Eddie's boys can."

"No bet. I've seen you run."

Mabel burped a giggle. "Come on, I need some incentive to go after him. Bet me something."

"No, Mabel. Let the cops catch him, if they can."

Sennett sidled up to them. "So who do you think won the pool?"

"I don't think any of us did," said Maisy. "Up until yesterday afternoon, I thought it was Katy or Alma who had done the deed. I'm pretty sure nobody else got it right."

They continued to watch Browning and his men pursue McHatton for the next minute or so through the graveyard until suddenly the villain came racing around a crypt near Clover's grave, charged over the mound of dirt beside the deceased's final resting place, stumbled and fell into the hole, landing on top of the casket and knocking himself unconscious.

Maisy and the others stepped to the edge of the grave and looked down at McHatton.

"Well, Eddie, it looks like you've got your killer dead to rights."

ABOUT THE AUTHOR

Larry Names has had 40 titles published to date, 25 of them novels, and the remainder non—fiction all dealing with sports teams or sports figures. He resides in central Wisconsin with his wife Peg on a family farm that has been in his wife's family since 1854. They have a son, Torry and a daughter, Tegan, four cats and an escape-artist horse, Lucky Moondancer. Larry has four children from his first marriage: daughter Sigrid, son Paul, daughter Kristin, and daughter Sonje.

The author was born in Mishawaka, Indiana and has lived in nine different states during his life and went to eleven schools growing up. He is an avid researcher and traveler.

Please visit the author's website: www.larrynames.com

Made in the USA
Charleston, SC
05 December 2012